Get Your House Right

Architectural Elements to Use & Avoid

Get Your House Right

Architectural Elements to Use & Avoid

MARIANNE CUSATO & BEN PENTREATH

with Richard Sammons & Leon Krier

Foreword by H.R.H. The Prince of Wales

IN ASSOCIATION WITH
THE INSTITUTE OF CLASSICAL ARCHITECTURE
AND CLASSICAL AMERICA

STERLING

New York / London
www.sterlingpublishing.com

STERLING and the distinctive Sterling logo are registered trademarks
of Sterling Publishing Co., Inc.

Library of Congress Cataloging-in-Publication Data Available

10   9   8   7   6   5   4   3   2   1

Published by Sterling Publishing Co., Inc.
387 Park Avenue South, New York, NY 10016
© 2007 by Marianne Cusato, Ben Pentreath, Richard Sammons, and Leon Krier
Distributed in Canada by Sterling Publishing
^{c}/o Canadian Manda Group, 165 Dufferin Street
Toronto, Ontario, Canada M6K 3H6
Distributed in the United Kingdom by GMC Distribution Services,
Castle Place, 166 High Street, Lewes, East Sussex, England BN7 1XU
Distributed in Australia by Capricorn Link (Australia) Pty. Ltd.
P.O. Box 704, Windsor, NSW 2756, Australia

Art direction: Edwin Kuo and Rachel Maloney
Book design and layout: Patricia Childers

Manufactured in the United States of America
All rights reserved

Sterling ISBN-13: 978-1-4027-3628-5
        ISBN-10: 1-4027-3628-2

For information about custom editions, special sales, premium
and corporate purchases, please contact Sterling Special Sales
Department at 800-805-5489 or specialsales@sterlingpublishing.com.

CONTENTS

ACKNOWLEDGEMENTS

THIS BOOK BEGAN AS A SERIES OF FAXES in 2000 between Andres Duany, Leon Krier, and Marianne Cusato, cataloging many common mistakes found in today's traditional architecture. Over the years that series of drawings grew and evolved through many formats into the book that you are holding today. It has been a lengthy process, but a worthwhile journey, and one only made possible with assistance from many friends and colleagues along the way.

We are grateful to H.R.H. The Prince of Wales for his interest in the book, and to Paul Kefford and Manon Williams in his office.

Thank you to Anne Fairfax, Diane Dorney, Rick Mullin, Jim Taylor, and Seth Weine for their reviews and comments to several of our early drafts; to Julie Trelstad for recognizing our potential, and to Anne Barthel, our editor, for her tireless work in bringing this book to print.

Hank Dittmar, Ben Bolgar, and Saad Ghandour of the Prince's Foundation have been supportive, as have Paul Murrain, Russell Versaci, and many other colleagues. Special thanks are due to Paul Gunther, Christine Franck, Henrika Taylor, Steve Semes, and Briana Miller of the Institute of Classical Architecture and Classical America.

We would like to thank our many mentors who have guided our education and inspired our love of architecture—Milton Grenfell, Charles Morris, Thomas Gordon Smith, Duncan Stroik, Richard Economakis, Victor Deupi, Norman Crowe, Cara Caroccia, and Michael Lykoudis.

Irina Woelfle and Deborah Slaunwhite were of special importance in the final stages of this book. Irina's counsel and friendship have been invaluable. Deborah's calm and dependable personality have kept Marianne in business while finishing the book. Thank you also to Mark and Cristi Pledger for their friendship throughout the entire process.

Finally, we owe a very special thank-you to Andres Duany. From the days of the first faxes to today, Andres's guidance and support has been instrumental in the development of this book and in our work.

CLARENCE HOUSE

In a world of ever-increasing homogenization and standardization, where ever more pettifogging rules and regulations suck out the character, charm and spiritual meaning from every pore of our human experience, the need to champion a living tradition of building and cultural continuity could not be more vital. As such, this splendid book has appeared at a very timely moment.

At long last, we are witnessing an increasingly widespread appreciation of the value of building in traditional ways. Across the world architects, town planners and builders are looking once again to time-honoured classical and vernacular sources as their inspiration for building today.

Sadly, it is all too apparent that despite our best intentions the traditional buildings that are being constructed today do not always feel 'right'. Why is this? So often, they seem to fail in the small details – the proportion of a window, or a badly-detailed door surround, or in a mistaken or short-sighted choice of materials.

As Leon Krier writes so eloquently in his introduction to this book, the problems stem from an appalling interruption in the teaching of basic traditional skills. During the last century, architects and builders lost much of the innate knowledge – both theoretical and practical – that had been built up by their forefathers for generations. It is a hard task indeed for us to re-educate ourselves, and to learn again the way in which our ancestors managed to build so beautifully, yet economically, and in sympathy with their local surroundings. This wonderful book should, I hope, make the task very much easier.

The project was the inspiration of a young American architect, Marianne Cusato, who wanted to explain in simple language exactly what the builder needs to know and her beautiful drawings form the core of this book. Her energy in promoting good traditional design in the United States, most recently with the marvellous Katrina Cottage, seems to know no bounds! I am delighted that three people who are well known to me have joined her in this task: Leon Krier, of course, needs no introduction, but it is no surprise to me that the master-planner of my own development at Poundbury, in Dorset, should be as skilled at understanding the small details as much as the bigger picture! Richard Sammons, an alumnus of my Foundation's first Summer School, and one of many wonderful classical architects practising in America today, has a particular expertize in the theories of proportion and historical construction; and Ben Pentreath, also an alumnus, has worked for my Foundation for the Built Environment in London. I am enormously proud that someone so adept and skillful, and with a real gift for design and draughtsmanship, should be working alongside my Foundation, and also at my development at Poundbury, to help stem the tide of brutality and ugliness which has been the hallmark of the 20th century.

I should like to congratulate all these remarkably sympathetic practitioners for producing such a complete – yet concise – book, from which I confess I have already learned a great deal! It should prove invaluable not only to builders and students, but – I suspect – to many architects. As the traditional architectural movement continues to grow around the world, and particularly in America, it is heartening to see a renewed appreciation for the finer details of old buildings and natural materials. It is my heartfelt hope that this book will help to re-establish a thriving – and genuinely authentic – practice of traditional design and building in our own time.

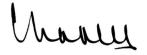

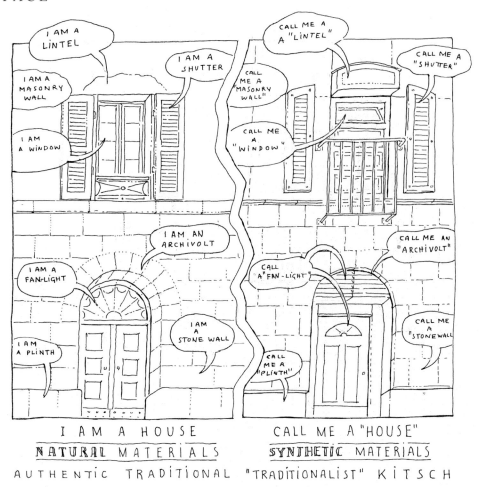

AMERICANS VISIT FALLINGWATER in religious awe, but when they choose a home, they turn for inspiration to Williamsburg and Mount Vernon, to the vernacular and classical models. Despite sustained efforts to re-educate the public according to modernist ideals, traditional designs have never ceased to dominate residential architecture in the United States. And yet even though "houses of the future" no longer look futuristic, the modernist propaganda has done lasting damage. The scandalous truth is that the vast majority of architecture schools today simply do not teach the theory and practice of traditional house design. Worse, they have erased the subject from their technical, intellectual, and artistic horizon.

The battle cry "Bauhaus instead of our house" has rallied the profession. It blinds it to environmental problems, to the reality of the housebuilding industry, and, paradoxically, to the taste and wishes of most house buyers. It is as if architects were trained to serve an alien people on a distant planet. They themselves go on living, working, and vacationing in traditional environs, but don't see the irony when it is put to them. Instead, a student or teacher who shows more than a passing interest in traditional concepts and techniques will be isolated from the academic cocoon like a blasphemer in theology class.

Imagine the fate of plain English if American schools ceased to teach the common language and began to ostracize its speakers. This is exactly what traditional architectural disciplines have been subjected to for more than two score years. The institutional attrition helps to explain the fact that the last half-century has, despite its unparalleled material wealth, produced the most debased traditional building styles in recorded history. The ill-sized, the ill-fitted, the ill-designed and ill-constructed, have become the norm in a field that represents a large part of the gross national product and absorbs much of family savings. The triumph of kitsch sensibility—the culture of the mean, the synthetic, and the fake—may be seen as the unintended results, the distorted mirror image of modernism.

Ironically, the most serious threat to traditional culture today comes no longer from modernism itself, but from "traditional" simulacra. Architectural analphabetism produces stunning, sometimes comical results. Discussing this book in a prestigious Washington, D.C., hotel, the authors overlooked the new pool house with its twelve sparkling Tuscan columns erected upside down, standing on their capitals. This scandal didn't raise an eyebrow among the fine clientele, nor did it cause headlines. Such and more serious mistakes in construction and design are now so common that they have become the signature of our time, a style with specific characteristics.

Curiously, the mistakes are "cultivated" with conviction; they are frequent and repetitive, they are stubbornly and sometimes proudly committed by all building trades, by professionals and amateurs. They are built by house builders and bought into by house buyers. They have spread ineradicably across five continents and through almost all cultures. How can such confusion triumph so completely without causing organized reactions or public protest? And why don't the buildings themselves collapse under the weight of their misconception?

Traditional and classical architecture can be thought of as a language—a grammar of constructing buildings from natural materials such as wood, stone, earth, sand, lime. Mistakes in joining, laying, or framing these materials become quickly evident through uncontrollable behavior, settling, cracking, or collapsing; even a genius cannot build a lasting mistake out of nature's materials. But synthetic materials (concrete, steel, wood derivatives, plastics) and their specific joining techniques (casting, gluing bolting, soldering, nailing) allow anyone to realize foolish forms without facing immediate ruin. When these materials and techniques are used to ape traditional designs, technology and semantics go inevitably on a collision course, ending in grinding—and lasting—incongruities.

To iron out the resulting anachronisms is taxing to an individual's capacities. The authors of this book have all tried and failed too often. It is sheer despair that has brought them together to draft ways out of the maze. The problems illustrated here are at once of a formal and technical nature; they are not, as ideologists claim, of a philosophical kind. Nor are they so complex as to be beyond the grasp of practical intelligence. To build a fine traditional house isn't that much more of an effort than to make a mess of it. It requires, more than anything, aesthetic sense, knowledge, judgment, and a passion for joining materials into meaningful forms that bring true and daily enjoyment to those who look at them, use them, and live in them.

In this book we do not belabor the reasons for what is nothing less than a cultural catastrophe, nor do we want to make converts for what can seem like yet another cause. Instead, we offer a primer to help those people who are already passionately convinced of the good sense of traditional building. The latter is neither a religion nor a mystery. It is about techniques and means of solving building problems with elegance and intelligence. Its solutions are self-evident and rational, practical and lasting, and when guided by talent, they are blessed with grace.

Leon Krier

WHY YOU NEED THIS BOOK

THIS BOOK IS FOR EVERYONE: everyone who wants to design, build, or live in a traditionally designed home.

Often, when we look at new traditional buildings, we can sense when a design is "off," but we can't put our finger on why. This book is a resource to help you articulate why a house feels right or wrong—why it strikes you as classic, solid, and timeless, or why it appears to be an unconvincing imitation.

The Language of Architecture

Traditional architecture is a language of its own. Like any language, it has a *vocabulary* (the building elements, such as windows, doors, and eaves) and *grammar* (the rules that we use to put the elements together). Designing a building without understanding these rules is like forming a sentence without understanding syntax. Without the foundation of basic knowledge, the results can be garbled, sometimes beyond recognition.

Get Your House Right teaches you how to speak this language and how to read it in every house you see. It is based on the premise of learning by looking, because it is often easiest to learn from our mistakes. By illustrating where common mistakes happen, and showing you how to avoid them, we'll help you train your eye to see the difference.

You do not need training in architecture to use and appreciate this book. Along the way, we may assume you have some knowledge of buildings and their structural components, but as we go along we will also impart a lot of information about the essential elements of your house, how they work together, and how to use them appropriately. If you're a homeowner, shopping for a home or commissioning a design, you will gain insight into the key elements that define the look and feel of a house. If you're a professional designing or building a house for a client, you will learn the specific details that make these key elements work.

1.1 The Language of Classical Architecture

Like any language, architecture has a vocabulary and a grammar. All of the buildings illustrated below are classical, not just because of their elements (the "vocabulary"), but because they are arranged by a common set of rules (the "grammar").

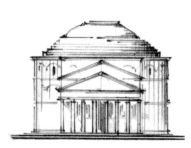

The Pantheon, Rome

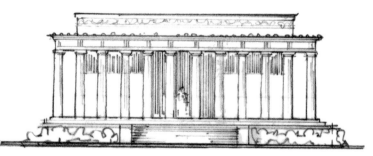

The Lincoln Memorial

Throughout this book are illustrations that serve as examples of good design decisions and bad ones. We will refer to the illustrations as if you are learning by doing—constructing and deconstructing each element of your house on the page, so that you don't have to do it on site. We will show you the techniques of design and construction you should *use* and those you must *avoid*. And we will immerse you in the language of classical architecture so that "speaking" it becomes second nature.

Building to Last

As the revival of traditional building in America continues to gain momentum, examples of the new classical architecture can be seen in almost every city. Nowhere has this transformation been more dramatic than in residential development. From across the country the message is clear: People want to live in traditional houses (and they will pay a premium to do so).

The benefits of traditional architecture and urbanism are more than economic. Architects, city planners, builders, and above all, homeowners are realizing that a sense of community can derive from well-designed and properly built places: the *social capital* of good design. Equally important are issues of environmental responsibility and sustainable development, vital for the well-being of future generations.

But good intentions alone cannot create good design, and all too often, new work being produced just doesn't "feel" quite right. Getting it right requires an understanding of the language and a realization that traditional design is not merely a matter of sticking on columns or applying trim here and there. To be successful both on paper and in the field, we have to build intelligently, understand historical precedent, and use local materials to create authentic, long-lasting architecture with a whole that is greater than the sum of its parts. This book will show you how.

A Georgian villa

A Charleston sideyard house

A Williamsburg cottage

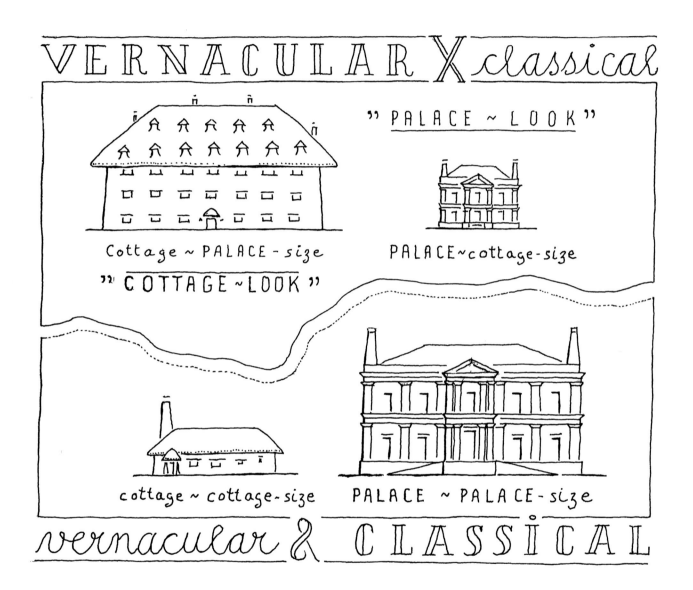

VERNACULAR ✕ classical

" PALACE ~ LOOK "

Cottage ~ PALACE - size

PALACE ~ cottage - size

" COTTAGE ~ LOOK "

cottage ~ cottage - size

PALACE ~ PALACE - size

vernacular & CLASSICAL

Chapter 1

NINE THINGS YOU NEED TO KNOW

The world of traditional architecture is rich and satisfying, but it can appear complex and confusing at first. This book is about explaining the details of traditional design. But before we look at the fine grain, we begin by looking at the big picture, and at the nine essential things you need to know.

WHAT YOU NEED TO THINK ABOUT (EVERYTHING)

For decades, too many decisions about how we live have been made in isolation from one another. Thoughtless zoning has created mono-cultures of single-use development that have made us over-dependent on cars and fossil fuels and led us to plan for roads rather than people. An epidemic rise in health problems, both physical and mental, and the collapse of the old values of community have taken their toll on many American towns and cities. More and more, people are noticing that all the problems are related. Thankfully, planners, architects, local politicians, and the general public are now recognizing that if we design more sensitively, the benefits will be felt for generations.

Long-term solutions begin with understanding how your own home fits into the greater community. Most builders start the design of a building with a drawing of the plans and elevations at $1/4''$ scale—and they stop there too. But a successful building requires a larger frame of reference. From the macro to the micro level, we need to appreciate the interconnectedness of our work with the world around us.

Think about the Planet

The single most important issue for future development is sustainability: meeting our needs in the present without jeopardizing our resources for the future. But sustainable design does not just mean installing double-glazed windows or thicker insulation, and it doesn't *just* mean using eco-friendly products such as solar energy panels or "green roofs" on which plantings take the place of shingles or tiles. All these things come into play, but they are valueless if we don't make a far deeper contribution to supporting our fragile environment.

The first step is to build for longevity. Our houses need to be built to last—and that isn't just a question of durable materials. They need to be places in which we love to live over time. That's how a building proves its worth, not just in the short term, but forever. It's been said that it's a lot harder to knock down a beautiful building that everyone loves than an ugly one that no one cares about.

Think carefully about the materials that you use. Remember—whether you're a designer, a builder, or a homebuyer—that good materials are worth paying for. Be responsible in your specifications and look for materials that can be maintained for many years to come, that won't just deteriorate and end up in the trash.

1.2 What You Need to Think About

In a word: everything. To be authentic, the design of a building needs to incorporate big-picture themes with attention to both the arrangement of the façade and the details.

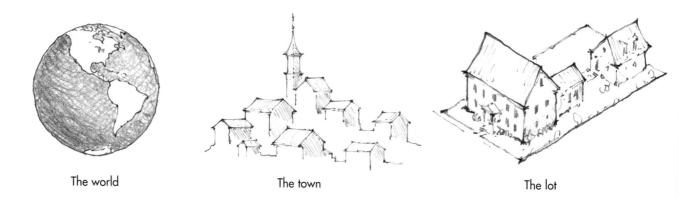

The world   The town   The lot

Think about the Town

Buildings are more than units in which to live or work. Collectively, they can make up towns and cities. When we think about the places we admire most, we are often thinking not about individual buildings, but instead about the way in which they relate to one another.

A group of plain three-story townhouses creates a marvelous *street* in New Orleans or Charleston. In a set of simple Craftsman bungalows in the Chicago suburbs, generous porches create a sense of community, a wider sense of belonging to a place.

Now compare those groupings to the typical post-war suburban tract. None of the houses relate to one another. A wide road (designed for cars, not people) leads inexorably from one placeless development to the next. But these houses and this road did not just spring up out of the ground by themselves. They were masterminded, budgeted, financed, and constructed—by professionals who had lost the old art of building towns.

Think about the Lot

Closer to home, think carefully about how your house is placed on its lot. Is there an old tree, or the line of a street, or the height of your neighbors' ridgeline to respond to? Are there local materials to respect? On a street of clapboard houses, would you want to build something in brick? Where will you position the garage or carport—on the street front? Or would it be better tucked behind the house, so that you have *windows* looking out at the world passing by?

Work to define the space you have with courtyards and gardens. The smallest spaces can also be the most private if they are designed properly. Suburban tract developments waste acres of land simply because the individual lots are not designed to define space, so achieving any sort of privacy requires building houses further and further apart.

Don't build the first thing that comes into your head. Don't swallow a tiny lot with a huge, dominating building. Think about your surroundings, and how each and every building can enhance or diminish them. Make sure you're not one of the villains!

The house

A window

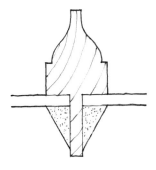

The details

Think about the Façade

Only now that you have thought about the big picture is it time to look at the building itself. The façade of your building is its public "face", quite literally. In the course of this book we will return many times to different considerations that shape the façade: design of windows and doors, their relative proportions, treatment of the roof, eaves, and chimneys.

Don't think about your façade in isolation from the rest of the building. Think carefully about what sort of rooms you want at the front and back of your house. Think in terms of solar orientation, use, and privacy: for instance, would you like your bedroom to receive direct afternoon sunlight, even if the south side of your home faces the street? But then check that the rooms work together to make a beautiful, well-proportioned elevation. Do you want a symmetrical façade? Do you prefer a more organic quality? Either way, your end result should be balanced. It should have a simple inevitability about it, so that you couldn't move anything at all without making it go wrong.

And most importantly, don't stop here with the design of the elevation; keep going and look closer.

Think about the Details

You may not believe that the details of window proportion or the thickness of a glazing bar could really make the difference between a building appearing right or wrong. In the biggest scheme of things, that may be right; we certainly don't want to be accused of failing to see the forest for the trees. But nonetheless, the small details do matter. Why?

It's the approach to details that makes something feel authentic. People recognize and respond to *the real thing*. What creates this elusive "authenticity", which makes us strive to own a particular brand of watch or jeans or eat a certain type of food? It's not just glossy advertising. It's in the details—the care and attention with which something is put together (the jewels in the watch, the stitching on the coat). Get these wrong, and it's not the "real thing" anymore. It is exactly the same in architecture.

The Elements of Authenticity

Authenticity is *not* about how old something is. It is about how well it is made and whether it is created with genuine understanding of its form and its function. Authentic traditional building depends on getting the details right without losing sight of the big picture. To do this successfully, keep these key concepts in mind as you plan every facet of your house.

HOW TO USE THIS BOOK

As we explained at the beginning of this chapter, architecture is like a language. It has a vocabulary (the windows, doors, eaves, etc.) and a grammar (the rules that we use to assemble elements). Each chapter addresses a different element of the house, from the big-picture ideas to the finest details, looking at both the vocabulary and the grammar of architecture.

Because so many of the ideas we discuss are repeated themes throughout the book, we have included a layer of cross-references to help you navigate between topics, so you can read from cover to cover or skip from section to section.

WARNING: Don't take this book too literally. In some cases we are very direct about a detail to use or avoid, in other cases the issue is not as black and white. Often, the "use" example is one of many good alternatives. Due to logistics and limited pages, we were not able to illustrate every option. Use this book as a point of departure. Don't take it too seriously or too literally. Use it to learn the language. Then use what you have learned to break all of the rules and have fun.

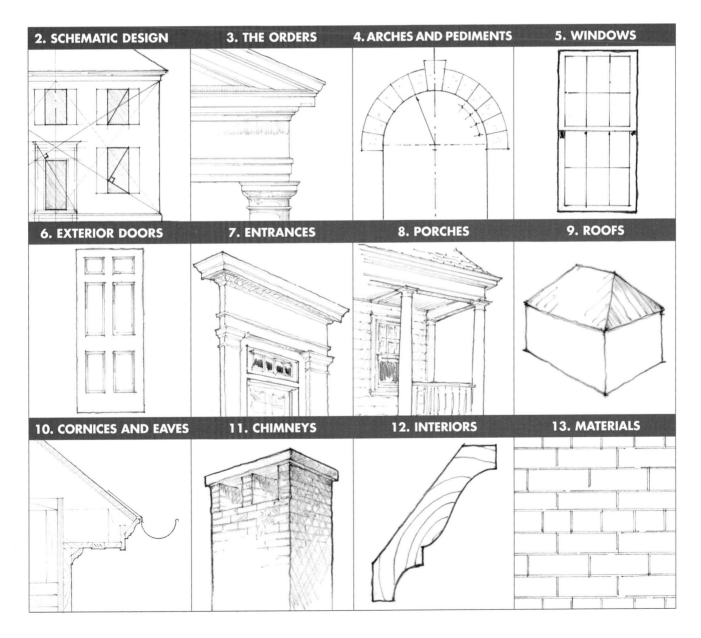

2. SCHEMATIC DESIGN
3. THE ORDERS
4. ARCHES AND PEDIMENTS
5. WINDOWS
6. EXTERIOR DOORS
7. ENTRANCES
8. PORCHES
9. ROOFS
10. CORNICES AND EAVES
11. CHIMNEYS
12. INTERIORS
13. MATERIALS

1.3 **Does Your Design Add Up?**

AVOID

Don't use a design in which the individual elements don't relate to each other. Successful building design is more than randomly assembling pieces and parts.

USE

A design is successful when the whole is greater than the sum of its parts, with each element sized, scaled, and located in relation to the other elements of the building.

(1) MAKE THE WHOLE GREATER THAN THE SUM OF ITS PARTS

Thinking about the building as a whole is very important. The most beautiful design element—a finely detailed door surround, well executed eave return, or elegant bay window—will look out of place if it is not integrated with the rest of the building.

Everything should add up to create a harmonious composition where nothing can be changed without spoiling the design. It's about achieving balance and harmony visible from a distance, so that nothing dominates the building unnecessarily—no huge dormers, no ridiculous columns, no giant garage doors.

Figure 1.3 shows two similar houses: both have five bays with a gable roof, pediment porticoes and gable dormers. From down the street, 1.3 (top) is going to look unbalanced, because the elements bear little relation to one another. The windows are poorly spaced, the dormers overpower the windows below, and the portico overpowers the entire house.

By contrast, 1.3 (bottom) shows a house that has a balanced composition. The windows are rationally spaced, away from the building's corners. The dormers are modest and scaled in relation to the windows below. The entry surround contributes to the design without overpowering it. A pair of chimneys terminates the composition. Even from a distance, these details and relationships will be apparent.

The chapters ahead will discuss fine details one by one, from windows to chimneys. But first, think of your building as a *whole composition*. Don't let the individual elements or planning requirements take over and throw the composition out of balance.

The Squint Test

How will your design look from across the street? Stand back from your drawing and squint your eyes. What stands out? Where does your eye go?

In a balanced composition the hierarchy of elements is clear. Generally, the focus should be on the front door. If the design is unbalanced, the eye is confused and does not know what to look at first.

(2) KEEP IT SIMPLE: LESS IS MORE

Don't do everything at once. It was the modernist architect Mies van der Rohe who coined the phrase "less is more." When it comes to 1970s glass office towers, some may agree with Robert Venturi's brilliant counter-attack—"less is a bore"—but in traditional housebuilding, we can actually learn lessons from this idea.

Much beauty in traditional architecture arises from balance: emphasizing some elements while simplifying others. This creates a *hierarchy* within the house, focusing energy on the most important parts. The goal is to create a building that is interesting but not overwhelming and confused. Of course, many traditional buildings *do* have wonderful decoration. But it is all placed within a context that respects the hierarchy of the building—its importance within the town, and the importance of each elevation, and the importance of each element in the façade. The key to achieving this balance comes from knowing when to pull back and when to add more.

Most traditional architecture is surprisingly simple. A Nantucket saltbox or Southern Greek Revival farmhouse rarely has many specifically "architectural" elements. Its success is derived from *proportion*, *scale*, *harmony*, and *good detailing*. Simple buildings allow the builder to spend money where it is required: a generous eave, better quality brick, a substantial masonry chimney, and a simple, well-designed door surround.

Today, very often people mistakenly think that a house needs a lot of "detail" to make it "traditional." A bunch of expensive and vacuous bits of vaguely classical trim are ordered, ready to be tacked on here and there. This is a total waste of time and money.

It is not necessary, or even practical, to put every element on every building. Save the budget and spend it where it counts. Remember that good *proportion* does not cost more and use this to your advantage.

Make a commitment to yourself to do only what you can afford to do well. Doing less, but doing it really well, is always better than trying everything and doing none of it well enough.

1.4 **Less Is More**

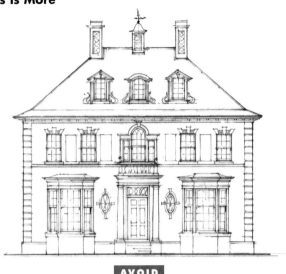

AVOID

Don't use every element you can think of in a single building. Even if each element is well detailed, it can be too much for the composition.

USE

The beauty of traditional architecture comes from simplicity and hierarchy. Focusing your energy (and budget) on the most important elements of the house will create a calm composition that feels right.

1.5 **Structural Common Sense**

Does your design stay true to traditional materials? Could it stand on its own? Are post and beam in balance?

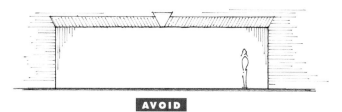

AVOID

Avoid long spans that could not stand without hidden structure. The eye recognizes that this brick lintel would fall down.

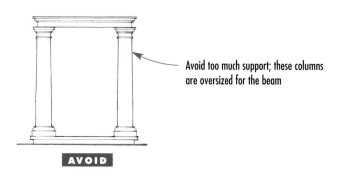

Avoid faux rustication patterns that would collapse if the wall were actually made of stone

AVOID

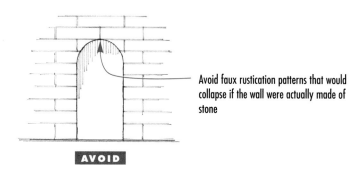

Avoid too much support; these columns are oversized for the beam

AVOID

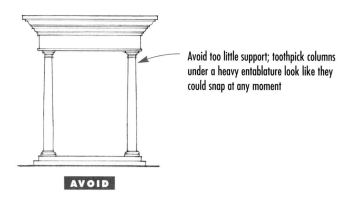

Avoid too little support; toothpick columns under a heavy entablature look like they could snap at any moment

AVOID

(3) DESIGN WITH COMMON SENSE: STRUCTURE CHECK

Modern construction methods have freed us from many of the constraints that shaped traditional building elements in the past. No longer bound by the limits of wood and stone, we can span long distances with thin members or cantilever large platforms out from a wall.

This is all very well for a skyscraper or airport terminal, but not appropriate for a traditional house. If you want an authentic design, remember the structural capacities of traditional materials, even when you're using hidden structural elements to support them.

Stay True to Materials

Wood spans further than masonry and requires less support. Masonry is stronger, but its openings are narrower because it is more difficult and expensive to span long distances in stone construction. You can avoid many mistakes by remembering the practical reasons behind traditional designs and staying true to your materials.

Size Posts and Beams Correctly

Are your columns sized correctly to carry their loads? Figure 1.5 (second from bottom) illustrates columns that are unnecessarily large for the beam that they are carrying. The outsized columns make the composition look like a cartoon. In the drawing below it, the columns are *undersized* for the entablature above, giving the feeling that at any moment they might snap in two from the weight that they are carrying. In both cases the imbalance between post and beam creates a design that is unconvincing, because it lacks structural common sense.

Not-So-Common Sense

Using common sense in design has become not so common. This is one reason why so many new traditional buildings look like cartoons. A detail will be disruptive to your design if it doesn't make sense and at least *look* like it could work.

(4) DESIGN WITH COMMON SENSE: PRACTICALITY CHECK

Most elements of a traditional building originate from necessity. The width of an opening, roof pitch, depth of the eave projection, or detail of a drip molding: all have a good practical basis.

Today, many of these once functional elements have become largely ornamental. Plastic weather-proofing, for example, protects exterior walls from water as well as a deep eave projection. With function no longer an issue, design has often lost sight of a basic tenet of good traditional building—that it should be fit for purpose.

Could It Really Work?

Always think of the practical requirements of and reasons for the elements you are using, and then ask yourself, could it really work? Is it *believable*? If you are unconvinced, the chances are anyone else judging your house will be unconvinced as well.

Shutters were historically used for security and to provide protection from weather. Today, they are frequently installed too small to cover the windows and glued onto the wall several inches from the jamb (1.6 top). Why bother? If you are going to use shutters, at least make them *look* as if they could work.

Is It Really Necessary?

Figure 1.6 (center) shows a small gable "pop-up" above a window. But note that the head of the window is *below* the eaves line. If the window doesn't ride above the eaves line, why go to the trouble and expense of making the mini-gable? It's clearly not required for a good practical purpose, such as making room for a window within a sloping roof.

When it comes to balconies, canopies, or other projections, be sure the loads are visually transferred to the ground. Don't use anything that looks like it needs to be held up by the proverbial "sky-hook" (1.6 bottom). It doesn't matter if an element is engineered to the highest standards—it's perception that counts.

1.6 Practical Common Sense

Could your design really work? Is it necessary? Does it feel right?

Avoid shutters that could never close. These are obviously vinyl planks nailed to the wall. Why bother?

Avoid gratuitous pop-ups. A traditional building rarely has architectural details that don't serve a purpose.

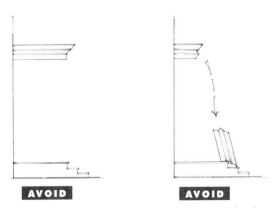

Avoid cantilevered door surrounds held up by a "sky-hook." Always use brackets to support projecting details and visually transfer the load back to the ground.

1.7 **Shadow and Texture**

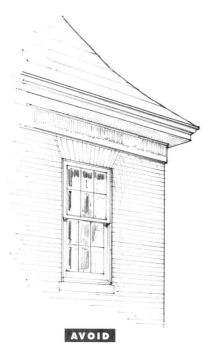

AVOID

Avoid wire cut brick and flush mounted windows (along with the absence of planting) give the wall the appearance of a thin veneer.

USE

Create rich texture by choosing materials such as handmade brick, setting the window back to create a reveal, and using sensitive landscaping.

(5) DESIGN WITH TEXTURE: SHADOW AND LANDSCAPE

Why do so many new buildings appear flat and static while older buildings are rich and interesting? Old buildings come alive in the texture of a brick, the shadow from a window reveal, or the softening of a creeping vine. Two buildings that look identical on paper can feel completely different once built, depending on the selection of materials, the detailing of elements, and the landscaping.

Shade and Shadow

A house's striking patterns of light and shade arise in part from practical requirements. Traditional load-bearing walls were thick, so the jambs at an opening were deep, throwing a longer shadow. Likewise, substantial eaves were used to throw water far from the walls and foundation. Among more formal elements, even a simple door surround, chimney cap, or any projection from the wall plane gives texture to a façade.

Many new buildings look bland by comparison. The most obvious difference is seen at the windows. Setting the window back even a few inches gives the house depth and makes it feel substantial. Projecting muntins, to separate panes of glass, give the building scale and add more shadow. New windows, by contrast, are typically placed flush with the exterior, their muntins flat and clipped on to one side only. To the eye, this makes the difference between seeing the exterior walls as substantial construction and seeing them as a thin, inauthentic veneer. Ensure that your moldings have enough depth and structure to work convincingly, with clear definition between highlights and shadow lines.

Landscape and Hardscape

Even a well-built house will look absurd if it is marooned in a sea of asphalt or bright red concrete pavers. Think carefully when specifying hardscape: consider using rolled gravel instead of asphalt, bricks rather than concrete pavers. Avoid brightly colored materials—natural, stone-colored materials always look more sympathetic. *Always* specify materials that will age well.

(6) DESIGN FOR PLACE: APPROPRIATE MATERIALS AND DETAILS

Traditional architecture has developed over time in response to specific climatic and environmental conditions as well as regional trends. While all traditional buildings share common approaches to design, their appearance and detailing can change considerably from region to region. A Georgian building in New England has the same proportional system and design elements as a Georgian building in the South. Yet the buildings are very different. For example, the eaves projection in the New England house would be greatly reduced to let in as much light as possible during darker winter months. The Southern house would need deeper eaves to block the hot sun and cast away water from summer storms.

Historically, choice of material, likewise, varied from region to region. Twentieth-century industrial production, together with a general decline in attention to the uniqueness of local environments, turned design in a catastrophically different direction. Now buildings from Texas to Alaska are assembled using the same pre-packaged components, the same flat roofs, and requiring the same extensive mechanical systems to keep them cool in summer and warm in winter.

The traditional building should be designed to work with the local climate, not to combat it with mechanical engineering and synthetic materials. Specify local materials wherever possible, instead of shipping (for thousands of miles) generic products that bear no regional relevance.

Respect for the local environment, climate, and geology is integral to traditional architecture. We need to create new buildings that respond as beautifully today as in the past to a local "sense of place". It is these variations that make a building feel authentic and appropriate. Without them it can look like it has landed from outer space.

1.8 Using Appropriate Materials

Use materials and designs appropriate for your climate and region.

Colonial

Large central chimneys kept New England Colonials warm; in Mid-Atlantic Colonials, the chimneys moved to the outside walls.

Deep South or Caribbean

Hipped roofs allow for broad eaves to shade four sides of the house; deep verandas capture breezes.

Mediterranean

Less humid climates deal with heat through massive construction and blinds to regulate sunlight; tile roofs require a low pitch, good for climates that do not have heavy rainfall.

Arid

In very hot climates with low rainfall, flat-roofed adobe buildings with small windows work with local weather and materials.

1.9 SUVs and Urbanism

The building industry has more impact on the environment than the automobile industry. Cars may contribute to global warming, but only because roads are planned in a way that requires people to drive several hours a day. Building compact communities with connected roads and a mix of uses will not only improve our quality of life, but also greatly reduce our dependence on fossil fuels and combat global warming.

1.10 Sustainable Building Design

The most sustainable design is one that people love and want to maintain over time. This extends beyond individual buildings or materials. It speaks to the communities that we build.

(7) BUILD SUSTAINABLE DESIGNS

We are coming to a new awareness of the impact we humans are making on the environment and the planet as a whole. Disturbing reports of global warming and its long-term implications have become commonplace in the mainstream media. The only things more depressing that the constant deluge of news on the topic is our ability to ignore the issue, first, because we can't see the literal effects in our day-to-day lives, and second, because most of us feel helpless to do anything to effect change.

But it is within our means, in our own lifetime, to implement a change in society that will reduce if not reverse the damage that we are doing to our planet. In large part, we can make this change through the building industry, in the designs of our cities and towns and in the way we build our houses.

Planning for Sustainability

Today when we hear about "green" or sustainable architecture, we think of specific building products such as green roofs or solar panels. These are important elements of sustainable design, but they are not enough. Green design needs to start at the level of city planning. We need compact, walkable, mixed-use communities that reduce our dependence on the automobile and fossil fuels. This is not to say that we should eliminate cars, but simply that it should not be necessary for the average American living in a new suburban home to get on the freeway to get coffee in the morning.

But to be truly sustainable, we need to do more than look at our cities. We need to think about the individual design of each building. All too often in recent years, "green" architecture has turned into a showcase for products—but as we mentioned on the first page of this book, the most sustainable building of all is one that people love and don't want to tear down.

To make a building sustainable in this way, we need to start with a timeless design. And achieving a timeless design means looking at the details and understanding the principles of traditional architecture. Timeless may not always mean traditional, but it finds its roots there: as with most things in life, you have to know the rules before you can break them.

(8) LEARN THE VOCABULARY

The elements we've looked at so far are pieces of the big picture, and they are all important—not only for traditional architects but for *all* designers. We think that traditional design comes up with the best solutions to a lot of these problems. And we certainly believe that unless they have been considered you can't really call your building traditional.

Chapter 3 will delve deep into the foundation of traditional architecture: the classical Orders, from Tuscan to Corinthian. Although most people think it refers only to a column, an Order is actually a complete set of integrated elements: pedestal, column, and entablature. These parts give a building its system of proportion, setting the cornice height and determining the design of most elements, such as door surrounds, window lintels, and eaves. If classical architecture is a language, the Orders are the grammar that makes it coherent. Every element within the Order has a name, from the column to the smallest moldings—the real vocabulary of authentic design—and it's difficult to design a traditional building competently without knowing these basic definitions. Before you can use and apply the elements, you need to know what they are called.

You'll find a glossary at the end of this book, and we will define less common terms as we go along. But for now, there are several definitions that are critical to our discussions. Take time to study the relationships of the parts. Commit them to memory, because it is in the application of these elements that most—if not all—of the common mistakes are made.

1.11 Learn the Definitions

In an age before hidden structural solutions and modern synthetic materials, each element of a building had to serve a specific and crucial function. Every element of classical architecture derives from those rigorous requirements, serving the building's most basic need: to stand up and shed water.

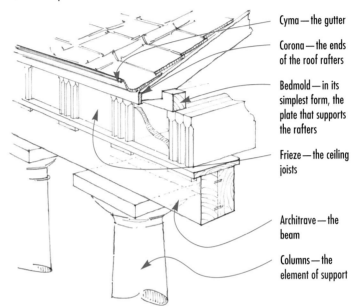

Cyma—the gutter
Corona—the ends of the roof rafters
Bedmold—in its simplest form, the plate that supports the rafters
Frieze—the ceiling joists
Architrave—the beam
Columns—the element of support

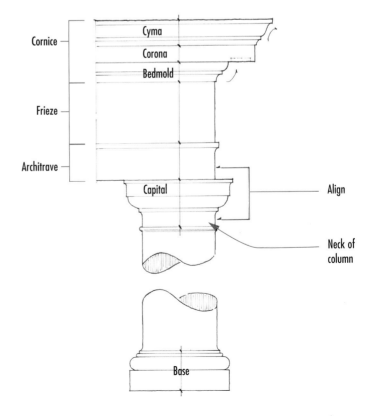

(9) DO ALL OF THIS BECAUSE IT MATTERS

You might be asking yourself, what on earth are these people talking about? The size of a shutter, shade and shadow, city planning, and now the vocabulary of the Doric Order? What is going on? Why does all of this matter?

It matters because design matters. Design makes a difference. Design principles, from the big-picture issues of the planet to the details of the Orders, work together to create the places we call home. What's more, the value of a place grows exponentially when the design is more than functional. Design cannot be quantified on a spreadsheet, but it absolutely can help the bottom line.

Many of the points that we have made in this chapter and will make throughout this book may seem minor, but they matter nonetheless. They matter because these are the details that transform the dialogue around the sale of a house: instead of selling square footage and a tick list of "features," we are creating communities with social capital.

The Vitruvian Triad

Architecture, the art of building, has the power to transform a shelter into a home. But architecture requires balance—a mix of function, economy, and aesthetic, or, as the Roman architect Vitruvius put it, "firmness, commodity, and delight." This timeless premise, first written in A.D. 20, remains today at the heart of good design.

Firmness

Good design must work well and last long. It must be sustainable in its construction, in its location, and in its ability to remain in service over time as its uses change.

Commodity

Many beautiful designs have been drawn on paper over the years. But architecture is about building, not just drawing. A good design must also be a design that can be built. Traditional details may cost more to get right; this is why it is important to carefully choose the elements in your building and use only designs that you can do well. Be smart about where you use expensive elements and simplify other areas of your design.

Delight

Vitruvius knew it. Design matters. Beauty may be in the eye of the beholder, but authentic details and materials, appropriate to place and based on fundamental principles of structure and proportion, resonate with every eye.

Where to Go from Here

In this chapter, we have covered the whole spectrum—everything it takes to get your house right. Keep these principles in mind as your read the rest of the book. Think about the big picture and think about the details; in the balance of the two you will find good design.

CHECKLIST

Secrets of a Successful Design

1. Make the Whole Greater than the Sum of Its Parts

❑ Is everything balanced?

❑ Is the building organized under one roof?

❑ Does anything dominate (dormers, portico, garage doors)?

2. Keep It Simple: Less Is More

❑ Can you find the front door?

❑ Is there meaning, hierarchy and focus to your design?

❑ Are the important areas emphasized?

❑ Does it pass the 'Squint Test'?

3. Design with Common Sense: Structure Check

❑ Is the design true to traditional materials?

❑ Are posts and beams correctly sized in relation to each other?

❑ Could it work without hidden structure?

❑ Are loads transferred to the ground or are you employing the "sky hook"?

4. Design with Common Sense: Practicality Check

❑ Is it believable?

❑ Could the shutters work?

❑ Are elements necessary or are they gratuitous?

5. Design with Texture: Shadow and Landscape

❑ Does the selection of materials enrich the texture of the building?

❑ Do windows and eaves help to define the building by creating shadows?

❑ Is there landscaping to soften the building?

❑ Does the landscape palette make sense for your region?

6. Design for Place: Appropriate Materials and Details

❑ Does it respond to local climate?

❑ Does it use local materials?

❑ Does it enhance sense of place?

7. Build Sustainable Designs

❑ Is the urbanism around the house sustainable?

❑ Is the design timeless in nature?

❑ It is built for long term?

8. Learn the Vocabulary

❑ Do you know the names of the elements you are using?
(If you don't know the name, you're probably not using it correctly.)

9. Do All of This Because It Matters

❑ Does your design balance Firmness, Commodity, and Delight?

❑ Have you created mere shelter or real architecture?

How does your building score?

Chapter 2

SCHEMATIC DESIGN

"Schematic Design" is the first phase of any architectural project. This is the stage where we start with a blank sheet of paper and begin the process of developing the basic composition of the house. In this phase of the project, special emphasis is given to balancing aesthetic goals such as massing, architectural style, and layout of the plan with practical constraints such as site and budget.

SCHEMATIC DESIGN

SEVERAL BASIC DESIGN IDEAS need to be thought about from the start. Get them right, and everything else (from selecting the right materials to working up the details) tends to fall into place. Get them wrong—and however much effort you put in later, the house will still feel wrong. This part of Schematic Design really has to do with what we call "composition." Its importance cannot be overemphasized. It is the difference between creating mere shelter and a building of real beauty.

The goal of composition is to find unity in design; to create a work in which nothing can be added or subtracted without affecting the integrity of the whole. This is what is meant by the phrase "the whole is more than the sum of the parts." Designing, in plan and elevation, needs to be more than putting together a collection of elements. By combining the elements in thoughtful ways, so that each contributes to a bigger picture, we can create buildings that are often very simple in their details but where everything works together to make a beautiful whole.

Beauty in building comes from five elements: Order, Proportion, Hierarchy, Balance and Scale. These are words deep in meaning, yet difficult to define. However, to give ourselves a common frame of reference, we will try to define them.

- **Order:** The rationale behind the design; the sequence of space; the way in which the building is read and how it is experienced.
- **Proportion:** A system for the arrangement of parts that relates all the elements of the design to one another.
- **Hierarchy:** Placing the emphasis on the most important elements of the building through primary, secondary and tertiary elements. Hierarchy guides the eye and helps us understand the building—for example, allowing us to find the front door or recognize the primary rooms without even thinking.
- **Balance:** The relationship between parts of the building, making sure that the "weight" of each part is evenly distributed. Balance is most obvious in a symmetrical façade, but is perhaps even more important in asymmetrical design.
- **Scale:** The relationship between the sizes of different elements. Scale lets us read how large a building is, as well as the individual elements that compose that building. Scale is not to be mistaken for size. Elements of completely different sizes can share the same scale, if they are detailed consistently.

A successful design thinks about these elements in parallel with the program (requirements for the plan such as number and type of rooms and proposed square footage), the budget, and the site constraints. Good architecture is about balancing the practical and the ideal—which is the reason why so much traditional architecture is so satisfying. In its essence, traditional architecture is simply this combination of beautiful and practical.

It is true that in some cases getting the details of traditional architecture right can increase the cost of a building. But good proportions and order in the design don't cost more; in fact, they are often more economical than the alternatives. They simply require knowing a few rules of thumb and designing with the intent to create beauty.

2.1 Schematic Design

In this stage of the project, all the constraints—material, financial, and site—are resolved, together with architectural composition, to result in a building that is both fit for purpose and beautiful in itself.

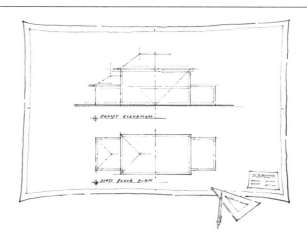

2.2 **Massing to Use**

A simple plan is not only practical, but also has its own innate repose and beauty. These diagrams show examples of how to work your extensions and additions sympathetically. The top row shows narrow-front houses, the bottom shows wide-front houses; both types show extensions off the back and to the side. In all examples the houses have a clearly defined main structure and smaller wings that work in harmony with the primary mass of the house.

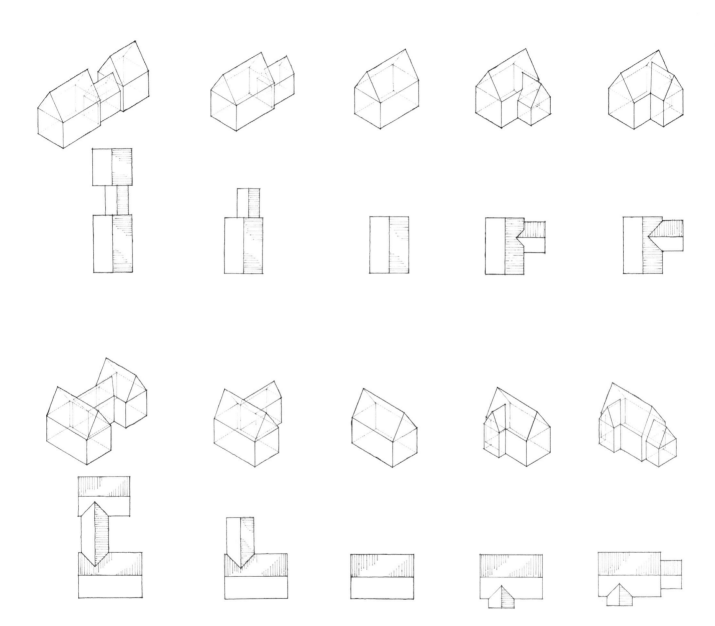

2.3 **Massing to Avoid**

Avoid a relentless number of extensions and gables that swell from every corner of the building and designs where no thought has been given to organizing the masses under a simple, coherent roof form.

McMansion massing

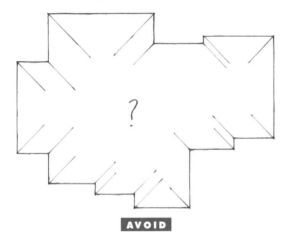

AVOID

Avoid a floor plan that results in a complicated roof plan; it will be difficult to build and create a chaotic streetscape.

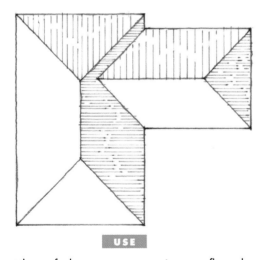

USE

Think about the roof when you are arranging your floor plan. Assemble the rooms coherently in a way that that can easily be covered without complicated hips and valleys. The house will be easier to build and will contribute to the streetscape.

MASSING AND THE STREETSCAPE

The first step in designing a building is to determine the massing: the way its volumes are put together. Simple forms are easier to understand; a house with complicated massing that generates endless hips and gables will lack focus and have a confused hierarchy. The best details in the world cannot save a building that has lost control of its form.

Design from the Roof Plan Down

To start, determine the primary mass of the building. At its simplest, a traditional house is often a square or rectangular box, more interior space, add regular volumes that resolve into the primary mass. Don't let the secondary masses get larger than the primary volume of the building.

The massing of a building is determined in the first stages of design, while the floor plans are still being resolved. The fatal flaw of the McMansion is that the floor plan is usually a jumbled combination of rooms—with little or no thought given to the roof plan above. These complicated forms become a framer's nightmare, but still worse, from the point of view of the streetscape, they are an aesthetic mess.

A helpful design strategy is to work back and forth between the floor plan and the roof plan. As rooms are added, make sure that the combination of spaces can be easily resolved under one roof.

Think about the Neighborhood and Streetscape

In the same way that a successful building design is more than a collection of individual elements, a successful neighborhood design is more than a collection of buildings.

In a traditional neighborhood, houses work together to create streetscapes. Rather than each building generating all its own interest, traditional buildings work together to create outdoor rooms. Every building doesn't need to be a focal point. In fact, if you try to make each building a focal point, the opposite occurs, and nothing stands out. Suppress the urge to add extra steps and complicated massing; the only thing that it will add to your building is cost.

2.4 **The Streetscape**

AVOID

Avoid houses that attempt to contain an entire streetscape in a single building elevation through complicated massing and by treating materials like wallpaper. McMansions compete with each other and take away from the street as a whole. Each house attempts to be the center of attention, making it impossible for any one of them to be noticed.

USE

Think about how your house looks in a streetscape. Every house does not need to have every element or be the center of attention. Successful streets have buildings that work together to create a larger composition, which gives the feeling of being in a graceful outdoor "room".

2.5 **Front-Loaded Garages**

In some cases the site plan requires the house to have a front-loaded garage. If this is the case, mitigate the presence of the garage on the street by pushing the front of the garage back behind the front of the house.

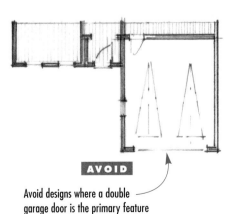

AVOID

Avoid designs where a double garage door is the primary feature of the front elevation.

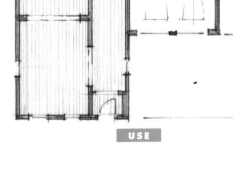

USE

When using a front-loaded garage, set the garage back a minimum of 6 feet, but ideally 18 feet, which allows a car to sit in front of the garage without stepping out in front of the house. Also, avoid double-wide garage doors, because they accentuate the horizontality of the garage.

2.6 **Start with the Roof Plan**

Design from the roof plan down, not from the floor plan up. Think about the volumes of the house before you get locked into a floor plan that cannot be covered with simple forms.

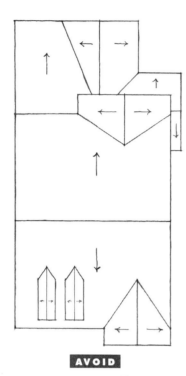

Avoid roof plans with complex geometry and an awkward combination of slopes.

AVOID

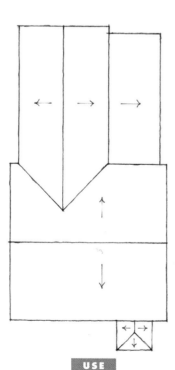

Use simple volumes that are easy to cover with a roof; limit the number of roof slopes.

USE

DESIGNING THE ENTIRE BUILDING

A common mistake in contemporary traditional architecture is to simplify the massing, yet still cover the building with every conceivable building element. Remember, KEEP IT SIMPLE—LESS IS MORE! Use restraint. Use fewer elements, but do the ones that you are doing really well. Spend money on material, rather than wasting it trying to add interest everywhere.

Massing and Style

The massing of a building relates closely to its architectural style. Georgian and Federal houses are simple symmetrical boxes with varying details by style. On the other hand, more organic or informal styles of architecture (such as Tudor or Arts and Crafts) derive from a very different type of volumetric organization. Be true to the style that you are using by studying historical precedent and existing examples. Avoid attempting to create a Tudor manor around a Georgian box, or a Federal house out of a Craftsman cottage. They won't look right, however well detailed or whatever the materials specification.

Laying out the Roof Plan

In Chapter 9 we will go into more detail about laying out a roof plan. For now, the important idea to note is, as we say again and again, keep it simple. Avoid using multiple slopes within a single roof volume. A simple adjustment in a drawing to make your building read well in elevation on paper will not translate well into three dimensions in the field. If the roof is too high in elevation, then perhaps it is too deep in plan.

Another common misstep in laying out the massing is ignoring the secondary masses once the primary mass is set. Figure 2.6 (top) illustrates a building that makes this mistake. The primary volume of space works well, but little thought has been given to how the roof fits over the rooms in the back of the house. The result is complicated spaces that awkwardly crash into each other. A building must work in three dimensions. It is easy to forget that every line on paper represents a three-dimensional object that has to be built.

2.7 Keep the Elevations Simple

Don't try to fit a McMansion in the space of a small traditional home. Limit the number of elements; spend more time and money on the elements that you do use. Don't forget the side and rear elevations, but think of the building as a whole; be aware of the connection to the backyard as well as light and ventilation to interior rooms.

AVOID

Front elevation

Avoid too many elements in a single elevation, which throw off the scale of the building.

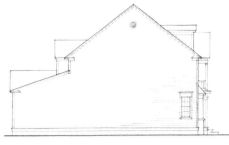

Side elevation

Avoid long blank side elevations without windows.

AVOID

Side and rear elevations

Avoid complicated massing, with too few windows.

USE

Front elevation

Use a small number of well built elements.

Side elevation

Don't forget the windows!

USE

Side and rear elevations

Use simple volumes that make the building a whole.

2.8 **Unity and Duality**

The relationship between opening and solid is crucial to the character of your building. Duality leaves the eye uncertain where to rest; unity creates harmony and a sense of natural repose.

1 bay: single opening, center void

2 bays: paired openings, center occupied by a wall, and each window of equal importance so the eye has nowhere to rest

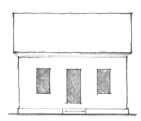

3 bays: symmetrical openings with windows balanced on either side, making the door clearly the most important element in the façade

5 bays: evenly balanced, symmetrical façade directs the eye very clearly to the center

THE CANON OF THE NUMBER

Composition, at its most essential, is concerned with the organization of *solid* (walls) and *void* (openings, doors or windows). The number of openings and the way they are arranged establish the character of the building at an early stage. In traditional architecture, this relationship is called the *canon of the number*. It depends on three key concepts: symmetry, unity and duality.

Symmetry

Symmetry is a well-known term for the exact reflection of shapes around a central (or "mirror") line. Much that's created in nature is symmetrical; and at a deep level, symmetry can be equated with beauty—not least, with regard to the human body or face. Symmetry, like proportion, is a unifying agent. It adds order and repose—or perfect balance—to a composition. For this reason, symmetry is a guiding principle of much classical architecture.

Unity and Duality

In any symmetrical building, there are two possible types of design. In one, the center is a void (often a door); in the other, the center is occupied by a solid (a wall or column).

The first type of design sets up what is called a *unity*. Unity always has an odd number of openings. The eye is led directly to the center, because this is the pivotal part of the composition. The second sets up what is called *duality*. Duality always has an even number of openings in a façade that create equal and competing centers. Because no opening is more important than its neighbor, the eye doesn't quite know where to rest.

Applying Unity and Duality

Harmonious composition seeks unity and avoids duality. For this reason, most classical facades have an odd number of bays. An even number of bays, reserved for secondary or side facades, help to emphasize the primary façade (2.8).

Prime numbers—numbers that can only be divided by themselves and 1—go one step further toward creating harmonious composition. Many classical buildings have 3, 5 or 7 bays. (13 is the next prime number, but that would be quite a large house!)

Larger buildings are often broken into a series of smaller bays. Avoid a rhythm of bays that sets up multiple centers across the façade. Instead use a duality on the side wings to focus attention on the center.

2.9 **Combining Unity and Duality**

The classical temple front has a clear centerline on the front door, making for a harmonious composition that clearly directs the eye. The side elevation has a central column, setting up duality on this façade. The eye doesn't know where to rest when looking at the side, so it quickly finds the front of the temple. This has the effect of further emphasizing the importance of the front door on the main elevation.

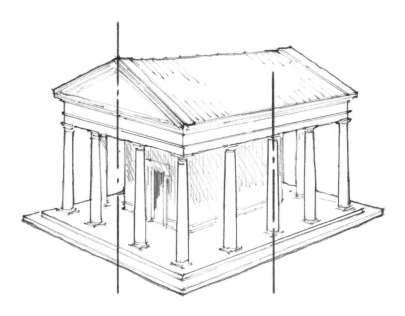

2.10 **Applying Unity and Duality**

On façades with seven or more bays, it is common to set a central bay forward, but be careful not to set up competing centers.

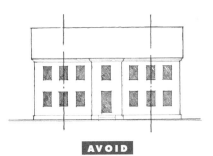 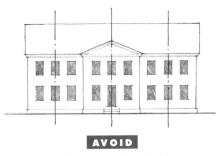 

AVOID	AVOID	USE
7-bay, 1-bay center	**9-bay, evenly divided**	**7 bay, 3-bay center**
Three-bay side wings with centers that compete with the front door	Side wings the same size as central bay, with their own centers, creating a double layer of competition for the eye	Paired bays on the side wings, clearly subsidiary to the front door

2.11 **Percentage of Opening**

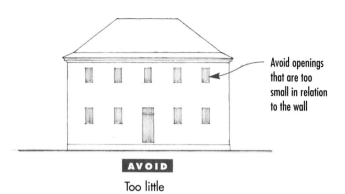

Avoid openings that are too small in relation to the wall

AVOID

Too little

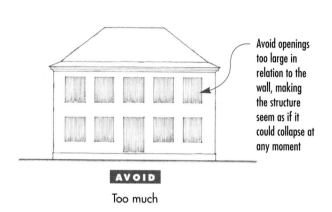

Avoid openings too large in relation to the wall, making the structure seem as if it could collapse at any moment

AVOID

Too much

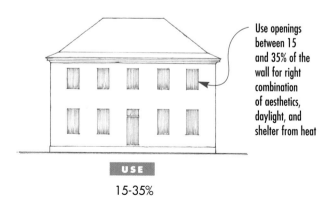

Use openings between 15 and 35% of the wall for right combination of aesthetics, daylight, and shelter from heat

USE

15-35%

THE OPENING AND THE WALL

Maintain the Structural Integrity

Consider the relationship of wall to opening (solid to void). Always try to maintain the feeling of a substantial wall structure. Traditional buildings did not have reinforced concrete or steel posts and lintels that could span long distances. Load-bearing walls required a structural integrity running from foundation to roof, with special consideration given to the strength of vulnerable areas such as the corner of a building. Openings punched in the wall presented the biggest threat to that integrity and their location within the façade was considered carefully.

Architects like Le Corbusier or Mies knew this. In fact, this is why their buildings appear just so revolutionary, with long strips of windows wrapping a corner or running floor to ceiling with no flanking masonry support. But the traditional building needs to follow rules of structural integrity and common sense based on traditional materials and methods.

Consider the Climate

Climatic considerations are very important when determining the size of your openings. As we will see time and again in this book, traditional design responds to not just a single concern but a variety of different requirements: practical, structural and aesthetic. It is interesting to see how regional variations inform the balance of wall to window.

In a Northern European city like Amsterdam, which has a temperate year-round climate but where daylight is at a premium, the canal houses have huge windows that take up as much of the wall as possible without compromising the structure. In Northern Africa, windows are kept deliberately tiny, so that buildings act like caves, staying cool in the summer heat and warm in cold winters. In America, such regional extremes are less distinct and are more dependent on the architectural style.

The 15-35 Percent Rule

Setting the percentage of wall openings to between 15 and 35 percent of the total wall area will balance good light quality in the house with visible structure, while leaving enough room for shutters if desired. As with all rules, there are exceptions: a sunroom or a large south-facing living room may have a larger percentage of openings, while windows on the north side of a building tend to be smaller. Figure 2.11 illustrates the progression of too little, too much and just right percentage of opening.

Vertical or Horizontal Windows?

The proportion of openings in traditional architecture varies, and it is difficult to provide hard-and-fast rules. More vernacular houses might have long, low openings, in contrast to the more formal, classical spirit provided by vertical sashes. But in general, traditional buildings have vertical openings. Horizontal openings can appear awkward on a house (2.12). Vertical proportions, by contrast, relate directly to the human figure, which was a vital design concern for the ancient and Renaissance architects who developed the patterns of classical architecture that we still use today (2.13).

Taking a common-sense approach provides a useful rule of thumb. A vertically proportioned window provides maximum light in relation to the width of the opening. The narrower the opening, the more economical the lintel required to span it—but the opening height can be whatever you like. Vertically proportioned openings tend, therefore, to make structural and economic sense.

Horizontal openings can be successfully used if there are vertical divisions within the overall span. This type of opening is commonly found in Arts and Crafts work and other less formal styles.

2.12 Proportion of Opening

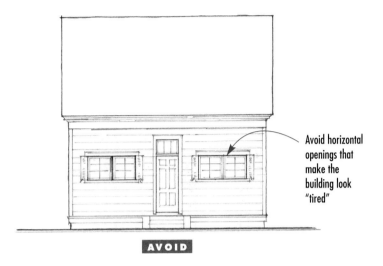

Avoid horizontal openings that make the building look "tired"

AVOID

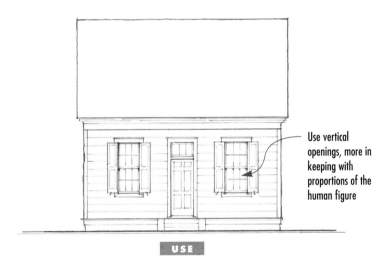

Use vertical openings, more in keeping with proportions of the human figure

USE

2.13 Window Proportions

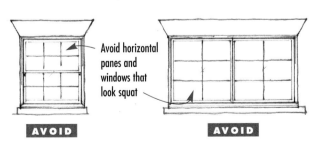

Avoid horizontal panes and windows that look squat

AVOID

AVOID

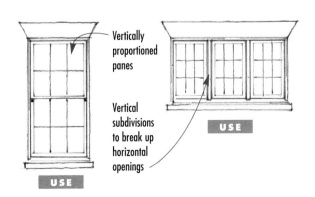

Vertically proportioned panes

Vertical subdivisions to break up horizontal openings

USE

USE

USE

2.14 **Arrangement of Openings**

Use a system of regulating lines to tie the composition together. In the lower design, window heads and sills align, and there is a coherent relationship between the proportions of the building and those of the window openings. The building appears harmonious; the whole is greater than the sum of the parts.

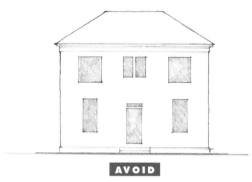

AVOID

Designs that lack a coherent relationship between openings

USE

Proportion of façade related to window openings within it

2.15 **Golden Section Rectangle**

In this classically pleasing proportion, the ratio of the whole to the larger part is the same as that of the larger part to the smaller.

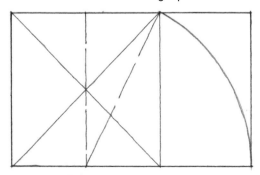

THE ARRANGEMENT OF OPENINGS

Regulating Lines

Applying a system of regulating lines across all of the openings and façade as a whole helps to create a harmonious composition. This ensures that all the elements of the elevation look coherent and relate to one another.

Figure 2.14 (top) shows a building with a random assembly of opening sizes and proportions. Even before the windows are divided, we can see that this building has a weak composition. Figure 2.14 (bottom), on the other hand, is tied together by a series of regulating lines. These diagonals relate the proportion and location of the windows to the door and its surround, as well as to the overall building.

The Golden Section

The Golden Section is a perfectly balanced asymmetrical division of a line in which the ratio of the smaller segment to the larger segment is equal to the ratio of the larger segment to the whole (the sum of the larger and smaller segments). Like *pi*, it is an irrational number that cannot be expressed in whole numbers, being approximately 1 to 1.618; that is, about 3 to 5 or 5 to 8. The Golden Section was first discovered and used in antiquity during the Golden Age of Greece. The numerical approximation of the ratio was embodied in the architecture and theory of the Italian Renaissance and rediscovered in the nineteenth century.

The ratio of the Golden Section creates a rectangle of universal beauty, which recurs throughout both natural and built environments (2.15). It can be a useful tool when laying out regulating lines on a building. Understanding and applying proportional systems is a complicated subject beyond the scope of this book; for now, the important lesson is that openings need to relate to the whole building, as well as each other.

Head and Sill Heights

Unless you've made a conscious design decision not to do so, all window heads and sills typically line through on a façade. Doors are unlikely to be as tall as a sash window, so their head heights can drop slightly from the windows, or the difference can be made up with a transom above the door. If the center bay has doors, one over the other, it can be nice to drop one of the door heights to keep the composition from becoming static. Be careful not to drop both doors, or the house will look like a sunken cake (2.16.)

As you work with window alignment in the elevation, watch that the windowsills don't get too high inside the rooms. On the first floor the typical distance from the floor is around 24″–30″. Second floor windows can ride a little higher, ranging from 30″–36.″ If the primary windowsills in a room are more than 36″ they will feel too tall (2.17).

Take the cornice into consideration when setting the heights of the windows. Ideally the second floor window heads will be set a minimum of 12″ below the bottom of the cornice or eave. This will allow the lintel or casing to be fully expressed and not cut short. If there is no room to do this, set the windows directly under the cornice. Avoid setting the windows more than 2″ or less than 8″ below the cornice, as this will visually cut the lintel short and make it look weak.

2.16 **Head Heights**

In general, align the head heights of doors and windows on elevations. In some cases, you may need to place doors at different heights; do so with care to avoid the "sunken cake" look.

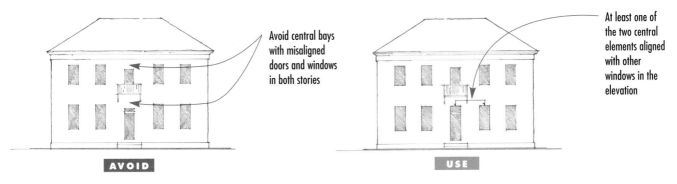

Avoid central bays with misaligned doors and windows in both stories

At least one of the two central elements aligned with other windows in the elevation

AVOID

USE

2.17 **Sill Heights**

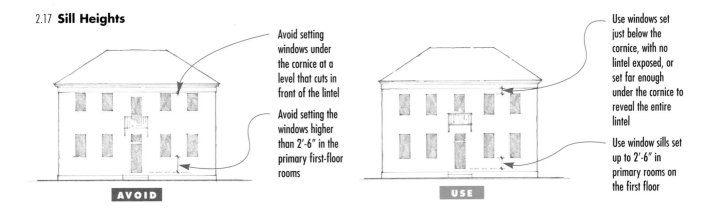

Avoid setting windows under the cornice at a level that cuts in front of the lintel

Avoid setting the windows higher than 2′-6″ in the primary first-floor rooms

Use windows set just below the cornice, with no lintel exposed, or set far enough under the cornice to reveal the entire lintel

Use window sills set up to 2′-6″ in primary rooms on the first floor

AVOID

USE

2.18 Punctuation

Every element of a building has a beginning, middle, and end. The end, or termination, is called a punctuation. The cornice punctuates the wall, the cyma punctuations the cornice, and a fillet punctuates the cyma. This layer of refinement is found in every element of the building as well as in nature.

2.19 Differentiation

Differentiation keeps elements from becoming dualities. Differentiated elements are similar in size and/or dimension, yet set apart by an emphasis in one direction or the other.

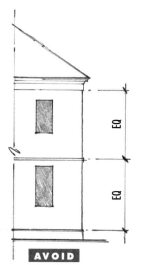
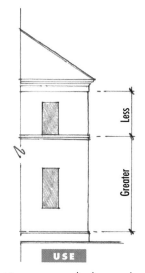

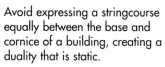

Avoid expressing a stringcourse equally between the base and cornice of a building, creating a duality that is static.

A stringcourse pushed up under the second-floor windows enlivens the façade and focuses attention on the more important floor.

PUNCTUATION, DIFFERENTIATION AND INFLECTION

Symmetry alone may make a façade feel a bit dull. The best facades have a combination of repose and movement. To keep the composition from becoming static, we add punctuation, differentiation, and inflection.

Punctuation

Few things in nature come to an abrupt end. They are almost always terminated in some way. In design (as in English grammar), we call this termination a *punctuation*. In nature, an arm is punctuated by a hand; the hand is punctuated by a finger; a finger is punctuated by the finger nail; and this in turn has its own small punctuation. Buildings have the same layers of refinement and punctuation (2.18).

Differentiation and Inflection

Differentiation and *inflection* introduce movement into the composition by creating hierarchy in some elements while deemphasizing others. Figure 2.19 (left) shows a two-story house with a stringcourse (horizontal band) equidistant from the cornice and the foundation. This design creates a duality because it is unclear which floor is more important. By differentiating between the two floors and inflecting the stringcourse up to just under the second-floor windows, we see that the primary focus of the building is on the first floor (2.19 right).

Window Inflection

Figure 2.20 shows the effect of inflection in window composition. This shifting of openings slightly off center creates subtle but enriching compositional relationships. In a five-bay house, the paired windows are inflected towards one another to create a less static rhythm across the façade. The largest space is left between the end window and the corner of the building. The second largest space is between the central bay and the first row of windows. The narrowest spacing is between the windows themselves.

Inflected windows have practical as well as aesthetic advantages. Often windows are inflected just enough to offset the exterior wall thickness, so they can be equally spaced in the room (2.21).

2.20 **Inflection**

A simple house will have even spacing between bays (below left). But inflecting the spacing slightly, giving a bit more breathing room to the center, makes the façade more interesting and emphasizes the front door (below right).

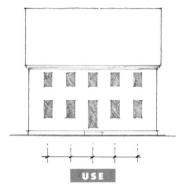

Equally spaced bays are fine, but can feel static.

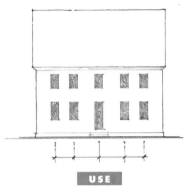

Inflecting windows places emphasis on the important elements of the façade.

2.21 **Inflection with Side Wings**

The windows on the left have been located in the center of the outside wall. Inflecting them slightly inwards reinforces the center of the house (and ensures that the windows will be correctly located inside the room).

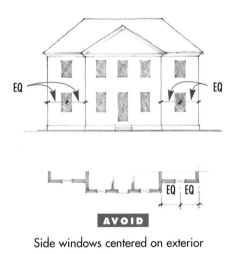

Side windows centered on exterior

Side windows centered in room

2.22 **Setting the Window Spacing**

To achieve harmonious spacing of windows, do the invisible-shutter test: Even if you are not using shutters, dot them on the elevation. If they overlap, the windows are too close; if there is a huge space between them, the windows are too far apart.

Avoid windows too close to the corners; they look wall-eyed

Avoid windows too close to the center of the house; they look cross-eyed

Windows evenly and correctly spaced feel harmonious

2.23 **Balancing the Fulcrum**

Find the center of balance for your building. In an asymmetrical design, the center of balance is usually not in the center of the composition.

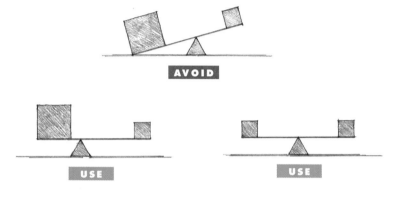

2.24 **Asymmetrical Composition**

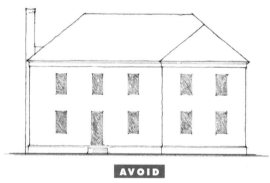

Avoid a symmetrical façade superimposed on asymmetrical massing, making the façade feel off balance (a problem compounded by the location of the chimney).

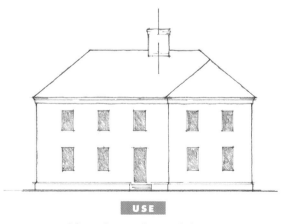

Repositioned front door and central chimney restore balance.

ASYMMETRICAL COMPOSITION

Asymmetrical buildings need to be composed just as carefully as symmetrical ones—perhaps more so, given that the asymmetry sets up complex compositional possibilities from the start. It is impossible to give too many hard-and-fast rules, because so much depends on the details of your design. But as you work, always remember to balance the visual weight of the composition.

Think of that simple experiment from school physics lab, using a fulcrum with a lever on it. A large weight near the fulcrum can be balanced by a smaller weight proportionally further away (2.23). Similar rules apply for architectural composition. Always consider the location of your "fulcrum", the center of the building, and keep the massing in balance around it.

The Two Layers of Asymmetrical Design

Asymmetrical compositions have two layers of design. The first layer is the massing and combination of volumes. The second layer is the arrangement of elements within each volume. A mistake that many make in this type of composition is to lay out asymmetrical volumes and fill them with symmetrically placed elements (2.24 top). This results in individual elements that are balanced, but an overall composition that feels weak. Instead, reinforce asymmetrical massing with an asymmetrical arrangement of elements (2.24 bottom). An asymmetrical arrangement of elements within each volume ties the composition together, each volume depending on the others to make sense. It is this interconnection that creates a whole greater than the sum of its parts.

Avoiding McMansions

McMansions are a prime example of asymmetrical composition gone wrong. They fail because the compositions are cluttered with volumes and elements attempting to create interest, rather than working together. Figure 2.25 illustrates two asymmetrical houses, one a McMansion, the other a small cottage. In the McMansion, several gables could be subtracted or 20 more added without an effect on the balance of the design. The cottage, on the other hand, feels balanced. Adding or taking away would need to be done skillfully or it would disrupt the composition.

Figure 2.26 illustrates another common type of McMansion, a series of classical design elements and volumes arranged asymmetrically. Avoid this type of design. It will never look like more than a cut-and-paste project. If you want an asymmetrical design, go all the way and design a building with asymmetrical volumes and elements. If you want a symmetrical building with classical details, design a symmetrical building with classical details. Do not attempt to merge these two types of building: the results are rarely good.

2.25 Asymmetrical Composition in Practice

The McMansion effect (top) has gables and extensions sprawling everywhere, but there is no logic or balance to the design; it could be added to indefinitely without making any difference. In the cottage (bottom), on the other hand, the asymmetrical elements are carefully weighted around the chimney to create a feeling of balance. Real skill would be needed to add to or take away from this composition without spoiling the design.

AVOID

USE

2.26 Symmetry or Not?

Another common McMansion effect is an asymmetrical volume with symmetrical, in this case "Georgian," details imposed on it. The composition of the house and its architectural details are fighting one another. If you want Georgian doors, windows, and details, use them—on a simple, symmetrical volume. This is intelligent use of traditional architecture, where the basic composition, the style, and the smallest details are related to one another to create a sensible, harmonious whole.

AVOID

USE

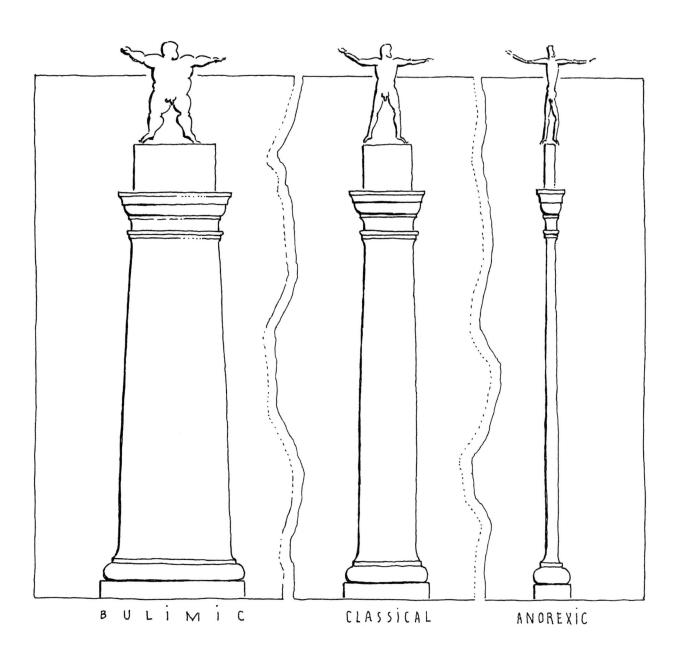

BULIMIC   CLASSICAL   ANOREXIC

Chapter 3

THE ORDERS

The classical Orders of architecture are the bedrock of traditional design. Across many cultures, and over thousands of years, the same underlying principles and details of design can be determined. While styles change, these essential characteristics have remained remarkably consistent. This chapter explains the basis of the classical Orders and the rules for getting them right.

THE ORDERS

THE ORDERS

THE ORDERS ARE THE FOUNDATION of classical architecture. Evolving through more than 3,000 years of experimentation and refinement, the Orders transform mere "shelter" into "architecture": the *art* of building.

In Chapter 1, we laid out the definitions of the basic elements that make up the Orders—the essential vocabulary of all traditional design. In this chapter, we'll help you understand the relationships between the elements and use them to get your design right.

What Are the Orders?

During the Italian Renaissance (circa 1420–1580), architects such as Alberti, Bramante, Vignola, and Palladio measured many of the structures of ancient Rome to produce a system of building that averaged their proportions into a series of ratios. Looking at the many hundreds of antique examples, they derived five basic types of building, which they called the Five Orders of Architecture. Tuscan is the heaviest in appearance; Doric is slightly lighter; and Ionic, Corinthian, and Composite are progressively more elegant and decorative.

Although the Orders are most familiar to us as the names of columns, they are not, in fact, just about columns. Even buildings without columns have an "order." The Orders are a system for the arrangement of all the necessary parts of a building, in a way that ensures harmonious proportion. They are a fusion of all the elements of construction—with a built-in proportional system. The Orders help us to size the height of a building, the projection of its eaves, the size and location of its openings, and the details such as door and window surrounds. Columns are merely the most refined and ornamental expression of this underlying order.

The Orders have very practical origins. Without any modern materials or hidden structure, ancient temples had to be carefully designed to stand up and to shed water. Aesthetics came into the equation when the parts of a building were refined to make them fit together beautifully.

The Tectonics of the Orders

Today, with modern materials and technologies at our disposal, our concern with the Orders is often as simple as specifying the right pre-manufactured column and constructing correctly detailed entablatures. But practical concerns are of paramount importance, because most mistakes that happen in contemporary uses of the Orders come from choosing the wrong elements or using the elements incorrectly. By knowing the vocabulary and remembering the original purpose of each element, you can avoid most mistakes that happen in contemporary uses of the Orders.

3.1 **The Classical Orders**

The Orders are a system of proportion that rigorously relates every element of a building in a harmonious whole.

3.2 **The Five Orders**

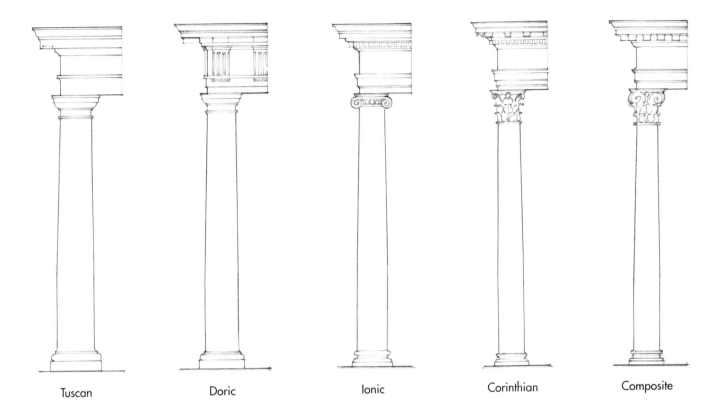

Tuscan   Doric   Ionic   Corinthian   Composite

NEED TO KNOW

The Five Orders: Further Study

The drawings on this page, and in this chapter as a whole, are just a starting point to show you the rich world of the classical Orders of architecture. This book tells you how to avoid all the common mistakes and navigate your selection of the right columns, building an entablature correctly, and so on. But for more advanced study, you need to know where to look next. Start with William Ware's *The American Vignola*, one of the best general texts available. William Chambers's *Treatise on the Decorative Part of Civil Architecture*

is an eighteenth-century text with very clear engravings showing many of the more complicated Orders in application. Finally, Andrea Palladio's *The Four Books of Architecture* shows you original Italian source material for many English and American Palladian buildings. Despite being over 400 years old, Palladio's books are simple to understand and full of easily comprehensible material. They are among the most influential architectural texts ever written.

3.3 **The Doric Order**

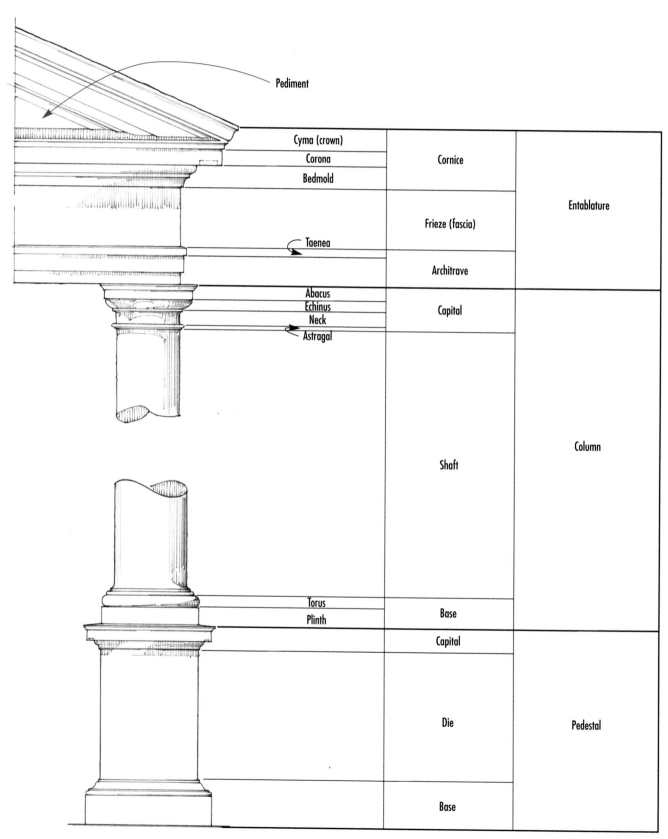

Pediment

Cyma (crown)	Cornice	Entablature
Corona		
Bedmold		
	Frieze (fascia)	
Taenea		
	Architrave	
Abacus	Capital	Column
Echinus		
Neck		
Astragal		
	Shaft	
Torus	Base	
Plinth		
	Capital	Pedestal
	Die	
	Base	

THE ORDERS

Organizing the Orders

Three successive horizontal bands organize the complete expression of an order: the pedestal (also called the *dado*), the column, and the entablature.

Pedestals

When setting out a classical building, the vertical proportions are calculated from a perfectly level line known as the *datum* (or dado). On an ancient building site, the datum was established—with no need for complex measuring devices—by setting up a trough of water at the top of the foundation wall; hence our expression "water-table."

At its simplest, the datum takes the form of a raised platform, often a flight of three steps known in ancient Greek as stylobate. In more complex architecture, the datum is the top of a more formal pedestal—the square base that sits beneath the column. The height of the pedestal is determined by the Order being used, and it gets progressively taller from Tuscan to Composite.

Columns

The column is divided into three parts: the base, the shaft, and the capital.

Bases

In the mists of antiquity, when the columns of temples and houses were presumably made of wood, a stone base was used to raise the end grain of the post off the potentially wet stylobate or datum. The bases of columns increase in complexity through the Orders.

The Greek Doric Order has no base as such—the base is the floor. In its simplest Tuscan form, the base comprises a square plinth and a half round torus. In all other Orders, a concave molding (called a *scotia*) is introduced between the convex torus moldings.

Shafts

The height of a column shaft is often expressed as a proportion related to its diameter. The diameter is defined by the dimension at the base of the shaft. The dimension becomes the module by which the proportions of all the other parts of the Order can be determined. The shafts of the columns get increasingly slender from the Tuscan (height roughly seven times diameter) to the Corinthian (ten times diameter).

Capitals

At the top of every column is the capital, literally the bearing plate that collects the load from the beams above. Like the column, the capital is divided into three parts:

At the top of the shaft, a molding called the astragal hides the joint between the column shaft and capital. Above this is the neck, round and vertical, which leads to a supporting molding called the *echinus*. The echinus visually mediates between the top bearing plate called the *abacus* (always square in plan) and the rest of the column (round in plan)—just as the plinth does at the base.

Entablatures

The next band is the *entablature*, which is in turn divided into three parts. The *architrave* represents a beam spanning between columns and forms the bond beam at the top of the wall. Except in the Greek Doric Order, the face of the architrave and the neck of the column should always align vertically **(see Installing Columns, page 52)**. At the top of the architrave is a fillet or other molding (typically an ogee or cyma reversa) that represents the location of the floor beams.

The *frieze*, above the architrave, is the band that represents the joists that span across the building. In the Doric Order, the ends of the joists are expressed in the form of *triglyphs* and *metopes*. Classically, the higher orders (Ionic, Corinthian, and Composite) often had continuous carving—either figurative (scenes of history or religion) or decorative (abstractions of leaves, flowers, or other organic forms). In some applications, the frieze had a convex shape known as a *pulvinated frieze*.

At the top of the entablature is the cornice, which protects the rest of the building from rain and provides a suitable compositional punctuation at the top of the building. In its simplest form, a cornice need be nothing more than the projecting rafters of the roof. As the Orders evolve the cornice becomes more complex, but it always retains three essential parts:

The *bedmold*, at its simplest, is a plate spanning the joists—or beams—of the frieze. The *corona* forms the drip, which forces water to drip beyond the foundation line, thus preventing water from running down the face of the building. The cornice is crowned by the *cyma*, which represents the gutter and terminates the Order.

3.4 Comparison of the Orders

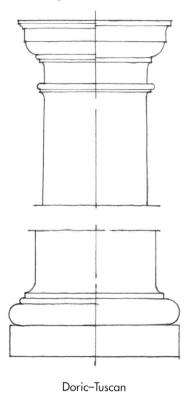

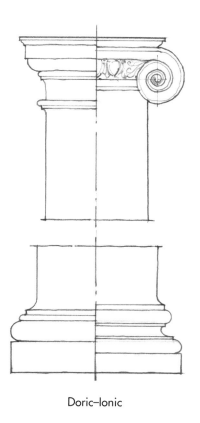

Doric–Tuscan   Doric–Ionic   Doric–Corinthian

3.5 Proportions of the Five Orders

Names of Features			Greek Doric		Tuscan		Doric		Ionic		Corinthian & Composite	
ENTABLATURE 1/4 TO 1/3	Cornice	CYMATIUM / CORONA / BEDMOLD	**2**	½	**1¾**	¾	**2**	¾	**2¼**	7/8	**2½**	1
	Frieze			¾		½		¾		6/8		¾
	Architrave	TÆNIA		¾		½		½		5/8		¾
COLUMN 1	Capital	ABACUS / ECHINUS / NECKING		½		½		½		1/3 (1/2)		7/6
		ASTRAGAL										
	Shaft		**4–6**		**7**	6	**8**	7	**9**	8	**10**	8⅓
		CINCTURE										
	Shaft	BASEMOLD / PLINTH	None			½		½		½		½
PEDESTAL 1/3 ±	Cap	CORONA / BEDMOLD	No pedestal but three steps the **STYLOBATE**		The **Cap** is one ninth the height of the pedestal							
	Die				**Pedestal** ⅓ (Vignola)							
	Base	BASEMOLD / PLINTH			The **Base** is two ninths the height of the pedestal							

3.6 The Tectonics of the Orders

Tectonics is the study of the elements of construction. In an age before hidden structural solutions and modern synthetic materials, each element of a building had to serve a specific and crucial function. Remember this diagram and refer back to it when you use the Orders. Knowing the origin of the elements you use will help you avoid many mistakes.

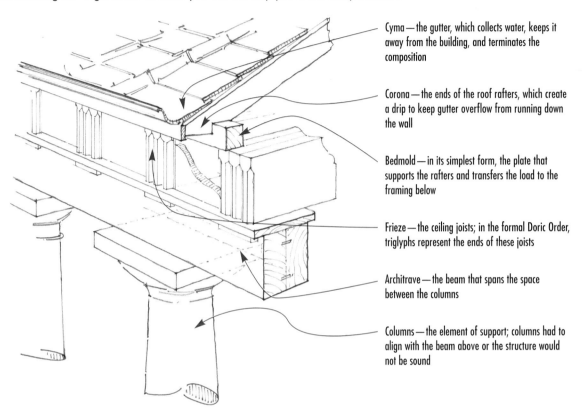

Cyma — the gutter, which collects water, keeps it away from the building, and terminates the composition

Corona — the ends of the roof rafters, which create a drip to keep gutter overflow from running down the wall

Bedmold — in its simplest form, the plate that supports the rafters and transfers the load to the framing below

Frieze — the ceiling joists; in the formal Doric Order, triglyphs represent the ends of these joists

Architrave — the beam that spans the space between the columns

Columns — the element of support; columns had to align with the beam above or the structure would not be sound

NEED TO KNOW

Tectonics: The Elements of Construction

The study of the elements of construction is called *tectonics*—looking at the way buildings are put together (both in the big picture and in the small details). In an age before hidden structure and modern synthetic materials and building systems, each element of a building had to serve specific and crucial functions—both standing up and keeping the weather out. Today, reinforced concrete and complicated plastic flashings mean that builders have lost sight of the practical reasons behind so many elements of traditional architecture.

A study of tectonics essentially trains the eye to recognize the structural integrity behind the origins of classical architecture. Figure 3.6 shows a reconstruction of a typical ancient temple. The *columns* (vertical structure or wall) are

supporting an *architrave* (horizontal structure in the wall plane—lintels, beams, or wall plates). The *frieze* represents the ceiling joists, spanning across the building, with chamfered (or beveled) ends that in the Doric Order create *triglyphs*. The *bedmold*, shown in its simplest form, is the plate that supports the rafters. The ends of the rafters are covered by the *corona*, which forms a drip. The final element is the gutter or *cyma*.

By learning tectonics, you can see how each part of the classical building was derived from structural function. This is why buildings look wrong if a part is missed. Tectonics trains your eye to think about today's decorative elements from their original, structural point of view. It will help you avoid a lot of common mistakes.

The Greek Orders of Architecture

Some 2,500 years ago, architects in the Ancient Greek city states – especially Athens – created some of the most timeless and beautiful buildings ever made. Of the buildings on the Acropolis at Athens, Plutarch wrote, "They were created in a short time for all time. Each in its fineness was even then at once age-old; but in the freshness of its vigour it is, even to the present day, recent and newly wrought." The beauty of many Greek temples depends on their subtle and refined systems of proportion. The products of a deep respect for tradition, they embodied in stone the principles of *trabeated* wooden construction, in which the elements of earlier timber temple structures were expressed in the emergent stone architecture (**see Tectonics, page 41**).

The Greek Orders have some unusual features. The Greek Doric column has no base, and it is the only order in which the face of the entablature and neck of the column do not align (the entablature overhangs slightly, which curiously creates a visual sense of perfection). Greek pediments are shallower than Roman, and their pitch gets shallower the wider the building, as a result of the method of setting them out (**see Setting Out Pediments, page 82**). Their decorative features include such items as *anthemia* and *acroteria*.

Greek architecture tends to be severe and solid, although the higher Greek Orders—Ionic and Corinthian—are extremely refined and decorative. This powerful, simple aesthetic increasingly began to appeal to architects in the eighteenth and early nineteenth century, particularly in America where Greek buildings had an additional connotation of civilized and transparent democracy, suitably for the newly founded nation of the United States of America. Greek revival buildings can be found all over the United States, from grand buildings such as the Lincoln Memorial to simple Connecticut farmhouses.

Although Roman Orders are more typical in classical architecture, we will refer several times in this book to Greek Revival alternatives. When detailing your Greek Revival building, look at the popular nineteenth-century books written by Asher Benjamin for inspiration and correct profiles. Several of his titles are still in print today.

3.7 **Hexastyle Greek Portico**

Greek temples typically have low-sloped pediments and proportions that are heavier than in Roman architecture.

The Roman Orders of Architecture

Ancient Roman Architecture, in contrast to Greek, made use of *arches* and of *concrete* to create buildings that have a completely different architectural quality. Greek architecture (see opposite) is *trabeated*—that is, it uses posts and beams. The monumental structures of ancient Rome are *plastic*—in other words, they often look like they are made of concrete that has been poured into a mold. By using arched construction, the Romans were able to create buildings like the Pantheon—which for many centuries remained the largest single-span structure in the world.

Roman architects did not, of course, ignore the classical Orders, but very often they were applied to these massive structures rather than forming an integral part of the construction. The Roman Colosseum, for instance, makes use of superimposed Orders to give meaning to the façade of the building (**see Superimposition, page 66**).

Marcus Vitruvius Pollio was a Roman engineer and architect active around 46-30 B.C. Although not particularly well known during his own lifetime, Vitruvius's *Ten Books of Architecture* became enormously influential in later centuries. It is from him that much of our understanding of Roman building methods—and also of ancient buildings now lost—is derived.

When Italian architects such as Alberti and Bramante, and later Palladio, rediscovered the buildings of classical antiquity during the fifteenth and sixteenth centuries—the Italian Renaissance—they inevitably studied the buildings of ancient Rome rather than Greece. For 300 years it was Roman architecture that provided the model for new classical buildings. Only in the late eighteenth century did a shift in taste and learning mean that ancient Greek buildings once again become a model for classical architects. For this reason, most of the classical orders we see in Europe and in eighteenth century America find their origin in Roman design.

Unlike the Greek Doric, all Roman orders have a base, and in all cases the entablature aligns with the neck of the column. Because of the way they are set out, Roman pediments have a consistent pitch (approxmately 22.5 degrees) whatever the size of the building. And it is true to say that all Roman orders tend to feel more ornamented than their Greek equivalents.

Because of the power of the Roman Empire in the first place, and then the influence of Italian Renaissance architects some 1500 years later, Roman Orders are normative in Western classical culture. Learn them before looking at the differences and details of Greek temples and columns.

3.8 **Roman Triumphal Arch**

Roman architecture is more attenuated and vertical than Greek architecture. Romans invented the arch, which allowed them to span greater distances with bricks and small stones.

3.9 Comparison of Greek and Roman Doric Orders

In the Greek Doric Order, the architrave and frieze are heavier than the cornice; in the Roman Doric Order, the cornice and frieze are heavier than the architrave. The Greek Doric is characterized by a baseless column that does not align with the architrave above.

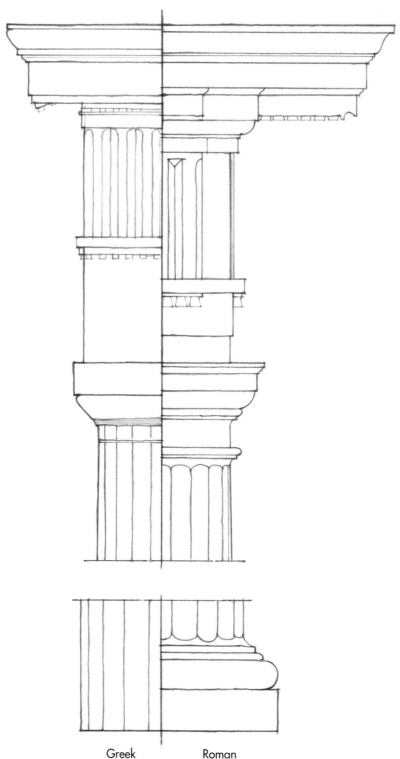

Greek   Roman

3.10 **Comparison of Greek and Roman Ionic Orders**

Similar to the Doric Order, the proportions of the Greek Ionic Order has a large architrave and frieze with a smaller cornice, while the Roman Ionic has a large frieze and cornice with a small architrave. The capital of the Greek Ionic is larger and more sculptural than that of the Roman Ionic Order.

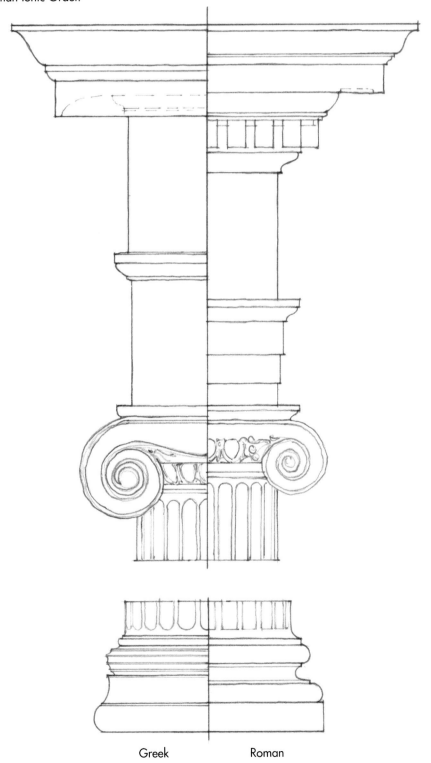

Greek   Roman

3.11 **Column Design and Detail**

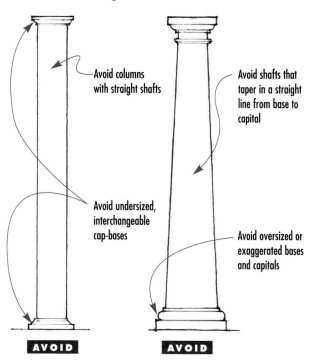

Avoid columns with straight shafts

Avoid shafts that taper in a straight line from base to capital

Avoid undersized, interchangeable cap-bases

Avoid oversized or exaggerated bases and capitals

AVOID   **AVOID**

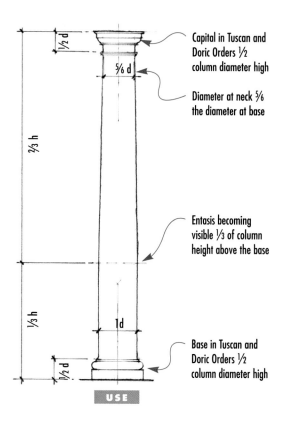

Capital in Tuscan and Doric Orders ½ column diameter high

Diameter at neck ⅚ the diameter at base

Entasis becoming visible ⅓ of column height above the base

Base in Tuscan and Doric Orders ½ column diameter high

½ d

⅚ d

⅔ h

⅓ h

1 d

½ d

USE

SELECTING COLUMNS

Unlike classical builders, who turned custom columns out of wood on lathes or carved them out of stone, today we typically order our columns out of catalogs. Navigating this process can be very difficult, because in most catalogs, only about 15 percent of the stock products available have authentic details; the rest are cartoons or caricatures of the classical Orders. The trick is recognizing the good designs and weeding out the bad. Here are some guidelines to help you choose correctly.

Look at the Details

Carefully examine the profiles of the capital and base of the column to verify that they are based on the profiles shown in 3.13. "Builder" grade columns tend to be badly detailed. "Architectural" grade columns based on designs by the architect Vignola will generally be right.

Entasis

Round columns should never have straight sides; only purchase columns that are narrower at the neck than at the base (3.11). In most ancient columns, the diameter decreased slightly in a continuous curve from the base to the capital. This reduction is called *entasis*. It gives the columns a grace that a straight-sided cylinder column lacks. In practice, entasis on the bottom third of the column is hardly visible to the eye. So typically, that bottom third is straight-sided, which allows adjustments to the height of the column on site with some ease.

Tuscan and Doric Orders

When specifying Tuscan and Doric columns, *avoid* the following pitfalls:

- Avoid too much or too little capital (3.12). The height of the capital and base should be set at $^1/_2$ the diameter of the column (3.13), with the diameter measured at the column's widest point. Any less or any more will not be in proportion with the column.
- Avoid the interchangeable cap-base (3.12). Although the capital and base have similar profiles, they are not exactly the same. Always check the difference.

• Avoid the round abacus. The abacus *is never round*. It is often mistakenly built round because the shaft is round. But it should always be square, to transition the round volume of the column into the architrave above (3.14).

Avoid the Obvious Slip-On Cap

Historically, columns were turned on a lathe, which meant that the entire column was one piece. Today, we rarely use wood or stone columns. Rather, we use new synthetic products, and the capital is a separate piece slipped onto the shaft. If the capital gets too large it will overpower the column and appear out of proportion (3.15). Look for a capital with a minimal step between the top of the shaft and the astragal (3.16).

3.12 **Tuscan and Doric Capitals**

Avoid miniature, interchangeable cap-bases

AVOID

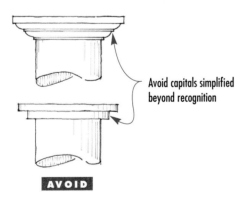

Avoid capitals simplified beyond recognition

AVOID

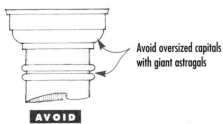

Avoid oversized capitals with giant astragals

AVOID

3.13 **Capitals and Bases**

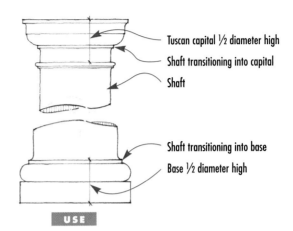

Tuscan capital ½ diameter high

Shaft transitioning into capital

Shaft

Shaft transitioning into base

Base ½ diameter high

USE

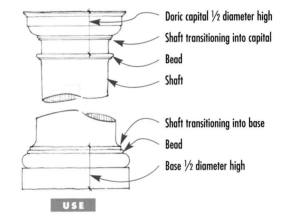

Doric capital ½ diameter high

Shaft transitioning into capital

Bead

Shaft

Shaft transitioning into base

Bead

Base ½ diameter high

USE

3.14 **Round and Square Capitals**

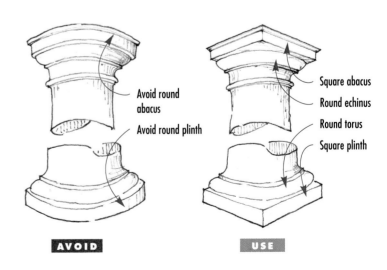

Avoid round abacus

Avoid round plinth

Square abacus

Round echinus

Round torus

Square plinth

AVOID   **USE**

3.15 **Slip-On Caps**

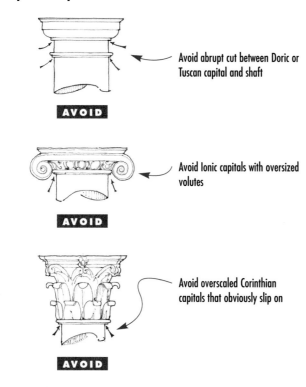

Avoid abrupt cut between Doric or Tuscan capital and shaft

AVOID

Avoid Ionic capitals with oversized volutes

AVOID

Avoid overscaled Corinthian capitals that obviously slip on

AVOID

3.16 **Capitals Correctly Connected**

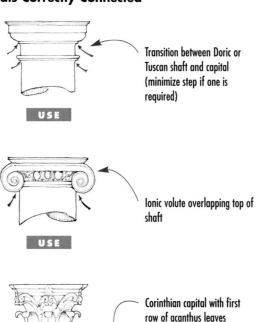

Transition between Doric or Tuscan shaft and capital (minimize step if one is required)

USE

Ionic volute overlapping top of shaft

USE

Corinthian capital with first row of acanthus leaves aligned with neck of column (capital should sit on shaft, never slip over it)

USE

Purchasing Columns

General

❏ Avoid "Builder" grade columns

❏ Use "Architectural" grade columns based on Vignola's Orders

❏ Avoid fiberglass columns. If you must use them for budget reasons, fill them partially with sand to make them feel solid.

❏ Avoid straight shafts; select shafts with entasis.

Tuscan and Doric Columns

❏ Avoid miniature and interchangeable cap-bases.

❏ Set the height of capital and base at 1/2 the column diameter.

❏ Never use a round abacus or plinth; use a square abacus and a square plinth.

All Orders

❏ Avoid oversized capitals that are obviously slipped on.

❏ Use capitals that transition into the shaft and are sized to fit the column.

❏ Avoid novel column types and cartoon versions of known types.

❏ Use only column designs closely based on the five Orders: Tuscan, Doric, Ionic, Corinthian, and Composite.

Caution Approximately 85 percent of the products available in most column catalogs are not fit for use. Specify with care and ask for cut sheets with details before you buy. Compare the details to this book first.

3.17 **Cartoon Design**

Avoid columns that have novel names or look like cartoon versions of well-known designs.

AVOID

The Charleston

AVOID

Cartoon Corinthian

AVOID

Cartoon Tower of the Winds

3.18 **Channels and Flutes**

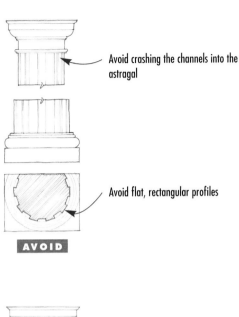

Avoid crashing the channels into the astragal

Avoid flat, rectangular profiles

AVOID

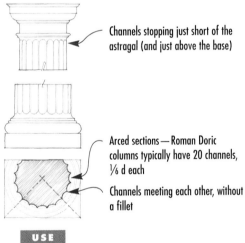

Channels stopping just short of the astragal (and just above the base)

Arced sections—Roman Doric columns typically have 20 channels, 1/6 d each

Channels meeting each other, without a fillet

USE

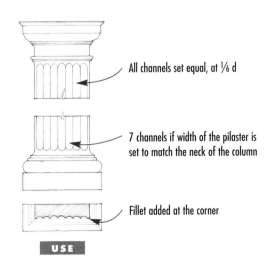

All channels set equal, at 1/6 d

7 channels if width of the pilaster is set to match the neck of the column

Fillet added at the corner

USE

Avoid stopping the flutes too low below the capital

Avoid mini scallops with large spaces between

Avoid machine-cut "routed" flutes

AVOID

Flutes stopping just below the capital (and just above the base)

Semicircular flutes, 24 per column, deeper than channels, separated by fillets

USE

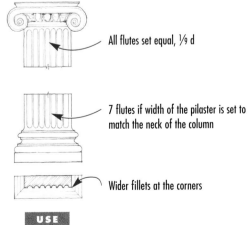

All flutes set equal, 1/9 d

7 flutes if width of the pilaster is set to match the neck of the column

Wider fillets at the corners

USE

3.19 **Terminating and Supporting Moldings**

The emphasis of a supporting molding, or bedmold, is upward. The emphasis of a terminating molding, or cyma, is outward.

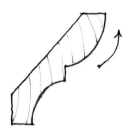 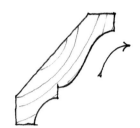

Supporting molding,
emphasis up

Terminating molding,
emphasis out

3.20 **Moldings in Practice**

Never place a corona above a cyma. Water hitting this design will run down the face of the building, and as a detail it looks awkward. Always use a cyma to terminate a composition, with supporting moldings to hold up the corona. Water hitting this design will drip away from the building, and the look is elegant and crisp.

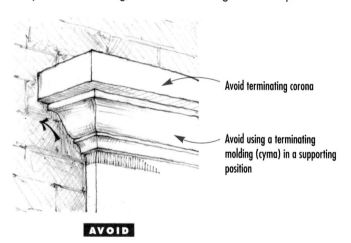

Avoid terminating corona

Avoid using a terminating molding (cyma) in a supporting position

AVOID

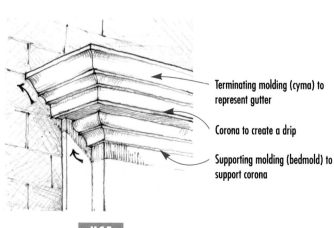

Terminating molding (cyma) to represent gutter

Corona to create a drip

Supporting molding (bedmold) to support corona

USE

MOLDING DETAILS

The two most common types of molding are *terminating* and *supporting* (3.19).

Terminating moldings have an outward emphasis. They are found at the top of a composition on a cornice (on a building's exterior) or crown molding (in the interior). They provide a visual termination for the design.

Supporting moldings have an upward emphasis and are used almost everywhere else. They visually transfer loads and provide support for the weight above.

When placing moldings, use common sense. When you are carrying a heavy box, what direction are your hands and arms facing? If you are like most people, the answer is up. This is the position that gives the most support. When you follow through after shooting a basketball, what position is your arm in? Most likely it will be out, away from your body. Imagine doing either of these activities with the reverse motions. It wouldn't work. The box would fall and the basketball would go behind you. Interchanging moldings has the same effect on a building.

Avoid the Terminating Corona

The purpose of the cornice is to keep water away from the building. In the days before modern synthetic materials, this was a paramount requirement for all buildings. In its earliest form, the cyma at the top of the cornice formed the gutter **(see Tectonics, page 41)**, and the corona below created a drip that kept any water overflowing the gutter away from the face of the building.

If the corona is placed above the cyma, you are in essence covering the gutter with the drip. The result is that water hitting the building will have nowhere to go but down the face (3.20).

A correctly assembled cornice is composed of a bedmold supporting the corona, which forms a drip and in turn supports the cyma. Water hitting this design will fall clear of the face of the building, and the design will look visually correct, too.

Moldings and Ornament

Throughout the Orders, ornament is commonly applied to molding profiles. As with most elements in traditional architecture, there is a purpose to how this ornament is applied. The combination of patterns and types of molding are typically determined by the profile of the molding. For instance, a leaf-and-dart motif is found on a cyma reversa, which is a supporting molding, because the profile of the molding matches the profile of the motif. And an egg-and-dart motif is found on a quarter round profile because both share the same shape.

Separating and Transitioning Moldings

The two other common molding types, in addition to supporting and terminating moldings, are separating and transitioning. Separating moldings can be concave or convex and begin and end with a horizontal emphasis. They are found in column bases and bead profiles. Transitioning moldings begin and end with an emphasis up and down. This type of molding is found in base caps and other elements where a transition between vertical surfaces is occurring.

3.21 **Ornament on Moldings**

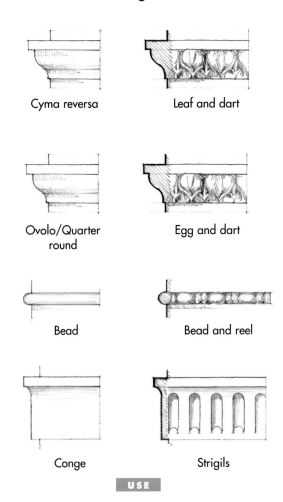

Cyma reversa   Leaf and dart

Ovolo/Quarter round   Egg and dart

Bead   Bead and reel

Conge   Strigils

USE

3.22 **Types of Moldings**

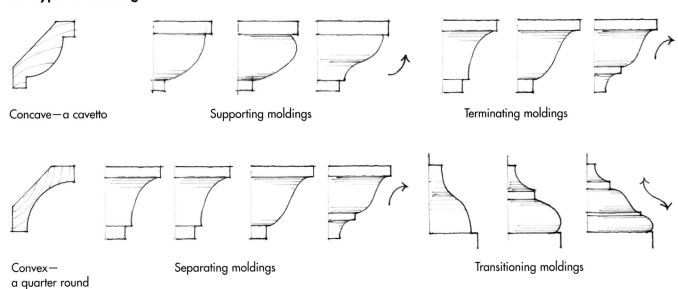

Concave—a cavetto   Supporting moldings   Terminating moldings

Convex— a quarter round   Separating moldings   Transitioning moldings

3.23 **Column Alignment**

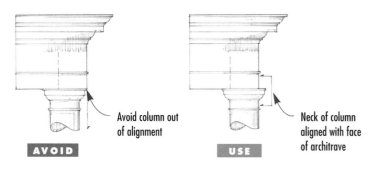

Avoid column out
of alignment

AVOID

Neck of column
aligned with face
of architrave

USE

3.24 **Column and Beam**

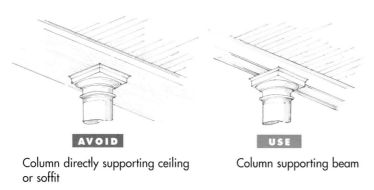

AVOID

USE

Column directly supporting ceiling
or soffit

Column supporting beam

3.25 **Column and Architrave**

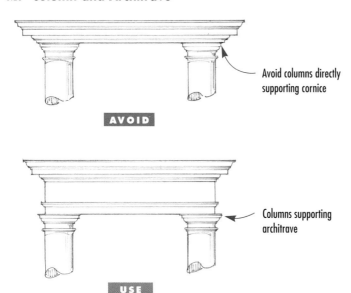

Avoid columns directly
supporting cornice

AVOID

Columns supporting
architrave

USE

INSTALLING COLUMNS

The most common mistakes made in traditional architecture have to do with the relationship between the column and what it supports. These mistakes happen because we forget the tectonic origins of the Orders or ignore the limits of traditional materials. When designing, remember to constantly ask the questions: Could this stand without hidden structure? And does it make sense? The practical solution is also usually the architecturally correct choice.

Align the Neck of the Column with the Face of the Architrave

Always align the *neck of the column* with the *face of the architrave,* front, back, and side (3.23). If the two are placed in any other way, the column will appear undersized and weak for its job. **(See Porch Planning, page 174.)** There is one exception to this rule. Greek Doric Orders do not quite align.

Avoid Columns Directly Supporting the Ceiling

Columns *only* support a beam or architrave. *Never* place a column supporting a flat ceiling or soffit. A column carries a point load. If it is supporting a flat surface, it will look as if it is going to poke through the ceiling at any moment (3.24). Columns need to support an architrave to make structural and visual sense.

Don't Omit the Architrave

Never let the cornice span the space between columns. The cornice evolved out of the top plate, rafter ends, and gutter. These elements are not spanning members. Without hidden structure, this arrangement of building elements would instantly fail. Always use a beam, or architrave, to span between columns. Beams both make good sense and look right (3.25).

3.26 Installing Columns in One Story

Think ahead. The relationships necessary to installing columns correctly are set on site long before the actual columns arrive on the job. It is easy to get it right if trades are coordinated at the beginning of the project and care is taken to set these relationships.

3.27 Installing Columns in Two Stories

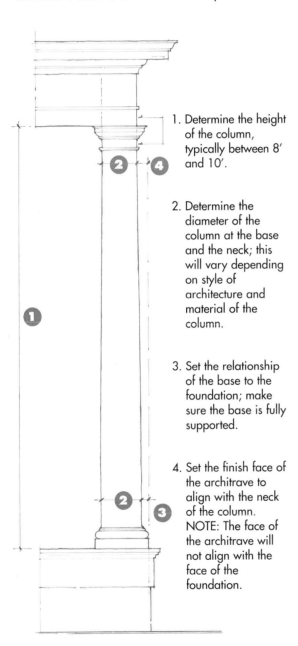

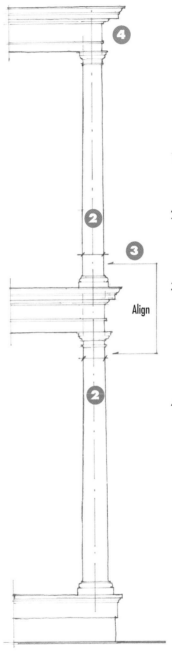

1. Determine the height of the column, typically between 8' and 10'.

2. Determine the diameter of the column at the base and the neck; this will vary depending on style of architecture and material of the column.

3. Set the relationship of the base to the foundation; make sure the base is fully supported.

4. Set the finish face of the architrave to align with the neck of the column. NOTE: The face of the architrave will not align with the face of the foundation.

1. Follow the steps for installing columns in one story.

2. Set the centerline of the second-story column to align with the first-story columns.

3. Set the diameter of the second-floor column, typically equal to the neck of the first-floor columns, but not in all cases; see Superimposition, page 66, for more information.

4. Determine how the porch will engage the building, incorporated in the room or a separate volume; for more information see Engaging the Building, page 176.

Typical Column Dimensions

8'– 0" high	10" d at Base	8" d at Neck
9'– 0" high	11" d at Base	9" d at Neck
10'– 0" high	12" d at Base	10" d at Neck

CHECKLIST

Installing Columns

- ❏ Does the neck of the column align with the face of the architrave?
- ❏ Does the column support a beam or an architrave?
- ❏ Have you used a beam or architrave to span the space between columns?

3.28 **Entablature Errors**

All entablatures should be made up of three elements—architrave, frieze, and cornice—in the right order at the right size. Within the cornice, remember the three primary divisions: bedmold (plate), corona (drip), and cyma (gutter).

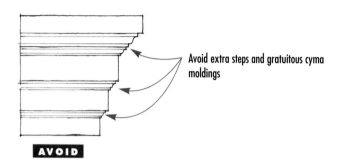

AVOID

Avoid extra steps and gratuitous cyma moldings

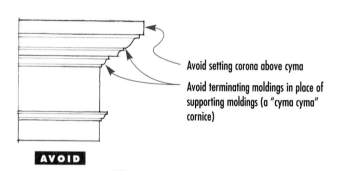

AVOID

Avoid setting corona above cyma

Avoid terminating moldings in place of supporting moldings (a "cyma cyma" cornice)

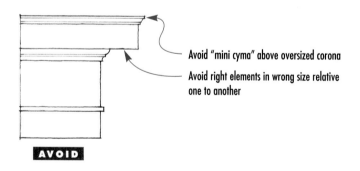

AVOID

Avoid "mini cyma" above oversized corona

Avoid right elements in wrong size relative one to another

CHECKLIST

Tuscan & Doric Entablatures

❏ Does your entablature have an architrave, frieze, and cornice?

❏ Is the cyma above the corona?

❏ Is there a drip under the corona?

❏ Is each element sized in relation to the others?

TUSCAN AND DORIC ENTABLATURES

Unlike the columns we have looked at in this chapter, a good entablature is impossible to buy off the shelf. There are many commercially produced entablatures available, but they are almost always incorrectly detailed. Never use them.

Fortunately, it is easy to construct a good entablature on site from readily available stock moldings. The two secrets to a successful entablature are:

• Arrange the parts correctly.

• Make sure their relative sizes are appropriate.

Getting the Parts in the Right Order

Think back to the Tectonics diagram in 3.2. The design of the entablature originates in structural common sense. You should always make sure that it is composed of:

CORNICE

on top of

FRIEZE

on top of

ARCHITRAVE

Don't use any other arrangement.

What Not to Do

Do not assemble random parts. Figure 3.28 (top) shows an entablature made up of a confused collection of moldings that don't relate to correct classical precedent.

Do not get the parts in the wrong order. Figure 3.28 (center) shows an entablature that has the right components. But they are arranged incorrectly, with a terminating molding used where a supporting molding should go.

Do not size the parts incorrectly. Figure 3.28 (bottom) shows an entablature that has the right components in the right place. But their sizes are all out of proportion.

What to Do

Figures 3.29 and 3.30 show the Tuscan and Doric Orders correctly laid out. Copy these exactly to avoid mistakes.

3.29 **The Tuscan Order**

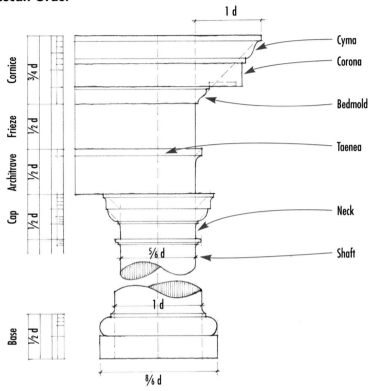

- Cyma
- Corona
- Bedmold
- Taenea
- Neck
- Shaft

3.30 **The Simplified Doric Order**

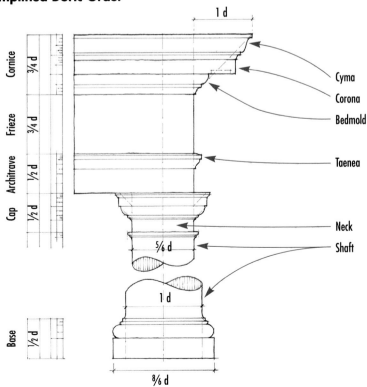

- Cyma
- Corona
- Bedmold
- Taenea
- Neck
- Shaft

3.31 **Triglyph Designs**

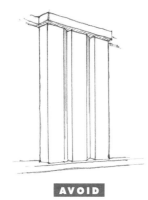

AVOID

AVOID

Channels cut the entire height of the triglyph

Routed-out or pressed-in details

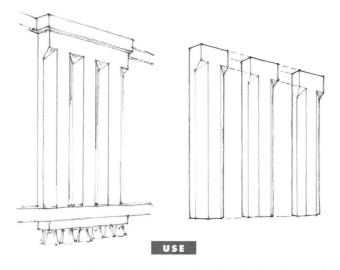

USE

Triglyphs made up of three boards with chamfered ends

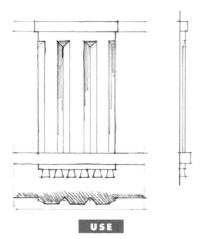

USE

Channels stopping short of the top of the triglyph; channels cut at 45 degrees

FORMAL DORIC ENTABLATURES

Doric entablatures can be enriched with details called—from the ancient Greek—triglyphs, metopes, and mutules. Using a formal Doric Order requires careful study of traditional precedent at a level of detail that is beyond the scope of this book. These two pages are only an introduction. Use caution in both design and execution. If your budget does not allow you to get the details right, it would be better to simplify the design than to cut corners.

Triglyphs and Metopes

In the original wood construction of ancient temples, triglyphs, located in the frieze, are assumed to have been the exposed ends of the beams, chamfered to produce the characteristic pattern **(see Tectonics, page 41)**. Between the triglyphs are metopes, which might hold sculpted representations of mythical, historical, or religious scenes.

Figure 3.31 (top) shows two common details to avoid. To detail the triglyph correctly, the chamfers are formed from 45-degree cuts in plan and should always stop short of the top of the triglyph. The element has a small cap, as shown in elevation. The triglyph can be constructed by combining three chamfered boards (3.31 center).

Setting Out Triglyphs

Figure 3.32 (top) shows the enriched Doric entablature in elevation. Start by centering the triglpyh (and the mutule above it) over the centerline of the column. The area between the triglyphs, the metope, should not be more than square—in other words, wider than it is high—and it should not be less than the width of the adjacent triglyph.

Mutules

Mutules are the projecting element above the bedmold. They represent the rafter tails and originally provided support to the deep Doric cornice. Mutules are always aligned on the centerline of the column, positioned directly above the triglyph. At external corners, a square recessed panel should be formed on the underside (or soffit) of the cornice, as shown in the plan and perspective drawings (3.32).

3.32 **The Formal Doric Order**

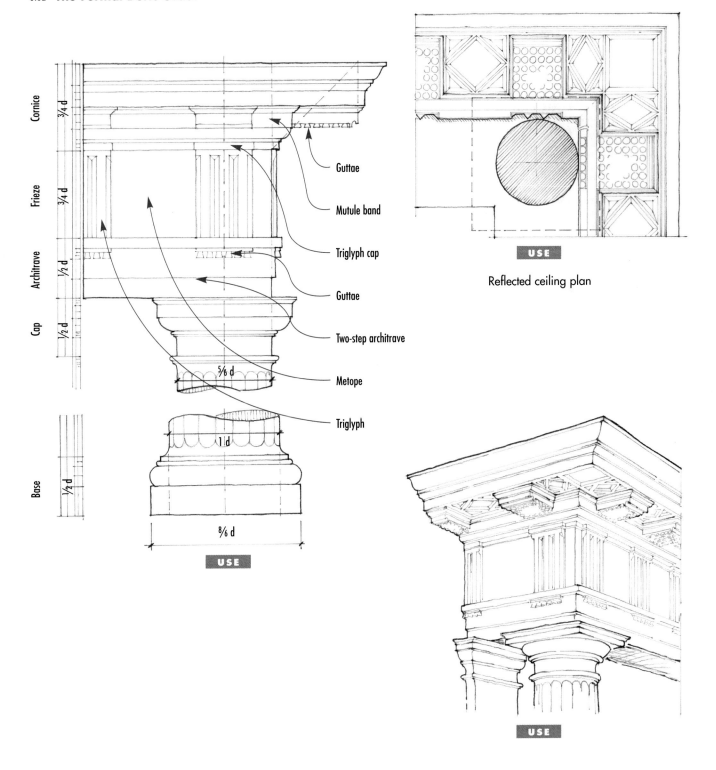

Cornice 3/4 d

Frieze 3/4 d

Architrave 1/2 d

Cap 1/2 d

Base 1/2 d

Guttae

Mutule band

Triglyph cap

Guttae

Two-step architrave

Metope

Triglyph

5/6 d

1 d

8/6 d

USE

Reflected ceiling plan

USE

USE

3.33 **Cornice Designs to Avoid**

Ornament is used to enrich a building. It is an extra, not a necessity. If you can't afford the correct details, leave them out.

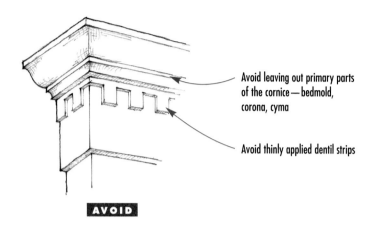

Avoid leaving out primary parts of the cornice—bedmold, corona, cyma

Avoid thinly applied dentil strips

AVOID

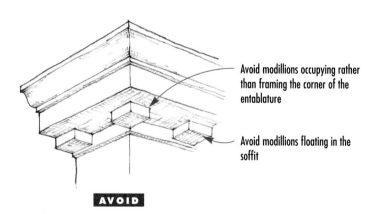

Avoid modillions occupying rather than framing the corner of the entablature

Avoid modillions floating in the soffit

AVOID

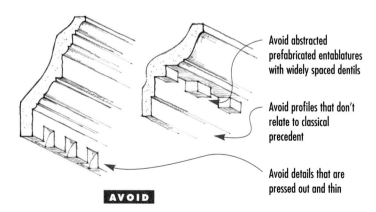

Avoid abstracted prefabricated entablatures with widely spaced dentils

Avoid profiles that don't relate to classical precedent

Avoid details that are pressed out and thin

AVOID

IONIC AND CORINTHIAN ORDERS

Capitals

Although the capitals of the Ionic and Corinthian Orders—the so-called "higher" Orders—appear complicated, if you look closely you see they are derived from the same basic system that controls the lower orders. In the Ionic capital, the abacus has morphed into the scrolls called volutes. In the Corinthian, if you look behind the foliate decoration (which is an abstracted version of acanthus leaves), you will find a bell shape that is merely the neck of the Doric capital stretched and flared. Do the same with an Ionic capital and the result is a Composite capital.

Entablatures

Like the capitals below them, the Ionic and Corinthian entablatures contain more elaborate, modeled detail than is seen in the Tuscan and Doric Orders. For this reason alone, you should be extremely careful when designing an entablature for these higher orders. Ionic and Corinthian entablatures have the addition of small blocks called dentils—so named because they look like teeth— and projecting brackets called modillions. (Some Doric Orders have dentils as well, but this is less typical.)

Ionic and Corinthian Entablatures to Avoid

Many "enriched" entablatures are commercially available, but no prefabricated detail can get close to the depth of carving and modeling required in a true application of these Orders. Details are usually simplified beyond recognition. Often they are formed from pressed wood or plastic, or the dentils may be formed from thin strips of indented wood stuck onto the frieze. Either way, the detail is far too shallow to look real and effective.

Modillions, too, are often misunderstood. There are careful rules for setting these out, as shown in 3.35. Compare this to the detail shown in 3.33 — the "McModillion" that floats incorrectly on the external soffit of the cornice.

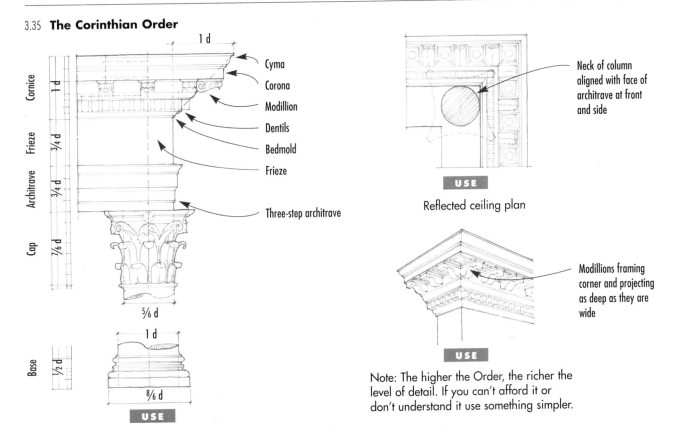

3.34 The Ionic Order

1 d

Cornice — 7/8 d
Frieze — 6/8 d
Architrave — 5/8 d
Cap — 1/2 d
5/6 d

Cyma
Corona
Bedmold
Dentils

Frieze
Two-step architrave

Volute

Base — 1/2 d
Attic base
1 d
8/6 d

USE

Reflected ceiling plan

Neck of column aligned with face of architrave at front and side

USE

Dentils framing corner and projecting as deep as they are wide

USE

3.35 The Corinthian Order

1 d

Cornice — 1 d
Frieze — 3/4 d
Architrave — 3/4 d
Cap — 7/6 d
5/6 d

Cyma
Corona
Modillion
Dentils
Bedmold
Frieze

Three-step architrave

Base — 1/2 d
1 d
8/6 d

USE

Reflected ceiling plan

Neck of column aligned with face of architrave at front and side

USE

Modillions framing corner and projecting as deep as they are wide

USE

Note: The higher the Order, the richer the level of detail. If you can't afford it or don't understand it use something simpler.

3.36 Elements of Support

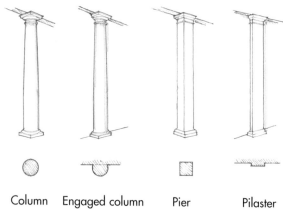

Column   Engaged column   Pier   Pilaster

3.37 Pilasters

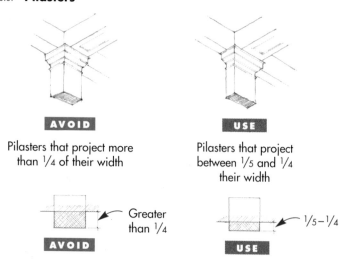

AVOID

Pilasters that project more
than ¹/₄ of their width

USE

Pilasters that project
between ¹/₅ and ¹/₄
their width

AVOID → Greater
than ¹/₄

USE ← ¹/₅–¹/₄

3.38 Engaged Columns

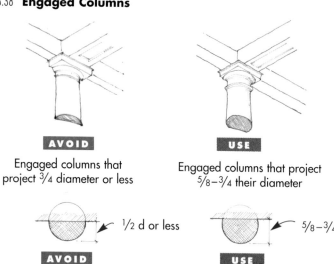

AVOID

Engaged columns that
project ³/₄ diameter or less

USE

Engaged columns that project
⁵/₈–³/₄ their diameter

AVOID ← ¹/₂ d or less

USE ← ⁵/₈–³/₄ d

PILASTERS AND ENGAGED COLUMNS

A column is a freestanding round shaft. A square column is called a pier. A round column attached to a wall is an engaged column; a pier attached to a wall is a pilaster (3.36). Pilasters and engaged columns provide visual support at the point where the entablature meets a wall.

Don't Make Pilasters Too Deep

Pilasters will look too chunky if they project too far. It is a common mistake to set the pilaster projection at half its width (3.37). The pilaster projection should be set between ¹/₅ and ¹/₄ of the width.

Don't Use Half a Column

On the other hand, engaged columns one-half a diameter or less will appear undersized and look as though they are being swallowed by the wall. Set the column between ⁵/₈ and ³/₄ of the diameter from the wall (3.38). The correct example shows how you will see the diameter of the column expressed. The small difference in plan will have a considerable effect in three dimensions. The shadow line behind the column provides definition and a sense of seeing the column as an object in the round.

Tapered Pilasters?

A very common question is whether to give pilasters entasis, or taper (see Entasis, page 46). There is no hard and fast rule, but typically pilasters, like the piers they are derived from, are straight-sided.

The key relationship to maintain is the alignment between the neck of the pilaster and the face of the architrave. To keep this relationship, set the dimension of the pilaster for the correct condition at the capital, and let the base be smaller than on the neighboring column.

Think in Three Dimensions

When you combine pilasters, engaged columns, and freestanding columns (3.39-3.41), keep in mind that architectural elements are rarely seen in true elevation, which is how a building appears in two dimensions on paper or when viewed head-on.

Once a building is built, it is very difficult to view it in true elevation, because a three-dimensional structure appears in perspective, which is to say that that front looks larger than the back. Round columns appear more slender in three dimensions because the diameter of a column remains constant regardless of the angle from which it is viewed. Piers and pilasters, on the other hand, appear wider when viewed obliquely because of their square corners.

CHECKLIST

Pilasters and Engaged Columns

☐ Is the depth of the pilaster set between $1/4$ and $1/5$ the diameter?

☐ Is the depth of the engaged column set between $5/8$ and $3/4$ the diameter?

3.39 Combining Columns and Engaged Columns

Match the diameter of the engaged column to the diameter of the free-standing column.

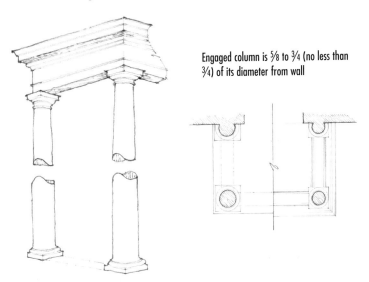

Engaged column is ⅝ to ¾ (no less than ¾) of its diameter from wall

3.40 Combining Columns and Pilasters

Set the width of the pilaster to match the neck of the columns; this maintains the alignment with the architrave.

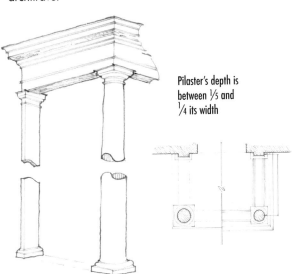

Pilaster's depth is between ⅕ and ¼ its width

3.41 Combining Piers, Columns, and Pilasters

Set the width and depth of the pier to match the neck of the column; set the width of the pilaster to match the pier and the neck of the column.

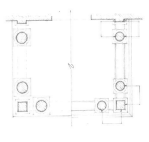

Depth of pilaster is ⅕ to ¼ its width

Bases of piers and pilasters are smaller than bases of columns

3.42 **Post Designs to Avoid**

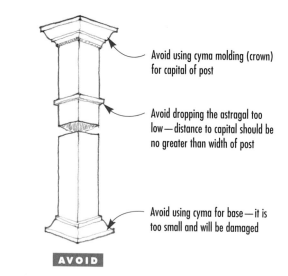

Avoid using cyma molding (crown) for capital of post

Avoid dropping the astragal too low—distance to capital should be no greater than width of post

Avoid using cyma for base—it is too small and will be damaged

AVOID

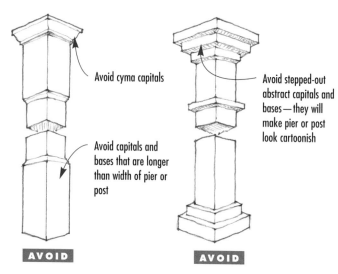

Avoid cyma capitals

Avoid capitals and bases that are longer than width of pier or post

Avoid stepped-out abstract capitals and bases—they will make pier or post look cartoonish

AVOID

AVOID

CHECKLIST

Piers & Posts

❑ Are both capital and base derived from classical columns?

❑ Is the astragal set high enough?

❑ Is the base low enough?

❑ Have you avoided using cyma moldings?

PIERS AND POSTS

A pier is a square column. In a formal design, the details can be worked out as they would be for the capital and base of a round column. Piers are typically straight-sided—that is, they don't taper. The diameter should be set from the neck. This gives the pier a smaller shaft at the base than a tapered column would have, and it makes the pier slightly smaller than any adjacent columns.

Posts are narrow piers, often used on back porches, screen porches, or breezeways. The detailing of a post is derived from the classical Orders, but represents a much less formal and often more economical option than a column or pier.

Details to Avoid

Figure 3.42 shows three common mistakes to avoid, and variations on these errors are endless. Stacked blocks of wood should not be used as capitals, nor should cyma moldings **(see Terminating and Supporting Moldings, page 50)**. Make sure that you don't make the implied "neck" of your pilaster appear stretched by placing the astragal too low.

Details to Use

Figure 3.43 shows how to construct a simple post from stock moldings. The capital is a base molding turned upside-down and topped with a cove. The astragal is a nose and cove molding, and the base is a flat board topped with a base cap.

Use the width of the post to determine the maximum height of the base and location of the astragal. Bases taller than they are wide should be avoided, as should astragals set too low.

Figure 3.44 illustrates a post closer in detail to the profile of a column. In this example the capital and base are formed out of bedmolds. Note that the base molding is larger than the capital molding.

Here the corners of the pier are chamfered, another option to create a more formal look. If you choose to add a chamfer, stop it short of both the base and the astragal for an authentic effect.

3.43 Traditional Post Profiles

Here a post is detailed more like a column, with chamfered corners that contribute to a more formal look.
The dimensions shown are for a 6"x6" post.

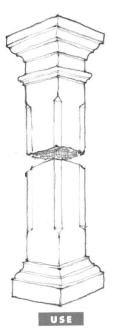

USE

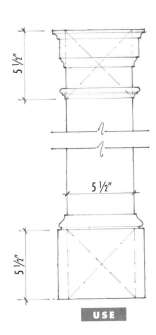

5 ½"

5 ½"

5 ½"

USE

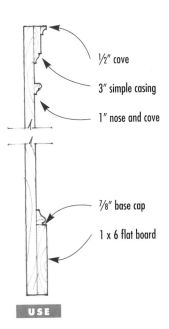

½" cove

3" simple casing

1" nose and cove

⅞" base cap

1 x 6 flat board

USE

3.44 Simplified Post Profiles

Less formal than a pier, a post can be correctly detailed as shown here. The capitals and bases on piers and pilasters, however, should be designed to match the profile of a column. The molding dimensions specified are for a 6'x 6' post; for larger or smaller posts, adjust proportionally.

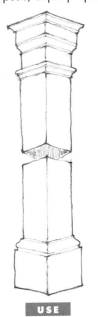

USE

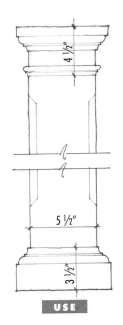

4 ½"

5 ½"

3 ½"

USE

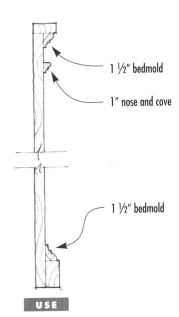

1 ½" bedmold

1" nose and cove

1 ½" bedmold

USE

3.45 **Intercolumniation to Avoid**

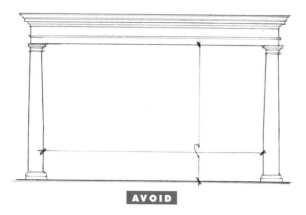

AVOID

Avoid long horizontal spans that are too long for the materials employed, and where the space between columns is wider than the height of the column (rule of thumb).

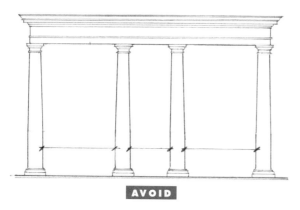

AVOID

Avoid inflection without focus created by narrow centers.

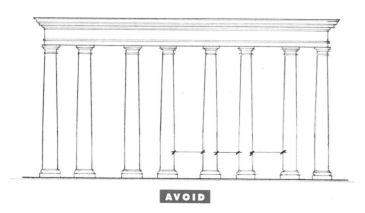

AVOID

Avoid ambiguously paired columns without clear distinction between the pairs and the spaces between them.

INTERCOLUMNIATION

The spacing of columns, or *intercolumniation*, affects both proportion and the perception of scale. In general terms, intercolumniation relates to the material strengths and limits of the lintel spanning between two columns. Lintels in wood can span further than stone, but they have limits too. Figure 3.45 (top) shows a span that the eye knows could not be achieved using traditional materials and construction.

Traditionally, intercolumniation was set by the diameter of the column. The number of diameters separating each column varied depending on the Order and the application. If you are using a formal Doric Order with triglyphs and metopes, it is important to maintain a module of spacing that directly relates to the diameter **(see Formal Doric Entablatures, page 56)**. In other cases, this strict attention to ratios is less important.

Height-to-Width Ratio
When setting intercolumniation, bear in mind the important visual relationship between the height and the width of the opening between columns. Generally, it looks better if the height of the opening is greater than the width.

Classical architecture tends mostly towards a vertical emphasis in composition. However, this is not a hard and fast rule. Plenty of historical precedent shows that horizontal openings can work well. They will make the building feel slightly more relaxed and "rooted" than a vertical design. Use judgment when setting out your columns and look closely at historical precedent for both the region and the style in which you are working.

Inflection
Adjusting the spacing of columns within a colonnade can add rhythm to what might otherwise be a monotonous long run. This adjustment is called inflection. Be sure that the largest opening corresponds to the most important element in your composition. Typically, this will be the center. For example, if your door is in the center, give its columns the widest opening (3.46 top).

3.46 **Intercolumniation to Use**

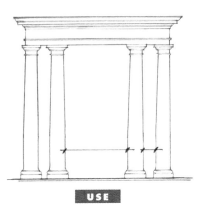

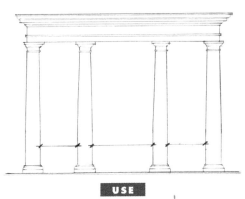

USE

USE

USE

Use narrow spans set at a reasonable width for the materials employed (wood spans farther than stone).

Clearly paired columns create a more formal effect.

Set a hierarchy of inflection that gives focus to the most important bay—typically the center, location of the front door.

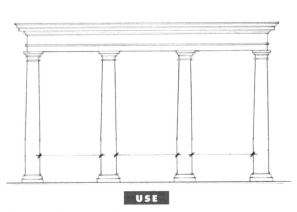

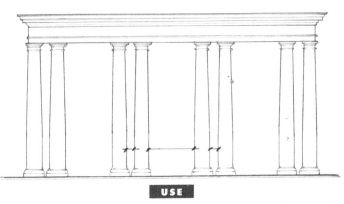

USE

USE

Space columns equally.

Clearly differentiate the spacing between the paired columns and the spaces between the pairs.

NEED TO KNOW

The Effect of Intercolumniation on Scale

The eye naturally understands the inherent structural capacities of stone; wider spans imply a smaller building than narrower spans. The columns are the same height and diameter in each of the drawings below. Widely spaced (left), they "read" as a door surround. Narrow intercolumniation (right) implies a giant temple front.

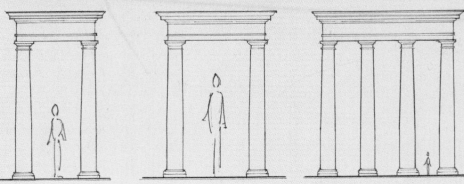

3.47 **Superimposition to Avoid**

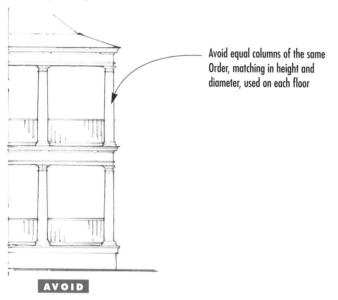

Avoid equal columns of the same Order, matching in height and diameter, used on each floor

AVOID

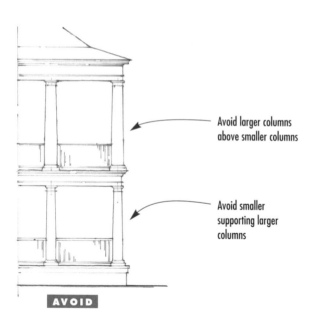

Avoid larger columns above smaller columns

Avoid smaller supporting larger columns

AVOID

CHECKLIST

Superimposition

❑ Is the first-floor column or pier larger than the second-floor column or post?

❑ Are the columns aligned along the same centerline, front and side?

❑ Are higher Orders (Ionic, Doric) above lower Orders (Tuscan)?

SUPERIMPOSITION

Superimposition is the name given to successive tiers of columns two, three, or more stories high. The ancient Romans made extensive use of superimposition, most famously at the Coliseum. Today, superimposed columns are more likely to be found on two-story porches. We have already outlined general rules for installing superimposed columns **(see Installing Columns, page 52)**. Here, we will look at design in practice.

Keep two principles in mind when superimposing columns: the lower floor must always be heavier than the upper floor and the centerlines of the columns must always align from floor to floor.

Two Common Mistakes

Avoid superimposing two identical columns, as shown in 3.47 (top). Because of the entasis **(see Selecting Columns, page 46)**, the second-floor columns will visually appear to be heavier, so the composition will look top-heavy.

If the first-floor height is lower than the second-floor height, take care with the column diameter. Normally a shorter column would have a narrower diameter, but it looks wrong for a small column to support a larger one, as shown in 3.47 (bottom). Instead, use a chunkier column or a square wood or masonry pier on the ground floor to create a hierarchy.

Variations to Use

For a three-story building (or taller), consider using a masonry ground floor with either round or elliptical arches or square piers. (Round columns can be set above square piers, but never the other way around.) Always set all columns, piers, and pedestals on the same centerline, both front and side. The neck diameter of the lower column should equal the base diameter of the upper column.

Always diminish the Orders in diameter, starting heavy and moving lighter. Higher Orders (Corinthian, Ionic) superimpose the lower Orders (Tuscan, Doric), so a natural diminution occurs, because of the Orders' increasing slenderness ratio.

3.48 **Superimposition to Use**

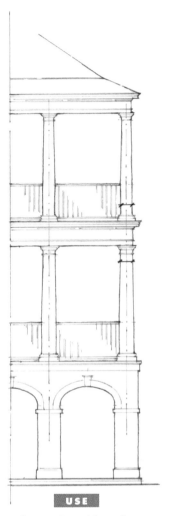

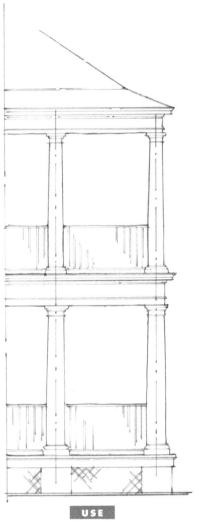

USE

Columns aligned from floor to
floor along the same centerline

USE

Diameter at the base of column
above matching neck of column
below set on the same centerline

USE

Thin columns or posts over
chunky columns or piers set on
the same centerline

NEED TO KNOW

Hierarchy of Support

- Heavier supports lighter
- Piers support columns
- Columns support posts
- Tuscan supports Doric, Doric supports Ionic,
  never the other way around. **(See also Double
  Porches, page 176.)**

3.49 Giant Orders to Avoid

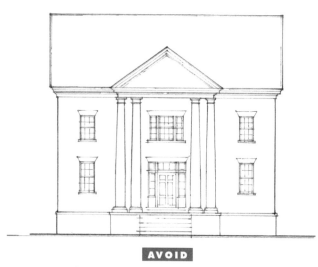

AVOID

Avoid thin and flimsy giant Orders that are underscaled for the building and entablature, without an architrave, and not detailed and sized in relation to columns.

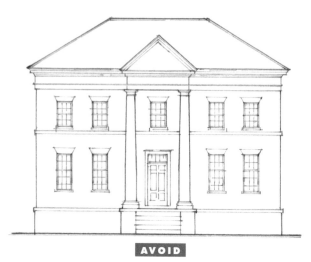

AVOID

Avoid using giant Orders with only two columns (they need at least four to feel right).

CHECKLIST

Giant Orders

❏ Have you set out the columns, entablature, and pediment according to the principles of the Orders?

❏ Do you have at least four columns?

GIANT ORDERS

A "giant" Order is a formal motif in which the column extends two (or more) stories high. Michelangelo first made use of giant Orders in the Renaissance, and they then became a common motif in grand eighteenth- and nineteenth-century construction. They are particularly common in Greek Revival buildings, where a large two-story temple-fronted main block would be flanked by one or two single-story wings to either side (3.50).

Because they allow columns to span more than one story, giant Orders make it possible to combine the formal language of the temple with contemporary practical requirements for multi-story building, while maintaining relatively low ceiling heights.

Designs to Avoid

When designing with giant Orders, don't forget the principles of the Orders in general. It is common to see buildings with giant Orders that appear too weak, even though they extend the height of the building. This is illustrated in 3.49 (top), where the sets of paired columns are too far apart for their height and the entablature is too small for the diameter of the column.

Figure 3.49 shows a design that is often found on suburban McMansions: the double-height pair of columns. This detail looks too vertical and thin for the house. Never use only two columns in a giant Order, always four or more.

Designs to Use

When using giant Orders, set them out like a normal temple front and size the columns and entablature according to the proportions of your selected Order. If you find this too heavy in appearance, then you may attenuate the order **(see Attenuated Orders, page 144)**. Attenuation involves stretching the height of an Order by up to one third while keeping the diameter (and entablature dimension) the same, thereby making the columns appear more slender and the building feel lighter and more elegant.

3.50 **Giant Orders to Use**

USE

The Greek Revival House

Use giant Orders with columns and entablature correctly scaled for the building. Use smaller Orders proportionally reduced on the same building. Make sure the giant Order has least four columns.

3.51 **Giant Orders Variations**

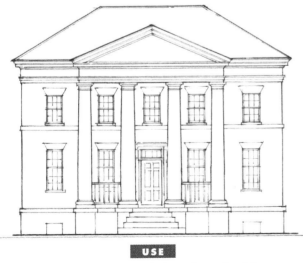

USE

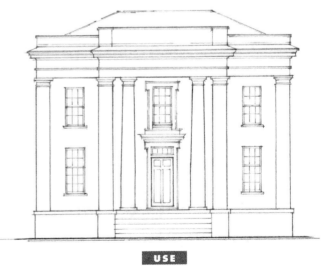

USE

Intermediate divisions to break down the scale of the building

Orders integrated throughout the building by changing into pilasters at corners

3.52 **Parapets to Avoid**

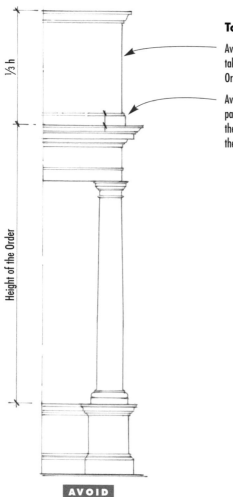

Too tall

Avoid setting the parapet height taller than 1/3 height of the Order below

Avoid undersized bases on the parapet—it will be eclipsed by the cornice when viewed from the ground

AVOID

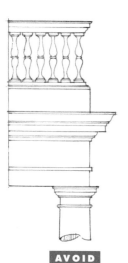

AVOID

Avoid balusters without a corner block.

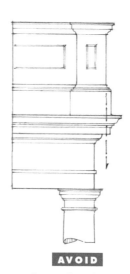

AVOID

Avoid extending the parapet over the cornice.

ATTICS AND PARAPETS

Attics and parapets occur above the cornice, either in place of or in addition to a pediment. In residential applications, attics and parapets are used on decks above porches to provide a railing.

Setting the Correct Height

Proportion your attic in relation to the entablature and column below. Figure 3.52 (top) shows what happens if you make the attic too large. Attics that are more than 1/3 the height of the Order below will appear to overwhelm the columns and entablature. Typically the attic is 1/5 the height of the Order, but this will vary depending on the specific design.

Figure 3.53 shows details for the attic in practice. The moldings should be laid out in the same way as for plinths, with a nose and cove at the base and a cap at the top.

Always Use Corner Blocks

Don't just let balusters run round the corner; they will look too insubstantial (3.52 bottom left). Always use corner blocks, called pedestals. The blocks can be left plain or paneled, as shown in 3.54. Depending on your application, use turned balusters or solid walls between the blocks.

Alignment

There are two conventions for the alignment of the attic. You can align the face of the pedestal with the neck of the column (3.55 right). This will mean that the base of the pedestal will project over the neck of the column and face of the architrave. Or you can align the face of the base with the neck of the column (3.55 left). This will lighten the appearance of the attic on the building.

The alignment that you select will vary depending on how heavy or attenuated you would like the parapet to feel in relation to the overall composition. In either case, the centerline of the column should align with the centerline of the pedestal.

3.53 **Parapets to Use**

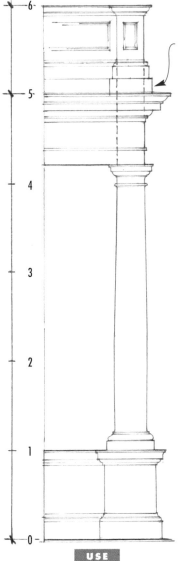

USE

Setting the height

Use a base visible above the cornice, +/- $^1/_5$ the height of the parapet

Set the height of the parapet, or attic, between $^1/_4$–$^1/_3$ the height of the column and entablature, not including pedestal, or $^1/_5$ the height of the Order including pedestal. Parapets can be lower than these dimensions, but should not be higher.

3.54 **Detailing the Panel**

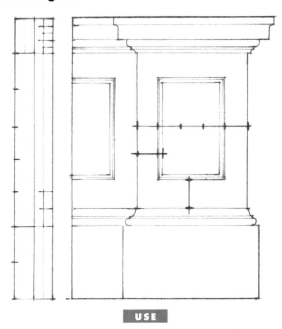

USE

Detailing the panel on a parapet is the same as detailing the panel on a door. Match the dimensions of the top rail and stiles. Make the bottom rail slightly taller. Parapets can be detailed in a variety of ways; study historic precedent for examples that suit your project.

3.55 **Corner Details**

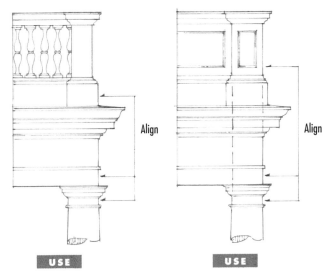

Align

Align

USE   USE

When using balusters, always use a corner block. Either set the face of the baseboard to align with the architrave and neck of column, or set the face of the parapet to align with architrave and column neck.

Note: When a parapet is located above columns, always align a pedestal over the column.

CHECKLIST

Attics & Parapets

❏ Is the height set in relation to the Order below?

❏ Have you used corner blocks?

❏ Does the centerline of the corner block align with the centerline of the column?

❏ Does the face (or the base) of the corner block align with the neck of the column?

AUTHENTIC·TRADITIONAL X SYNTHETIC·TRADITIONALIST

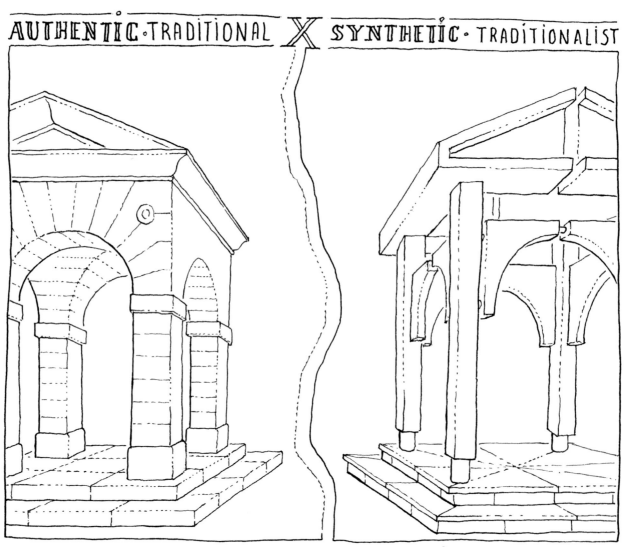

STRUCTURAL FORM & STYLE ANTI~STRUCTURAL

Chapter 4

ARCHES AND PEDIMENTS

Arches and pediments are two of the most typical motifs in traditional architecture. Though they themselves do not belong to the classical Orders, they appear in many elements of a building—from windows to doors to porches to roofs.

ARCHES AND PEDIMENTS

ARCHES WERE A ROMAN INVENTION. Greek architects used trabeated construction—that is, they raised horizontal beams on vertical posts or columns. This system, by its nature, limited the distance between columns to the length that a piece of stone or wood could span, unsupported, without cracking. But Roman engineers began to develop a system of arched structures that allowed them to span much greater distances.

An arch effectively overcomes the inherent weakness of stone by combining smaller pieces into a larger framework so that the forces of gravity are perfectly resolved and the structure remains stable. A properly constructed arch is an immensely resilient piece of construction, as witnessed by the survival of so many ancient Roman ruins, culminating in the Pantheon in Rome—effectively a giant arched building that for centuries remained the largest single-spanned domed structure in the world.

The Basics of Arch Construction

Today, because almost anything is structurally possible, we tend to lose sight of the common-sense *tectonics* of arch construction. It is from this oversight that most mistakes occur.

The basic tectonics of the arch, shown in 4.1, require an *impost*, or square starting block; *voussoirs*, the blocks making up the arch; and a *keystone*, the block at the top of the arch that, placed in last, binds everything in place and prevents the arch from falling in on itself.

It is good practice to stilt the arch: that is, to raise its center point a couple of inches above the top of the impost. This allows the arch to meet the support below vertically and keeps it from appearing to kick out at the sides.

Types of Arches

Arches come in several forms. The six most common types are illustrated in 4.3; the flat arch, elliptical arch, segmental arch, Tudor arch or four-point arch, semicircular arch, and Gothic or three-point arch. Although they vary in shape, these arches are all held up by the same tectonic principles. Their individual pieces work together and align to one or a small number of center points.

Classical Combinations

Romans incorporated the arch into the basic grammar of the classical language. Figure 4.4 shows a classical Order superimposed over an arch order, a style demonstrated most famously in the Roman Coliseum.

4.1 **The Arch**

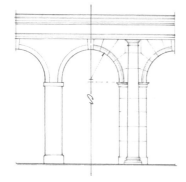

4.2 **The Pediment**

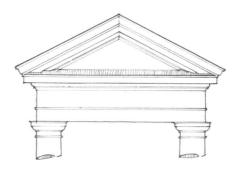

4.3 **Types of Arches**

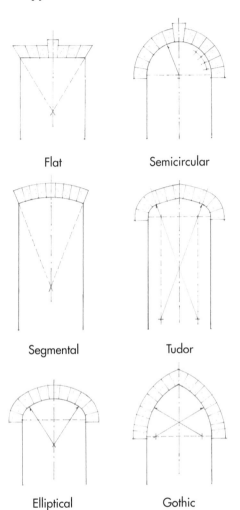

Flat

Semicircular

Segmental

Tudor

Elliptical

Gothic

4.4 **The Roman Triumphal Arch**

4.5 **Raking Cyma and Split Fillet**

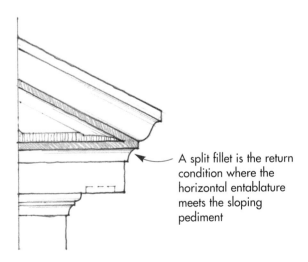

A split fillet is the return condition where the horizontal entablature meets the sloping pediment

Pediments

Another archetypal form of classical architecture, the pediment, is the formal expression of a gable-end roof; supported by a row of columns, actual or implied, it forms the "temple-front" motif we see in hundreds of thousands of buildings, from the Parthenon in Athens to farmhouses in Connecticut (4.2). The pediment has many applications in the traditional house, not only at the roof but also in door and window surrounds. It too must be detailed in keeping with the classical Orders, with a raking cyma and split fillet (4.5). The rules for setting out pediments are explained in the second half of this chapter.

4.6 **Semicircular Arches to Avoid**

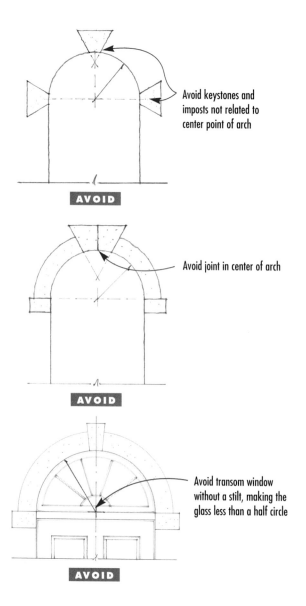

Avoid keystones and imposts not related to center point of arch

AVOID

Avoid joint in center of arch

AVOID

Avoid transom window without a stilt, making the glass less than a half circle

AVOID

CHECKLIST

Semicircular Arches

❏ Did you stilt the arch?
❏ Do all of the joints point to the center point of the arch?
❏ Are the imposts rectangular?
❏ Could it work without hidden structure?

SEMICIRCULAR ARCHES

Today, the details of an arch are often made up of decorative elements applied over hidden structure. But this is not license to design arches that could not stand up on their own. No matter how we build the actual structure, we need to maintain a common-sense approach to design. **(See Design with Common Sense: Structure Check, page 8.)**

Arches to Avoid

The rule of thumb is simple: If it couldn't stand without hidden structure, do not use it. Avoid the no-center arch with keystones and imposts that do not relate to the center point (4.6 top). Never put a joint in the center of the arch (4.6 center). If these designs were built out of stone without hidden structure, they would fall down.

Arches to Use

Study the example of 4.7 and note the following rules:
- Use rectangular imposts
- Stilt the arch by raising its center point two inches over the imposts
- Divide the arch into equally spaced voussoirs whose joints point to the center
- Set the keystone at the top of the arch with its joints pointing to the center

Figure 4.8 shows a more formal treatment. The keystone has been stepped and a profiled molding has been applied. And instead of delineated voussoirs, an architrave has been used to frame the arch. (The details of such an architrave should match the architrave of a typical door or window surround.)

Arched Windows

Adding a stilt to the arch grounds it into the vertical support below and keeps it from appearing to push out on the sides. When transom windows are inserted within an arch, stilting allows the glass to be a true half circle (4.9).

4.7 **Semicircular Arches to Use**

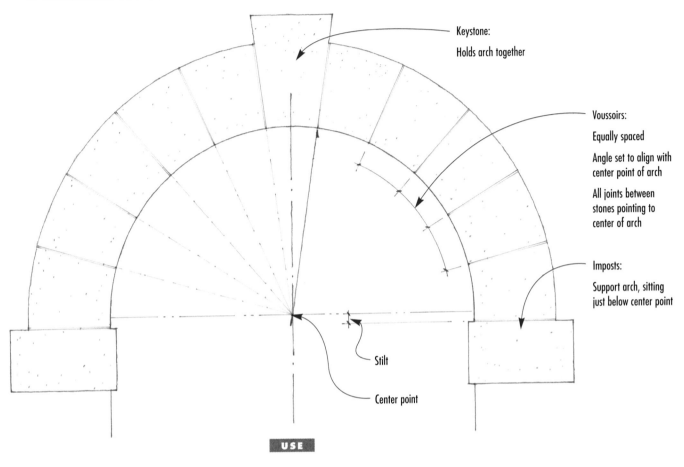

Keystone:

Holds arch together

Voussoirs:

Equally spaced

Angle set to align with center point of arch

All joints between stones pointing to center of arch

Imposts:

Support arch, sitting just below center point

Stilt

Center point

USE

4.8 **Semicircular Arch Variation**

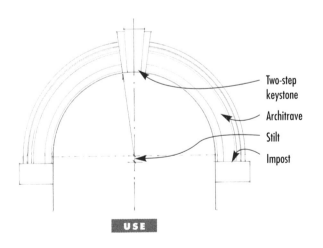

Two-step keystone

Architrave

Stilt

Impost

USE

4.9 **Semicircular Windows to Use**

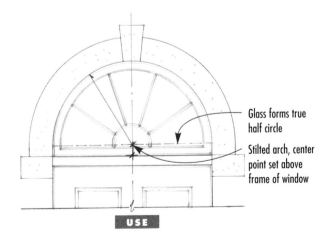

Glass forms true half circle

Stilted arch, center point set above frame of window

USE

4.10 **Elliptical Arches to Avoid**

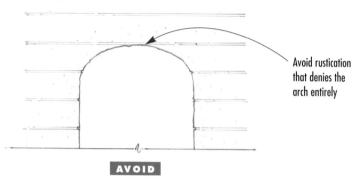

Avoid rustication that denies the arch entirely

AVOID

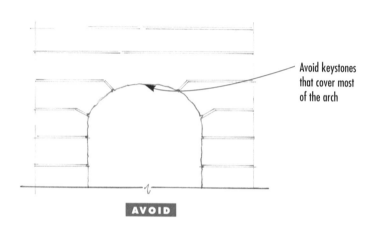

Avoid keystones that cover most of the arch

AVOID

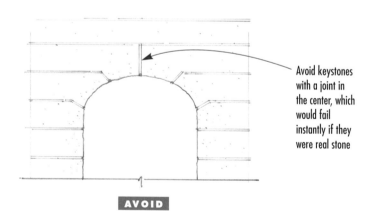

Avoid keystones with a joint in the center, which would fail instantly if they were real stone

AVOID

CHECKLIST

Elliptical Arches

- ❑ Did you stilt the arch?
- ❑ Did you lay out a regular ellipse, like 4.12?
- ❑ Are the imposts rectangular?
- ❑ Could it work without hidden structure?

ELLIPTICAL ARCHES

Ellipses are a convenient form of arch to use when the floor-to-floor height does not allow a full semicircular arched opening. The curves of an elliptical arch are also particularly graceful. For this reason, they became popular in the Federal period, when designers sought to accentuate long, elegant lines and curves. Elliptical arches were especially used in over-door locations, as shown in more detail on pages 136 and 137.

Details to Avoid

As with the regular semicircular arch, innumerable mistakes are made with elliptical arches, too many to catalog exhaustively here. The diagrams to the left show three examples that have gone wrong because the rustication denies the construction of the arch. In 4.10, the top design completely ignores the arch. The center design treats the arch like a cartoon. The bottom design undermines the structure by placing a joint at the most important location.

Setting Out an Ellipse

There are a number of techniques for setting out a true ellipse. Computer drafting technology and cutting machinery have made ellipses rather easier to form accurately in recent years, but some tried and tested methods are shown on the opposite page.

Figure 4.11 shows a three-centered elliptical arch. Though not strictly speaking a true ellipse, this arch can be set out relatively easily because it relies on two unvarying radii, as opposed to the methods shown in 4.12, where the radius of the curve is continuously changing.

The rules for elliptical arches are largely the same as for true semicircular arched openings. The arch should still be stilted, the voussoirs should still point to the center of the arch, and the keystone should act in exactly the same way. The arch should resolve with a vertical line at the springing point, just above the imposts. At its centerline, too, the radius line should just touch horizontal, as in an ordinary semicircular arch.

4.11 Elliptical Arches to Use

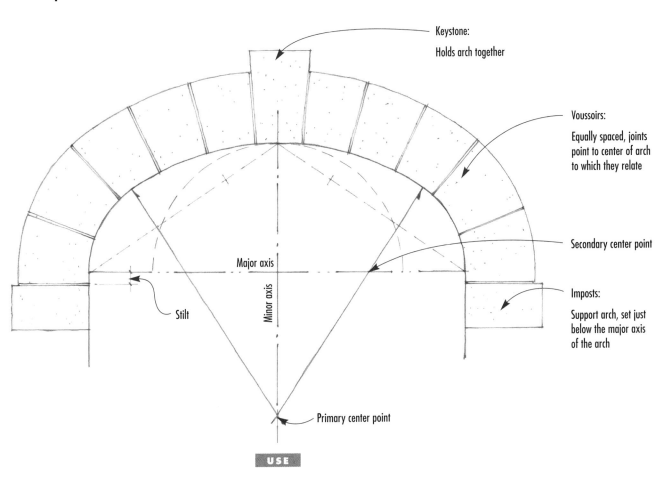

Keystone:
Holds arch together

Voussoirs:
Equally spaced, joints point to center of arch to which they relate

Secondary center point

Major axis

Minor axis

Stilt

Imposts:
Support arch, set just below the major axis of the arch

Primary center point

USE

4.12 Setting Out Elliptical Arches

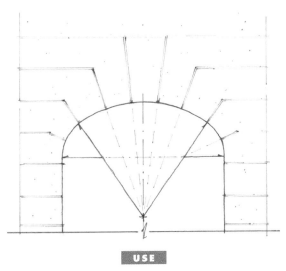

USE

Setting out the rustication

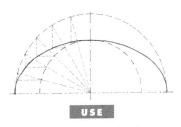

USE

String method

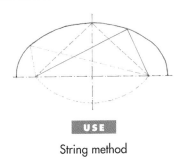

USE

Intersection method

4.13 **Arcades to Avoid**

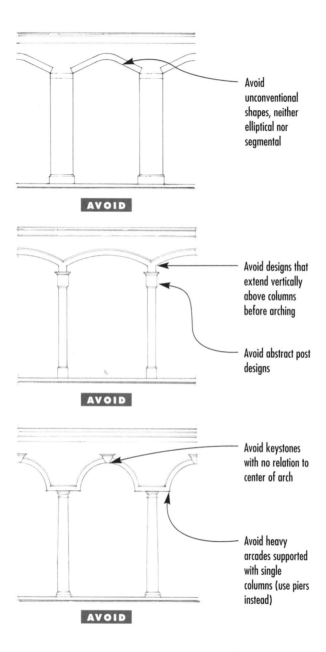

Avoid unconventional shapes, neither elliptical nor segmental

AVOID

Avoid designs that extend vertically above columns before arching

Avoid abstract post designs

AVOID

Avoid keystones with no relation to center of arch

Avoid heavy arcades supported with single columns (use piers instead)

AVOID

ARCADES

An arcade is composed of three or more arches in a series. It may directly employ the Orders (4.14) or use abstracted forms proportioned to fit the Orders, but without columns.

Some Common Mistakes

It would be impossible to catalog all the mistakes that are made with arches and arcades. Three very common examples are shown on this page. All of them ignore the basic rules outlined in the diagrams opposite.

Beware of the tendency, often seen on McMansions (and especially on McMediterranean McMansions), to clutter a building with arches and arcades. Don't fall prey to the illusion that lots of arches, or lots of different types of arches, make a building "classical." In fact, genuine classical buildings use arches with discretion. When it comes to arches, less is truly more.

Arcades to Use

When using the Orders on the arches that form your arcade, don't forget the vocabulary and the relationships of parts.

Figure 4.14 (top left) shows the same design as the diagram below it, but with the columns removed. It still speaks the classical language. You can see how the imposts, keystone, and entablature are related directly to the columns of 4.14 (bottom left), even though they are no longer actually used.

Figure 4.14 (top right) shows an *elliptical* arch on piers. Elliptical arches are employed where, for practical reasons, you need to maintain a certain clear width between the piers or columns but do not have the floor-to-floor height to fit in an entire half-round arch. The rules for setting out elliptical arches are shown in more detail on the preceding pages.

4.14 **Arcades to Use**

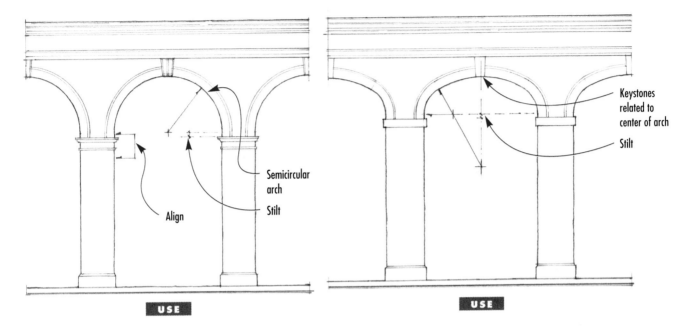

Semicircular arch

Stilt

Align

Keystones related to center of arch

Stilt

USE

USE

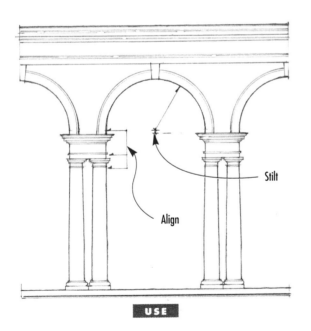

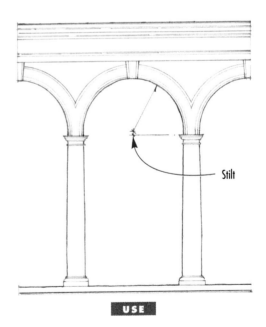

Stilt

Align

Stilt

USE

USE

4.15 **Pediments to Avoid**

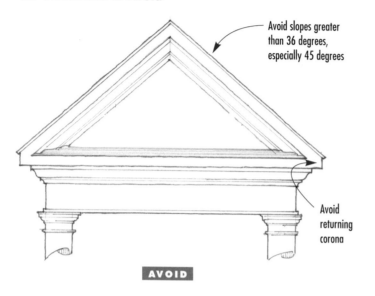

Avoid slopes greater than 36 degrees, especially 45 degrees

Avoid returning corona

AVOID

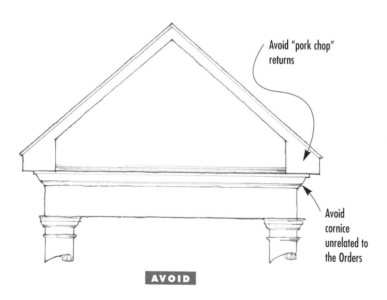

Avoid "pork chop" returns

Avoid cornice unrelated to the Orders

AVOID

SETTING OUT PEDIMENTS

The two most common methods for determining the slope of a pediment are illustrated on page 83. The method used by the Romans, shown in 4.16 (left), is the simplest technique because it requires only two steps. The slope that results from this method will be constant regardless of the width of the pediment. This slope is approximately 22.5 degrees.

Figure 4.16 (right) illustrates a more complex method used by the ancient Greeks. This geometry sets the slope in relation to the width of the pediment. Wider pediments will have a lower slope; narrower ones will have a higher slope, so that pediments on especially wide structures do not overpower the buildings.

The slope of the pediment, like every other element on the building, must relate to the overall composition and will vary depending on style. Greek pediments have lower slopes, while Georgian or Federal pediments have higher slopes.

It isn't always necessary to use case-specific geometry to set the slope of the pediment. Over time, practice has yielded a series of pleasing pediment slopes: 18, 22.5, 26.5, and 31.6 degrees.

Pediments to Avoid

Don't forget the Orders, especially in the cornice. The elements that make up the cornice of a pedimented Order are exactly the same elements that make up the cornices that we have looked at thus far in this book.

Figure 4.15 shows pediments with steep slopes and cornices that have departed from the classical Orders. A cornice is properly composed of a bedmold, a corona, and a cyma **(see Learn the Vocabulary, page 13)**. Be certain that your design contains each of these elements before you attempt to detail the pediment. Avoid setting the slope of the pediment steeper than 36 degrees, and take special care to avoid 45 degrees.

4.16 Pediments to Use

Roman construction

1. Determine the centerline of the pediment.

2. Set Point A on the cornice where the centerline intersects the cyma.

3. Using a radius set from Point A to the far edge of the cyma, draw an arc and set Point B.

4. Draw another arc, using the distance from Point B to the cyma as the radius. Set the top of the pediment at the point where this radius crosses the centerline.

   Note: The resulting slope is usually 22.5 degrees.

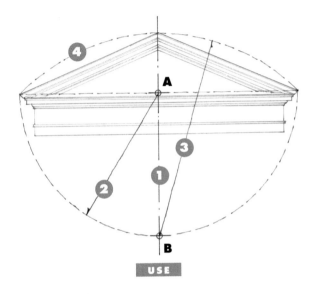

USE

Greek construction

1. Determine the centerline of the pediment.

2. Draw an arc, using the length of the cyma as the radius. Set Point A where this arc crosses the centerline.

3. Draw another arc, using the distance from Point A to the cyma as the radius. Where this radius crosses the centerline, set the lowest point of the cornice of the pediment.

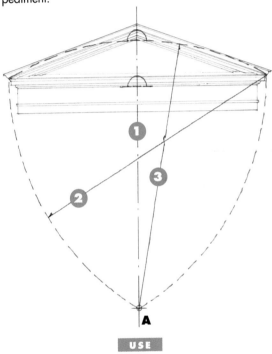

USE

4.17 Balancing the Pediment

When setting the slope of the pediment, take into account the proportions of the entire assembly. The area of the columns should be equal to the combined area of the entablature and pediment.

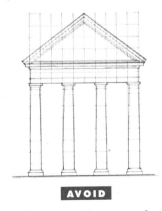

AVOID

Avoid pediments that are too heavy for the supporting columns.

USE

In a typical Roman temple, the area of the columns is equal to the area of the entablature and pediment.

USE

The heavier proportions of the Greek entablature result in a lower pediment slope to keep balance with the columns.

4.18 **Pediment Details to Avoid**

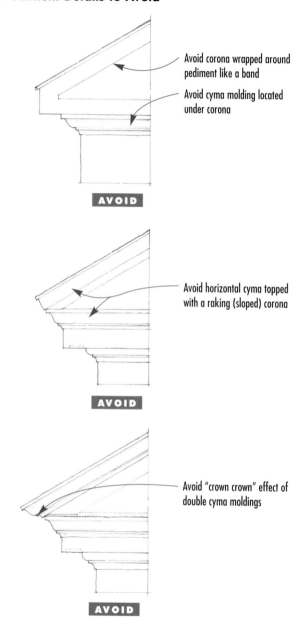

Avoid corona wrapped around pediment like a band

Avoid cyma molding located under corona

AVOID

Avoid horizontal cyma topped with a raking (sloped) corona

AVOID

Avoid "crown crown" effect of double cyma moldings

AVOID

CHECKLIST

Pediments

❑ Is the slope set at a calculated angle (not the same as the main roof)?

❑ Does the cornice have a bedmold, corona, and cyma?

❑ Does the raking cyma have the correct profile, different than the horizontal cyma?

❑ The horizontal cyma should not extend across the front of the pediment.

THE RAKING CYMA

Constructing a pediment requires using a raking cyma and split fillet (4.19). These moldings require different profiles in the angled moldings than in the horizontal members. This detail is complex to design and expensive to build. If it isn't within your means to get this right, it is better to simplify the design to a horizontal entablature. In chapter 10, devoted to the eaves of your building, we show a detail called the Poor Man's Cornice. This detail makes it possible to cut corners on the gable end of a house or a dormer on a roof, but if you are using a pediment on a door surround or formal element that is close to eye level, there are no shortcuts; only an authentic pediment will do.

Pediments to Avoid

First make sure that the cornice has the correct elements: bedmold, corona, and cyma. This will eliminate the possibility of ending up with a "pork chop" return (4.18 top) or raking corona (4.18 center).

Once the cornice is right, look carefully at the element that you angle. Note that in a correctly detailed pediment, the cyma does not carry across the entablature horizontally. Instead, it splits at the fillet and angles up the side of the building (4.19).

Carrying the cyma horizontally across the entablature, as well as at an angle, will result in a double cyma (4.18 bottom) or an extra corona. Both details should be avoided. On the side elevation the extra piece makes the cornice too heavy in relation to the other elements in the Order.

Constructing a Raking Cyma

The step-by-step construction of a pediment, showing the raking cyma, is illustrated on the opposite page. Critically, the profile of the horizontal cyma on the side of the entablature does not match the profile of the raking (angled) cyma; instead, the raking cyma is elongated, so that when the two moldings meet they form a clean miter at the corner.

4.19 **Pediment Details to Use**

A raking cyma is the key element when constructing a pediment. It describes the adjusted profile of the cyma molding as it extends up the angle of the pediment. The only way to make the geometry of the cyma resolve is to use two different cyma profiles.

1. Set the profile of the horizontal cyma molding

2. Draw the lines of the cyma up the angle of the pediment, making sure that the fillet is split

3. Dot in several equally spaced construction lines extending up the slope of the cyma

4. Draw lines perpendicular to both the angle of the roof and to the ground

5. Plot the profile of horizontal cyma on the sloping cyma

6. Connect the points to determine the profile of the raking cyma

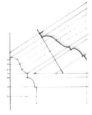

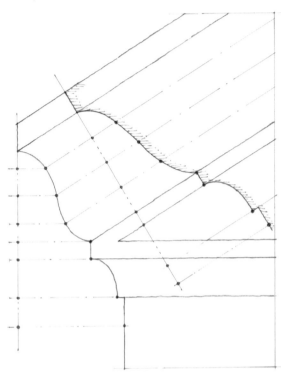

Constructing a Raking Cyma

Follow steps 1–6 to determine the profile of the raking cyma. The angled cyma will be more elongated than the horizontal cyma.

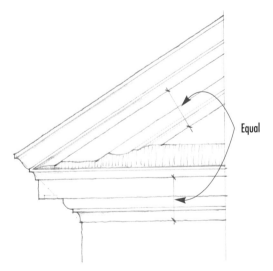

Constructing a Raking Cornice

A full raking cornice has all of the same elements of the horizontal cornice. After the angle of the raking cyma is set, repeat the raking profiles of the corona and bedmold to match the horizontal corona and bedmold.

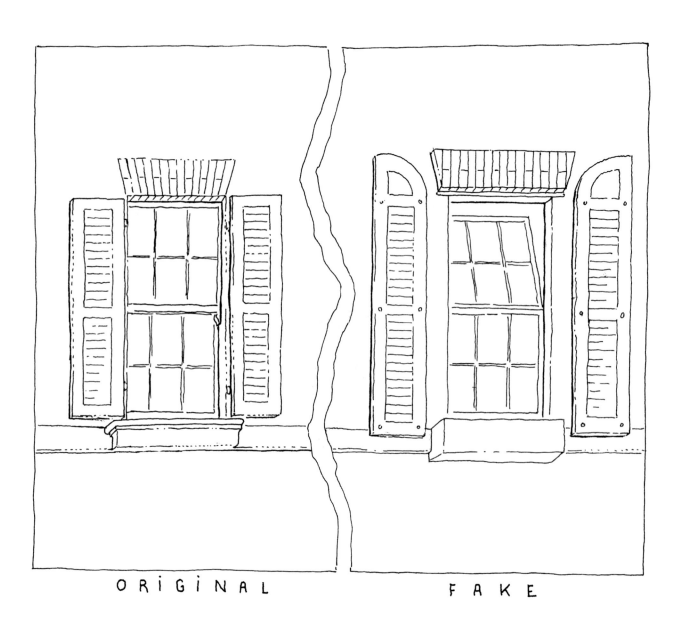

ORIGINAL

FAKE

Chapter 5

W I N D O W S

Windows are more than a means of providing light and ventilation. They are the "eyes" of the house. They connect it to the world around it, framing a view from the inside and offering a glimpse of interior life to the passerby. Windows, more than any other single element, will determine the character of your house.

WINDOWS

SINCE THE INTRODUCTION OF GLAZED OPENINGS in the medieval period, window design has gone hand in hand with technological developments. In the seventeenth century, wood or stone transoms contained very small leaded lights. The sash window arrived when the production of larger panes became possible in the eighteenth century, initially with multiple panes and thick glazing bars, and, as time progressed, with fewer panes and thinner muntins. Today, with technology that makes these structural limitations a thing of the past, we must choose windows more consciously and carefully than ever to create an authentic design.

In Chapter 2, we looked at the composition and design of openings as they appear from across the street—the "big picture." When choosing, buying, and placing windows, it is vital to familiarize yourself with these concepts. If you have not read that chapter, you should do so before proceeding here.

But getting your windows to feel authentic is about more than the big picture. As we find time and again, good building means thinking big first, then focusing on the details. The thickness of glazing bars, the way you treat a window surround, and how you build a dormer window: all these details will have a significant effect on the success or failure of the house as a whole.

Style and Window Design

The style of your building will determine the window size and the arrangement of the lights (the panes of glass in the window). A Georgian house might have large 9-over-9 windows with small individual panes, while a Federal house often has slightly smaller 6-over-6 windows, with larger individual panes. The variations of styles are too vast to explore in depth in this book, but the general principles apply across styles. We illustrate most of the examples with a 6-over-6 window in an opening with 2:1 proportions (5.1). As you design and detail your building, study historical precedent, then apply these principles as the style of your home dictates.

Where to Start

Successful window design achieves two goals. First, it reinforces the overall composition of the building by *unifying* the design. Second, it introduces a layer of *hierarchy* that adds focus to the primary floor and important rooms of the house. In a well-designed building, you can read the floor plan simply by looking at the elevation and the windows. Although these two goals—unity and hierarchy—appear to be contrary, they are not. This dual purpose is what makes an elevation dynamic.

Figure 5.2 shows a range of window types and light proportions. This chapter will explain first how to combine the window types correctly, then how to detail them.

5.1 **Windows**

The proportion, organization, and detailing of the windows on a house greatly impacts the appearance of the building.

5.2 **Double-Hung Windows**

3 over 6

6 over 6

6 over 9 (cottage style)

9 over 9

Triple hung

5.3 **Window Details**

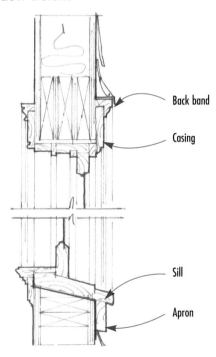

Back band

Casing

Sill

Apron

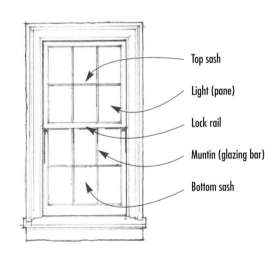

Top sash

Light (pane)

Lock rail

Muntin (glazing bar)

Bottom sash

5.4 **Window Shapes**

 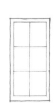    

Elliptical

Casement

Segmental arch

Lancet

Gothic sash

Palladian

5.5 **Glazing Bars**

Windows without glazing bars give a house a hollow look; glazing bars give it texture and human scale.

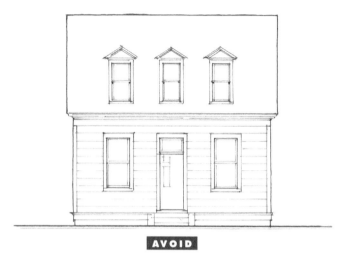

AVOID

USE

5.6 **Proportion of Lights**

Horizontal lights sit uncomfortably in a vertical window; vertical lights reinforce the proportions of the window and the house.

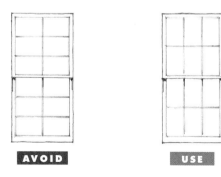

AVOID   USE

GLAZING BARS AND LIGHTS

Historically, large panes of glass were expensive because they were difficult to make and often broke during transportation. Glazing bars were used to divide the sash into small areas that were more manageable.

Today, although glass is available in almost any size—including huge sheets of plate glass—it is important not to omit the glazing bars. Windows without them often look like blank holes in a wall. The addition of glazing bars breaks down their size and gives the house texture and a sense of scale (5.5).

Vertical Proportion

Whatever the shape of your opening, it is important to keep the glazing lights *vertical*. Horizontal panes make a window appear squat and ugly, even if the window is well proportioned overall, because they conflict with the vertical shape of the opening (5.6).

Grouped and Paired Windows

When windows are paired or grouped together, keep the proportion and size of lights consistent to provide continuity of scale. Although the width of the opening can, and often does, change between the windows, make sure that the light size remains the same (5.7).

When to Omit Glazing Bars

Glazing bars *are* commonly omitted in some architectural styles, and occasionally left out for economy (fewer pieces in the window cost less). When you omit glazing bars from part of a window, do so vertically, not horizontally. That is, remove them from a lower sash and leave them in the top sash. Don't remove them from a center window while keeping them on the sides; this disrupts the continuity of scale in the design (5.8). Whatever arrangement you choose, use it consistently throughout the house.

Lights in Arched Windows

Be very careful when designing and selecting arched windows; they can easily overwhelm your design. Make sure that the division of lights is consistent throughout the entire window, with lights in the arch kept similar in size to those below (5.9).

5.7 Grouped and Paired Windows

Keep the size and proportion of lights consistent among windows in a group.

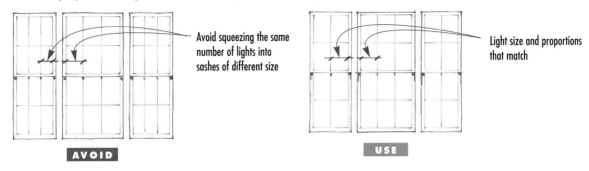

Avoid squeezing the same number of lights into sashes of different size

AVOID

Light size and proportions that match

USE

5.8 Windows without Glazing Bars

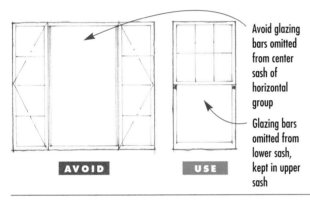

Avoid glazing bars omitted from center sash of horizontal group

Glazing bars omitted from lower sash, kept in upper sash

AVOID   USE

5.9 Windows with Segmental Arches

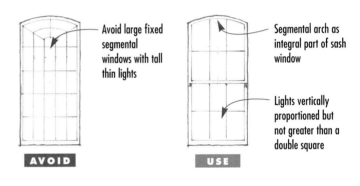

Avoid large fixed segmental windows with tall thin lights

Segmental arch as integral part of sash window

Lights vertically proportioned but not greater than a double square

AVOID   USE

5.10 Semicircular Windows

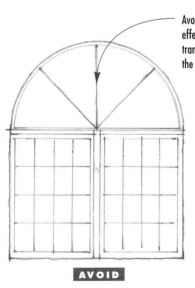

Avoid "wagon wheel" effect of large semicircular transom out of scale with the windows below

AVOID

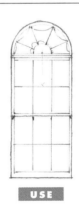 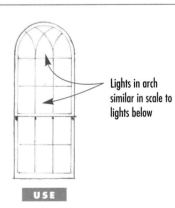

Lights in arch similar in scale to lights below

USE   USE

NEED TO KNOW

Glazing Bars and Scale

Glazing bars give scale to a building. But if they are not handled correctly, things can go wrong. Avoid too much variety in the glazing—both within each window and in the combination of glazing patterns in a group of windows. Don't lose sight of the big picture.

5.11 **Division of Lights on a Façade**

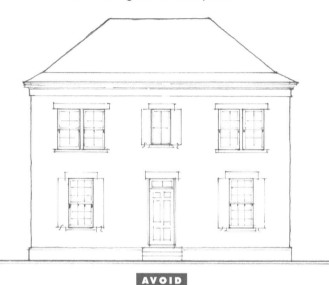

AVOID

Random collection of divisions that bear no relation to other windows on façade

USE

Coherent combination of divisions that reinforces composition of house

WINDOWS FLOOR TO FLOOR

The relationship of opening sizes and lights between windows on different floors can either unify or disrupt your composition. Use window and pane sizes to create hierarchy while maintaining a sense of balance between floors. Relate each window's opening and light proportions to the other windows and to the proportions of the building as a whole (5.11).

Organizing the Openings

Think about the façade, and all the windows in it, as a whole. Do not just "elevate the plan," that is, create the elevation by simply placing windows according to their function inside the house. The front elevation, in particular, needs care to create a unified appearance. Take a step back and look at the overall composition. In some cases you will need to make a choice between centering a window on a wall within a room and keeping the windows aligned on the exterior. Every situation is slightly different, but a strong and unified design will find a way to balance exterior alignment with sensible interior window placement in each room.

Relationships between Floors

The illustrations opposite show a series of relationships between windows on different floors. Although the differences are subtle, they will have an important effect on the success or failure of your building.

At worst, there is no relationship between the ground and first-floor windows. Never allow this to happen. A series of simple alternatives, to use where budget or supply issues do not allow something more complex, is shown next. Finally, look at the "best" examples. These have shared pane sizes or proportional ratios, ensuring a harmonious sense of unity between windows, while also varying the size of the openings, creating a sense of hierarchy.

5.12 Division of Lights from Floor to Floor

Bad:

Windows with more lights have hierarchy over fewer lights, yet larger lights have hierarchy over smaller lights. Here, the hierarchy is confused.

Better I:

Windows that share light size and proportion unite the composition, but the difference in height between these 6-over-6 and 9-over-9 windows can disrupt the façade.

Better II:

Using the same window on each floor can create a static effect. Use this combination cautiously.

Better III:

Use the same proportions for both floors, but vary the window size to preserve both the hierarchy and the unity. This option does not work in brick buildings where the width of the opening is fixed to a brick module.

Best I:

Use a cottage window (6-over-9) below a 6-over-6 window with the same light size and proportion.

Best II:

Set the opening size of the lower windows at a 2:1 ratio. With a 6-over-6 window, this creates lights that are golden sections, with height and width at a ratio of 5:3. Set the openings of the windows on the upper floor as golden sections also.

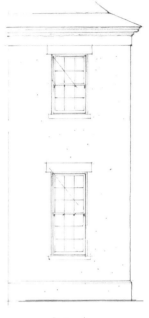

Bad

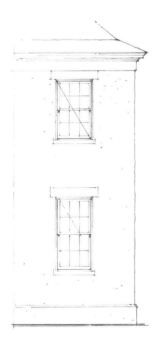

Better I

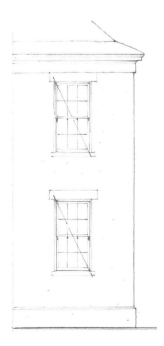

Better II

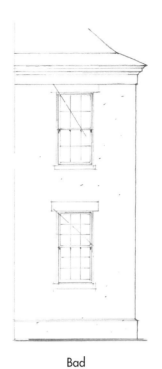

Better III

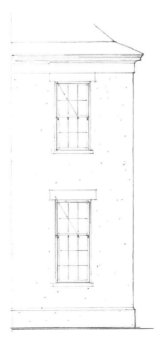

Best I

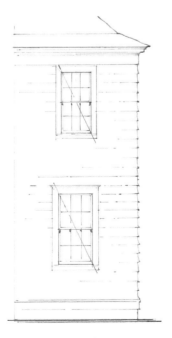

Best II

5.13 Division of Lights to Avoid

The images on these two pages illustrate two versions of a rear elevation of a townhouse. The principle here can be applied to any type of house: Avoid a collection of window divisions in a single composition that do not relate to each other.

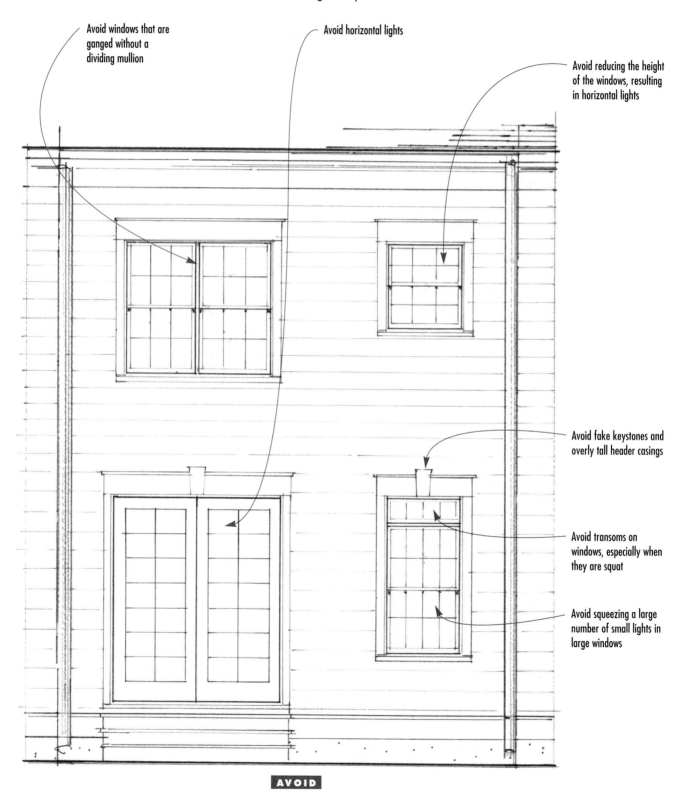

Avoid windows that are ganged without a dividing mullion

Avoid horizontal lights

Avoid reducing the height of the windows, resulting in horizontal lights

Avoid fake keystones and overly tall header casings

Avoid transoms on windows, especially when they are squat

Avoid squeezing a large number of small lights in large windows

AVOID

5.14 **Division of Lights to Use**

Relate the proportions of both opening and lights in all windows and doors in the building.

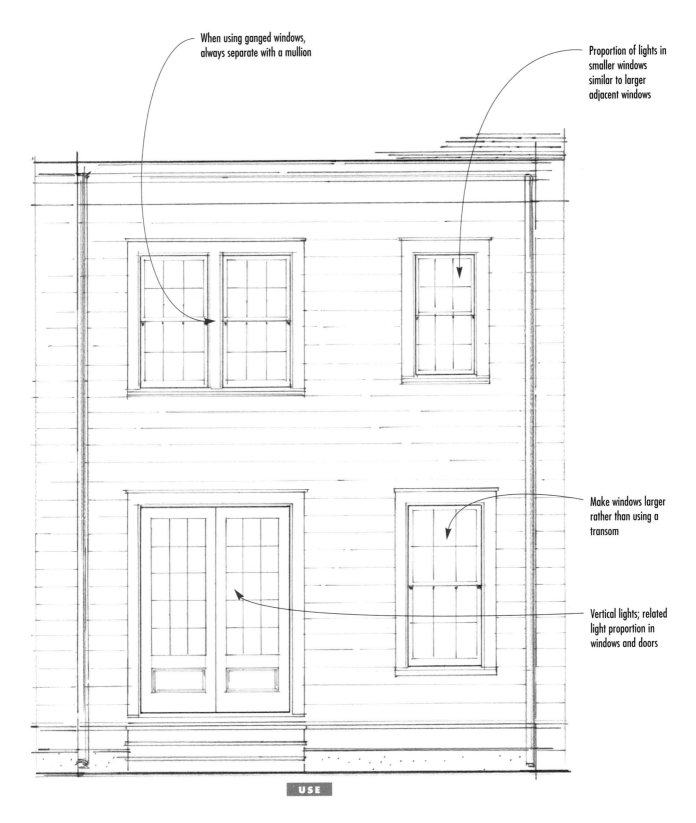

When using ganged windows, always separate with a mullion

Proportion of lights in smaller windows similar to larger adjacent windows

Make windows larger rather than using a transom

Vertical lights; related light proportion in windows and doors

USE

5.15 **Flanges, Casings, and Sills**

Modern windows often do not come with an integral casing and sill. Rather, they simply come with a flange, requiring the casing to be applied. When possible use a window with a casing and sill; if this is not an option, take special on-site care when installing the casing.

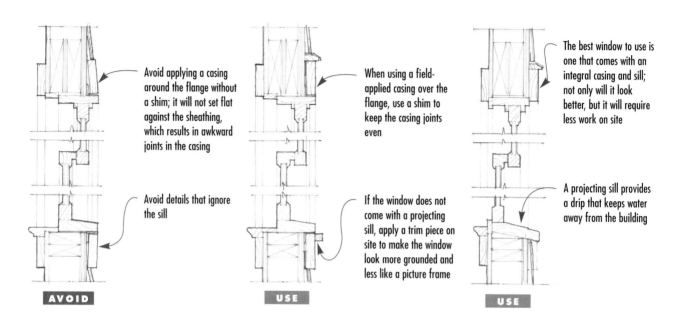

Avoid applying a casing around the flange without a shim; it will not set flat against the sheathing, which results in awkward joints in the casing

Avoid details that ignore the sill

AVOID

When using a field-applied casing over the flange, use a shim to keep the casing joints even

If the window does not come with a projecting sill, apply a trim piece on site to make the window look more grounded and less like a picture frame

USE

The best window to use is one that comes with an integral casing and sill; not only will it look better, but it will require less work on site

A projecting sill provides a drip that keeps water away from the building

USE

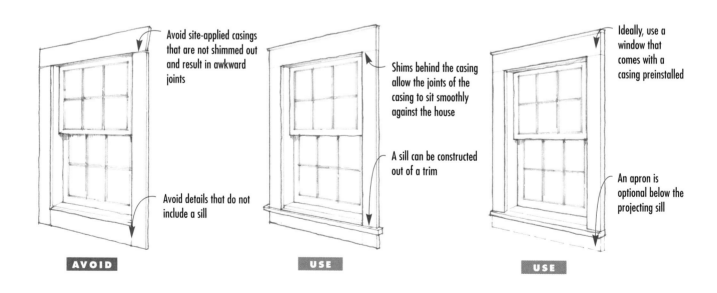

Avoid site-applied casings that are not shimmed out and result in awkward joints

Avoid details that do not include a sill

AVOID

Shims behind the casing allow the joints of the casing to sit smoothly against the house

A sill can be constructed out of a trim

USE

Ideally, use a window that comes with a casing preinstalled

An apron is optional below the projecting sill

USE

5.16 **Window Profiles**

Most windows available today derive to some degree from traditional precedent. The most successful designs are based closely on this precedent.

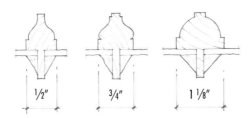

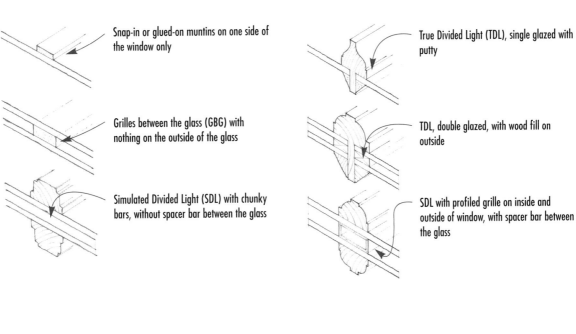

Snap-in or glued-on muntins on one side of the window only

Grilles between the glass (GBG) with nothing on the outside of the glass

Simulated Divided Light (SDL) with chunky bars, without spacer bar between the glass

True Divided Light (TDL), single glazed with putty

TDL, double glazed, with wood fill on outside

SDL with profiled grille on inside and outside of window, with spacer bar between the glass

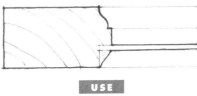

USE

Historic precedent

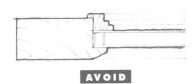

AVOID

Avoid profiles that project beyond the face of the window.

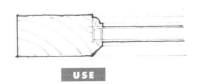

USE

Use profiles based on traditional window designs and construction techniques.

5.17 **Window Casings to Avoid**

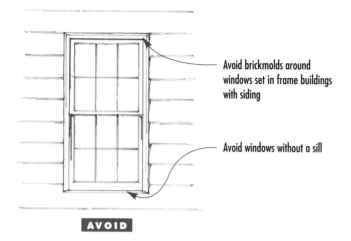

Avoid brickmolds around windows set in frame buildings with siding

Avoid windows without a sill

AVOID

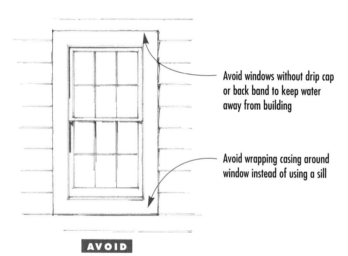

Avoid windows without drip cap or back band to keep water away from building

Avoid wrapping casing around window instead of using a sill

AVOID

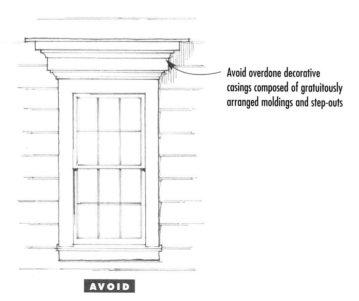

Avoid overdone decorative casings composed of gratuitously arranged moldings and step-outs

AVOID

EXTERIOR WINDOW CASINGS

The most common American window type is a sash window in a simple wood frame house. Exterior window casings serve two functions: they enrich the opening and provide additional protection from rainwater. The details of casing, lintel, and sill have a very important role in preventing water from entering at a vulnerable location.

Details to Avoid

A window needs a casing, both to provide a suitable visual "frame" within the facade and to protect the cut ends of the siding. Avoid using a brick mold in place of a casing, and don't forget the sill (5.17 top). As well as keeping water out of the building, the casing and sill visually engage the window with the house.

Avoid window casings that wrap all around the window and do not have a drip cap or backband (5.17 center). When water hits the casing, it will run down the face of the window rather than dripping away.

When dressing up a casing with moldings, make sure that the elements are in the right order. Always avoid the terminating corona (5.17 bottom). **(See Molding Details, page 50.)**

Details to Use

Figure 5.18 shows the same window, correctly detailed, in section and elevation. The crucial points to note are the drip cap and sill/apron. These are the minimum details that the window requires to do a good job of keeping water out. If you use a flat casing without a back band, make sure the casing is thick enough for the siding to resolve into the casing without exposing the end grain. Always use a visible sill; if you have ordered a vinyl or clad product made without an integral sill, add one on site.

Wood surrounds can have varying degrees of enrichment, depending on how much prominence you wish to give each opening on the elevation. Fully molded casings, with a bead and back band, add shadow and texture to the façade. In more ornate historical wooden buildings a frieze and cornice are added. If you are using this level of detail, make sure that the elements are in the right order. **(See Molding Details, page 50.)**

5.18 Window Casings to Use

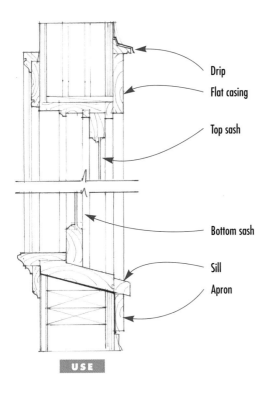

Drip

Flat casing

Top sash

Bottom sash

Sill

Apron

USE

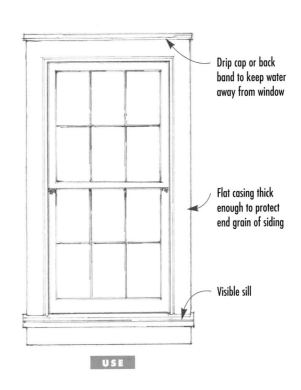

Drip cap or back band to keep water away from window

Flat casing thick enough to protect end grain of siding

Visible sill

USE

5.19 Window Casing Variations

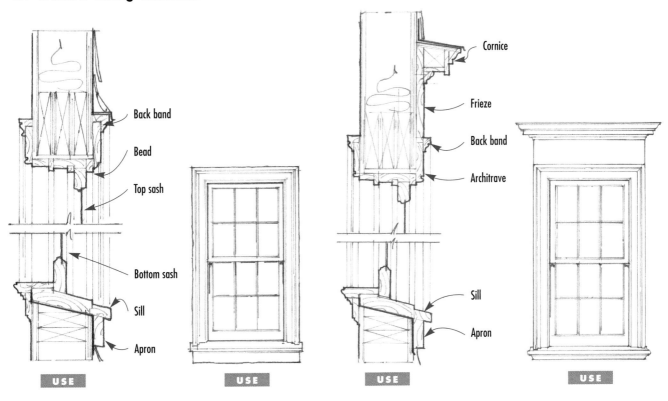

Back band

Bead

Top sash

Bottom sash

Sill

Apron

USE

USE

Cornice

Frieze

Back band

Architrave

Sill

Apron

USE

USE

5.20 **Masonry Lintels to Avoid**

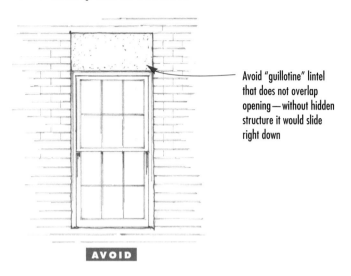

Avoid "guillotine" lintel that does not overlap opening—without hidden structure it would slide right down

AVOID

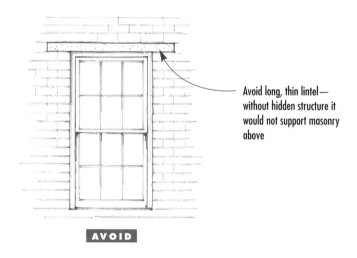

Avoid long, thin lintel— without hidden structure it would not support masonry above

AVOID

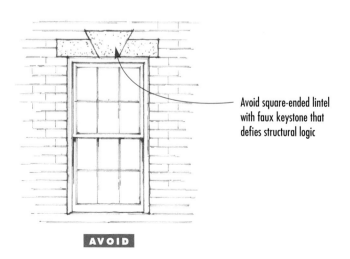

Avoid square-ended lintel with faux keystone that defies structural logic

AVOID

MASONRY LINTELS

Openings in masonry walls can be spanned in two ways: with lintels or with arches. Depending on the materials, lintels are the most economical for shorter spans. Arches, due to their structural qualities, can span further. **(See Arches and Pediments, page 74.)** The visual expectation for the size of a lintel is based on what was traditionally possible in masonry construction, without hidden structure.

Unlike the wood examples described on the previous pages, masonry construction does not require a frame around the opening to keep the weather out. As long as the window frame is well caulked and flashed at the sill and head, there should be no chance for rain to penetrate the opening, even if it is kept plain.

Lintels to Avoid

If the lintel has no overhang or bearing, it could never stay up without hidden structure. It would fall through the opening like the blade of a guillotine (5.20 top). A thin lintel is disturbing to look at because it too would fail without hidden structure; it could not support the weight of the wall above it (5.20 center).

Lintels to Use

Extend the lintel 4″ to 6″ on each side of the opening. Set the height of the lintel to twice the dimension of the overhang. Set the stone sill overhang at the same 2:1 ratio, two brick courses high, and let it project slightly from the face of the wall to allow for a drip molding (5.21).

Lintels with Keystones

In general, keystones should be used sparingly with lintels. On a normal-size window opening, a beam lintel is visually and structurally sufficient to span the opening. On the basis of the common-sense structure check, that's a good place to stop.

If your windows need particular emphasis, then add a keystone but make sure it is correctly sized and proportioned. It is best to use treat the lintel as a flat arch as shown in 5.22.

5.21 **Masonry Lintels to Use**

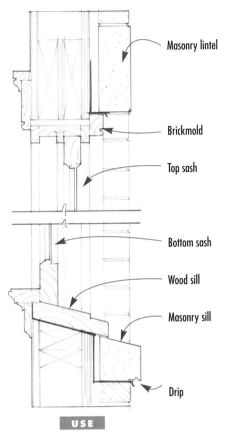

Masonry lintel

Brickmold

Top sash

Bottom sash

Wood sill

Masonry sill

Drip

USE

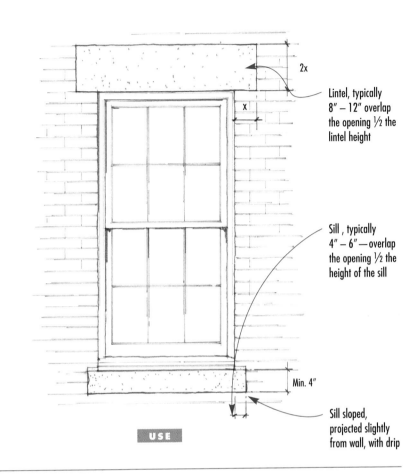

2x

Lintel, typically 8" – 12" overlap the opening ½ the lintel height

x

Sill , typically 4" – 6" —overlap the opening ½ the height of the sill

Min. 4"

Sill sloped, projected slightly from wall, with drip

USE

5.22 **Masonry Lintel Variation**

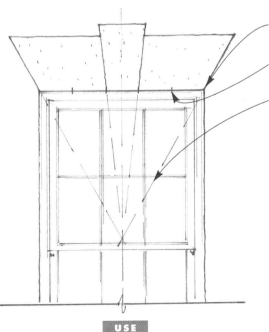

Angle set at 60 degrees or 72 degrees

Divide arch in five parts; assign center division to keystone

Set angle of keystone from the center point generated by the corner

USE

5.23 **Brick Arches to Avoid**

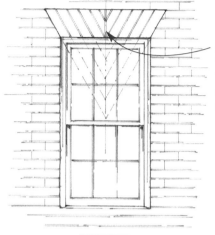

Avoid a No-Point arch with all bricks set at the same angle, resulting in a center seam

AVOID

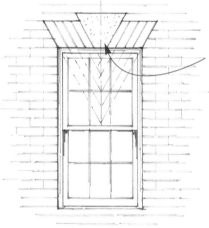

Avoid attempting to disguise the No-Point arch with a giant keystone

AVOID

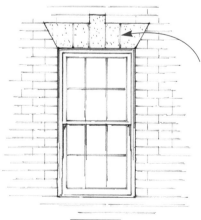

Avoid lintels with vertical joints, a design that denies arch structure and could never stand up on its own

AVOID

GAUGED BRICK ARCHES

A gauged brick or "jack" arch spans an opening with a series of tapered bricks. Each brick in the arch is formed at a slightly different angle, allowing all of the joints between the bricks to radiate from a single point at the center of the arch.

Jack arch "set-ups" are available from many brick manufacturers, but can be expensive. If budget is an issue, be careful when cutting corners. Some attempts to fake a gauged brick arch are transparent, while others can make convincing substitutes.

Details to Avoid

As an alternative to the tapered bricks of a gauged arch, manufacturers offer angled bricks that are substantially less expensive. Although this design appears to work in the corners, when the two sides meet at the center it is impossible to resolve the angles. The result is a joint at the center of the arch (5.23 top). This could never stand without hidden structure.

To hide the awkward seam, some manufacturers add a keystone (5.23 center). The problem here is that the angle of the keystone has to match the angle at the corners of the arch, making it too large and disrupting its structural relationship to the arch.

A real arch stands up through tension, each of the members working with the others to cross a span. If the joints don't reflect this relationship, the design will not feel authentic (5.23 bottom).

Details to Use

A true gauged brick arch is made up of tapered bricks with each joint angling to a single center point (5.24). If you use a keystone, set the angle from the center point (5.25 left). The angle at the corners of the arch varies depending on the design, but is usually either 60 degrees (as shown here) or 72 degrees.

An Economical Alternative

Use angled bricks that are resolved in the center with a single vertical brick (5.25 right). This design, ideal for small openings, is recommended only for side and rear elevations or outbuildings. The key to making it look right is to use a steep angle, 72 degrees or more.

5.24 **Brick Arches to Use**

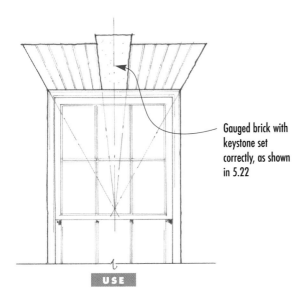

Gauged brick lintel

Brickmold

Top sash

Bottom sash

Wood sill

Brick rowlock sill

USE

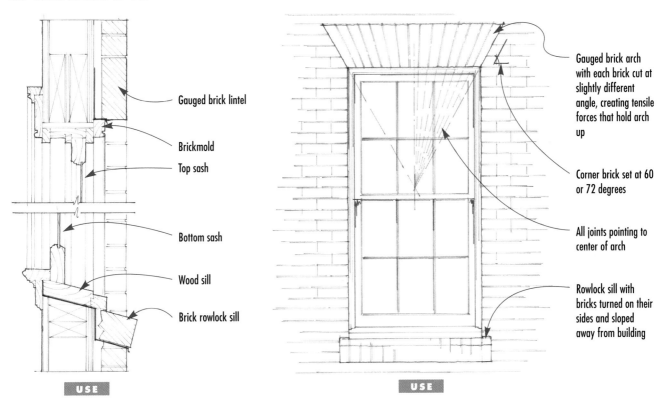

Gauged brick arch with each brick cut at slightly different angle, creating tensile forces that hold arch up

Corner brick set at 60 or 72 degrees

All joints pointing to center of arch

Rowlock sill with bricks turned on their sides and sloped away from building

USE

5.25 **Brick Arch Variations**

Gauged brick with keystone set correctly, as shown in 5.22

USE

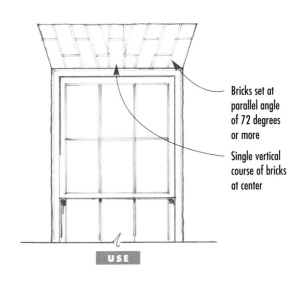

Bricks set at parallel angle of 72 degrees or more

Single vertical course of bricks at center

USE

5.26 More Brick Arches to Avoid

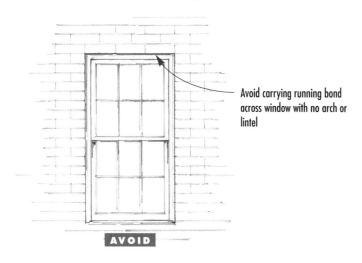

Avoid carrying running bond across window with no arch or lintel

AVOID

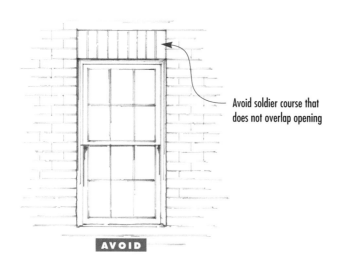

Avoid soldier course that does not overlap opening

AVOID

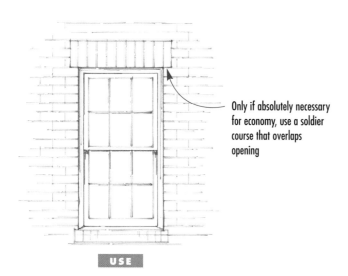

Only if absolutely necessary for economy, use a soldier course that overlaps opening

USE

OTHER BRICK LINTELS

The details that we have looked at for both lintels and gauged brick arches can be expensive, and in some cases the budget may not even allow for an attempt. Unfortunately, regardless of cost, the structure spanning the opening needs to be acknowledged in some form.

Alternatives to Avoid

Do not carry the running bond across the opening with no lintel or arch at all (5.26 top). If you are spending the money to build a masonry building, use one of the less expensive alternatives outlined in these pages.

The most economical way to express a lintel is to run a soldier course of brick above the opening (5.26 center). This solution should be avoided if at all possible, because it could never stand on its own. But if, for reasons of economy, none of the preferred designs is an option, a soldier-course lintel may be the least of the evils. If you use this design, make sure that it is wider than the opening by one or two bricks (5.26 bottom). This design would not stand without hidden structure either, yet at a glance it is more convincing than the other options illustrated here.

Alternatives to Use

Another excellent traditional alternative that does not require special bricks is to set regular bricks in a very shallow arch over the opening (about $2^1/_2''$ to $3''$ for a $3'\text{-}0''$ wide opening) and "feather" the joints between the arch bricks—that is, let the joints get slightly thicker towards the top (5.27). In this way, it is possible to form a good, simple arch without the need to cut bricks as you would for a jack arch.

Beware of Cutting Corners

Remember, in a brick building you must always acknowledge the structure above openings (5.28). It's best to use either a concrete lintel (as detailed in 5.21) or a true gauged brick arch (as detailed in 5.24). If you can't afford to express a lintel correctly, consider whether you can really afford to build in brick.

5.27 **More Brick Arches to Use**

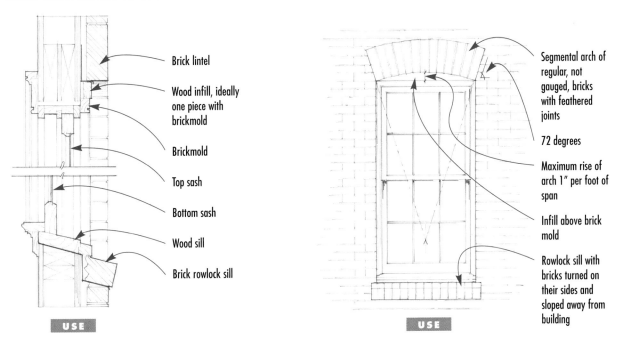

Brick lintel

Wood infill, ideally one piece with brickmold

Brickmold

Top sash

Bottom sash

Wood sill

Brick rowlock sill

USE

Segmental arch of regular, not gauged, bricks with feathered joints

72 degrees

Maximum rise of arch 1" per foot of span

Infill above brick mold

Rowlock sill with bricks turned on their sides and sloped away from building

USE

5.28 **Brick Arch Review**

Always acknowledge the structure above openings. If at all possible, express a lintel with one of the details shown here.

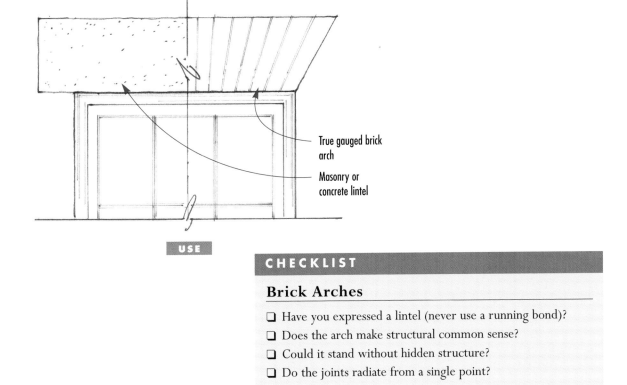

True gauged brick arch

Masonry or concrete lintel

USE

5.29 **Arched Windows to Avoid**

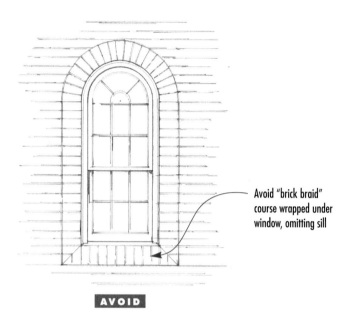

Avoid "brick braid" course wrapped under window, omitting sill

AVOID

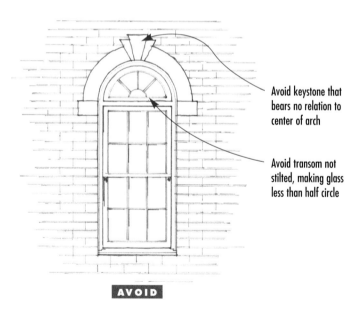

Avoid keystone that bears no relation to center of arch

Avoid transom not stilted, making glass less than half circle

AVOID

SEMICIRCULAR ARCHED WINDOWS

Arched windows can be a welcome addition to an elevation. But use them cautiously and sparingly. Before looking at the details, check that the openings are in scale with the composition of the building as a whole.

Most mistakes that occur in arched masonry openings can be avoided with an understanding of the basic principles of arch construction **(see Semicircular Arches, page 76)**:

- Stilt the arch slightly, that is, raise its center by an inch or two above the major axis—2″ for a 3′-6″ arch.
- Align all the brick joints to the center of the arch.
- If using a keystone, set it to the center of the arch.
- If using an impost, make it rectangular and set it just below the spring point of the arch.

Arched Windows to Avoid

Don't forget the window sill. The sill creates a drip to keep water away from the building, but it also forms a base for the window. Avoid omitting the sill and wrapping the brickwork all around the opening like a piece of braid (5.29 top). If you use a keystone, remember that its design must take the basic structure of the arch into account. Avoid the many variations that get this relationship wrong (5.29 bottom).

The stilt, important for any arch, takes on another useful function when the arch contains a window: it allows the glazing in the transom to be a true half circle. If it is not stilted, the arch will start below the bottom rail, resulting in a transom that is a segmental rather than semi-circular arch (5.29 bottom).

Arched Windows to Use

Remember the rules outlined above and apply them to achieve a properly detailed arch. Make sure that you use a masonry sill to act as a drip at the bottom of the window. Stilt the arch to resolve glazing even when there is not a separate transom (5.30).

There are two good, simple options for glazing arched windows. In 5.30, arches have been repeated to form a Gothic motif. Figure 5.31 shows a plain arched pattern, with muntins placed carefully to form panes of equal size.

5.30 **Arched Windows to Use**

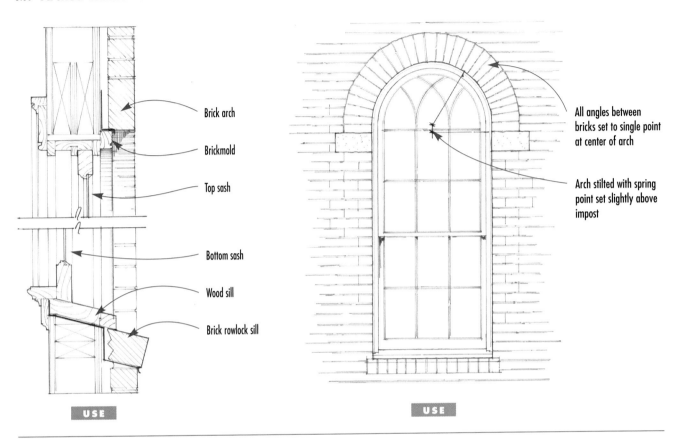

Brick arch

Brickmold

Top sash

Bottom sash

Wood sill

Brick rowlock sill

USE

All angles between
bricks set to single point
at center of arch

Arch stilted with spring
point set slightly above
impost

USE

5.31 **Arched Window Variation**

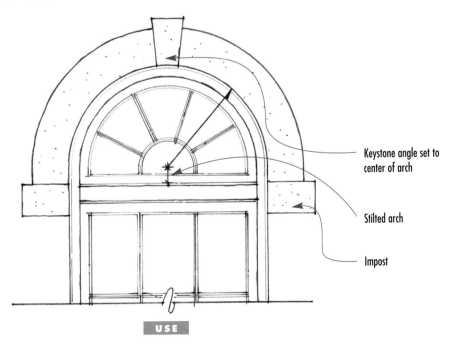

Keystone angle set to
center of arch

Stilted arch

Impost

USE

5.32 Palladian Windows to Avoid

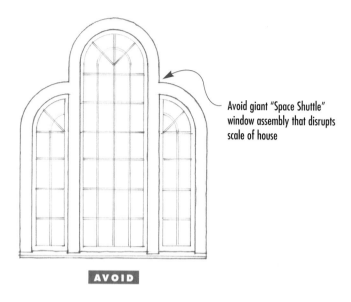

Avoid giant "Space Shuttle" window assembly that disrupts scale of house

AVOID

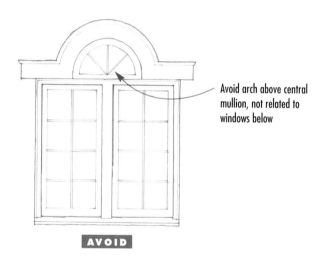

Avoid arch above central mullion, not related to windows below

AVOID

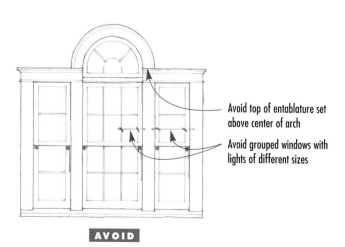

Avoid top of entablature set above center of arch

Avoid grouped windows with lights of different sizes

AVOID

PALLADIAN WINDOWS

Named after Andrea Palladio, the sixteenth-century Italian architect, Palladian architecture became popular in England and then America in the mid-eighteenth century. "Palladian" windows were frequently used on grander houses, but always reserved for the most prominent rooms.

The Palladian window is a central arch-headed window flanked by two side windows. Formal examples use columns between the windows and a full entablature at the window heads. Simpler buildings have a reduced version of the full-blown classical design.

Details to Avoid

Because they are so closely based on classical precedent, Palladian windows are very complex to lay out correctly, so some people unwisely aim for the general look. Figure 5.32 (top) shows a typical McMansion attempt to convey the impression of a Palladian window. *Never* buy a window like this. The "Space Shuttle" design, like the "Wagon Wheel," has become a ubiquitous element of many large suburban homes, but it looks absurd to the trained eye.

Simplified attempts at Palladian windows usually fall short as well. Figure 5.32 (center) would be much better without the arched window perched on top.

The window shown in 5.32 (bottom) comes closer, but the details don't work: the side lights do not match the center panes, and the arch should be an integral part of the upper sash, not an add-on.

Details to Use

Figures 5.33 and 5.34 show correctly detailed Palladian windows laid out using the classical Orders, with pilasters, full entablatures, and correctly stilted arches. In each, the glazing panes are the same width and height and the arch is an integral part of the top sash. **(See Learn the Vocabulary, page 13, and Arches and Pediments, page 80.)**

In some eighteenth-century buildings, Palladian windows were simple outside, with frames of plain stone or stucco blocks and the ornate detailing reserved for the interior. It is possible, as in 5.34, to simplify the detailing considerably and produce an authentic design.

5.33 **Palladian Windows to Use**

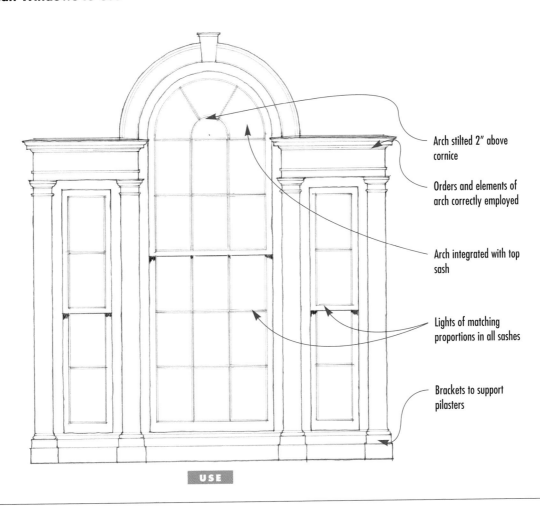

Arch stilted 2" above cornice

Orders and elements of arch correctly employed

Arch integrated with top sash

Lights of matching proportions in all sashes

Brackets to support pilasters

USE

5.34 **Palladian Window Variations**

USE

Simple beam and arch

USE

Matching light sizes and proportions, whether windows are small or large

5.35 **Shutters to Avoid**

Don't use shutters that clearly could not cover your windows correctly (or at all).

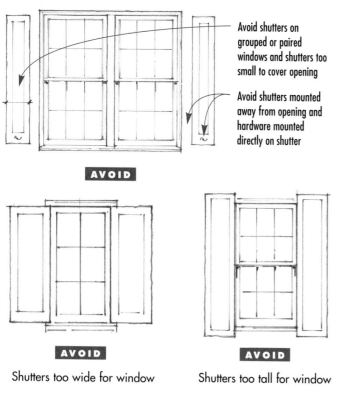

Avoid shutters on grouped or paired windows and shutters too small to cover opening

Avoid shutters mounted away from opening and hardware mounted directly on shutter

AVOID

AVOID
Shutters too wide for window

AVOID
Shutters too tall for window

5.36 **Shutters to Use**

Even decorative shutters should look as if they could work.

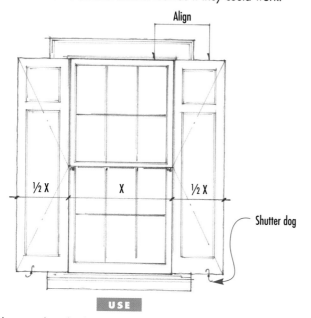

Align

½ X   X   ½ X

Shutter dog

USE

Shutters placed adjacent to window overlapping casing and sized to cover opening

SHUTTERS

Traditionally, shutters were used to provide security, privacy, and protection from the weather. Although shutters today tend to be used more for decoration, it is important that they not become a gratuitously applied ornament. At a minimum, they should *look* as though they could operate.

Working shutters offer several practical benefits. In recent years, many local building codes have begun to apply very strict hurricane requirements. Operable shutters with sheet metal backing meet many of these codes and save the cost of expensive impact glass. They can also greatly reduce the energy use of the house. Judiciously opening and closing the shutters, as people do in Southern Europe, can keep the house cooler during the hot summer months and warm during the winter.

Sizing Shutters

Avoid shutters on wide (grouped or paired) windows that could clearly never function (5.35). Likewise, avoid shutters that are too tall or too wide for the opening (5.35). A building will look better with no shutters at all than with shutters that are incorrectly sized. If your entire building has single windows with shutters and you are trying to accommodate a few double windows, either leave the shutters off the double windows or use folding shutters that extend to cover the entire opening.

When using shutters on a single window, align the top of the shutter with the top of the upper sash and the bottom edge with the base of the lower sash. Each shutter should be exactly half the width of the window, so that when closed, they meet exactly in the middle of the window (5.36). To cover a very small window, use a single-side shutter.

If your windows are arched, the shutters need to be arched to follow the profile of the opening. Avoid using square-head shutters on an arched opening (5.37).

Hardware

Use shutter hardware, such as shutter dogs and latches, on all shutters to enhance the feeling of authenticity, even if the shutters are not real. But use common sense when mounting the hardware. Never mount it directly in the center of the shutter so that it could clearly never work (5.35 top). Shutter dogs come in many designs and can be located on sides or at the bottom of the windows. Study precedent to find a design that works with your building.

Placing the Shutters

Never mount the shutters away from the window jamb (5.35 top). Instead, always install them adjacent to the window, as if they were operable. Never cover the shutters with a railing or balcony unless it is placed to allow the shutters to operate freely (5.38).

Shutter Styles

Many different stock designs of shutters are available on the market (5.39). Use shutters with rails, stiles, and a lock rail. The panels can either be solid or louvered. Solid panels, which are early eighteenth-century in appearance, typically give a more robust look to your building. Historically, the ground floor of a building might have had paneled shutters for security, while the upper floor had louvered shutters to capture breezes. The first floor shutters often had a square or rectangular panel at the top with a small decorative cutout, often to symbolize something important to the family that commissioned the house. A building project with a large budget might still use this detail today.

CHECKLIST

Shutters

- ❏ Are the shutters sized to cover the entire opening?
- ❏ Do they look as if they could operate?
- ❏ Do the shutters align with the top and bottom of the opening?
- ❏ Is the hardware located where it could be of use?
- ❏ Does the railing allow the shutter to work?

5.37 **Shutters on Arched Windows**
Always match the tops of the shutters to the arched window head.

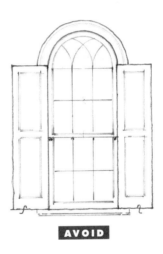 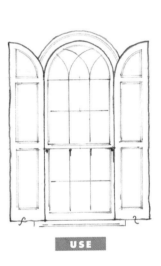

AVOID USE

5.39 **Shutter Styles to Use**

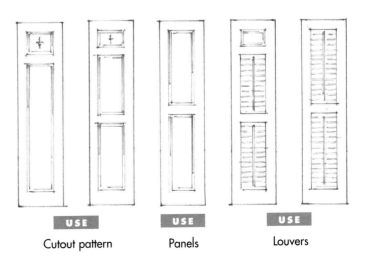

USE   USE   USE

Cutout pattern   Panels   Louvers

5.38 **Shutters and Common Sense**
Don't combine shutters with railings in such a way that they could not possibly function.

AVOID   USE

5.40 **Window Screens**

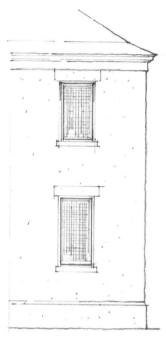

AVOID

Avoid screens that cover entire window, especially on front elevation.

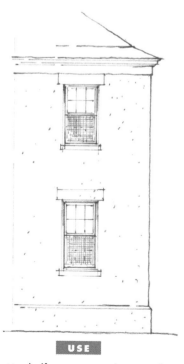

USE

Use half screens over lower sash or roll screen inside sash. Only use screens on windows that will be opened.

SCREENS

Window screens are unavoidable in any location that gets infested with insects in summer. Screens allow the sash windows to be opened fully to catch any breeze without letting insects in, particularly at night, when the lights inside attract them.

The trouble with screens is twofold. They can tend to give the house a "blank" look. As we discussed earlier in this chapter **(see Glazing Bars and Lights, page 90),** multiple panes give a sense of scale to a building, but the screen covers these and creates the appearance of large voids at the openings. Also, screens can make a house dark inside.

Screens to Avoid

Avoid using full-size exterior screens on every window on the house (5.40 top). If possible, avoid using exterior screens on the front of the house; limit their use to the side and back.

Where you do use screens, you can mitigate the effect on the house in several ways. Depending on design and budget, a single house may use more than one of the following options.

Screens to Use

One solution, using half screens over the lower sash only (5.40 bottom), keeps the scale of the window while offering ventilation. The half screens are also more manageable and easy to store in the winter. The only drawback is that the top sash cannot be opened. If full size screens are used, make them removable so you can take them down in the winter.

As an alternative, use interior rolling screens that fit completely into the jamb of the window when closed. This detail is more expensive; it also requires a deeper wall section to accommodate a thicker jamb.

Screen Material

Traditionally, houses had copper screens. Over time, the copper took on a light patina. Copper is the ideal material, but not always in the budget.

Some synthetic meshes available are dark and opaque and will block light passing through the windows. Look for a transparent material that is a light color and will not sag in the larger openings.

CASEMENTS

Casement windows preceded the development of sliding sash windows in the early eighteenth century. They are most often found on simpler or vernacular buildings, as well as in the English Arts & Crafts style of architecture, but are also characteristic of formal, classical styles in hot countries, where they combine particularly well with exterior louvered shutters to provide shade and breeze. A casement window is hinged on one side and swings open, unlike a sash window, which slides up and down in its jamb to open. Casement windows can open either inward or outward, depending on whether screens and shutters are mounted on the inside or the outside.

When to Use Casements

Although most American house styles use sash windows, casements can be found in styles such as French Norman, Tudor, and Mediterranean. Casement windows can also be mixed into houses with sash windows, regardless of style.

Sometimes it is nice to use casements over the kitchen sink because they are easier to open when you lean across the counter. They can also work well in small bathrooms or powder rooms where the opening would be too small for a well-proportioned sash window.

Casement windows can be successfully mixed with sashes in the same house as long as care is taken to relate light size and proportion. Avoid mixing tall, thin lights in casement windows with shorter, squatter sash lights.

Center Division

When using casement windows with two leafs, it is best to use a frame without a central mullion dividing the two. If it isn't possible to eliminate the mullion, try to find a detail that minimizes the width. It won't be noticeable when the window is closed, but when both sides are open, a large division in the center of the opening will be distracting.

Light Proportion

Figure 5.41 illustrates a range of light configurations and proportions. Each of these examples is good. As an exception to the light proportions we looked at in the beginning of this chapter, casement windows *can* have horizontal lights.

When determining the light proportion of a casement window, it's important to make sure that it relates to the other windows in the house and to the overall composition.

5.41 **Casement Windows to Use**

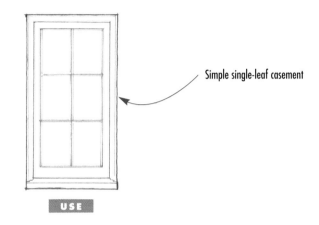

Simple single-leaf casement

USE

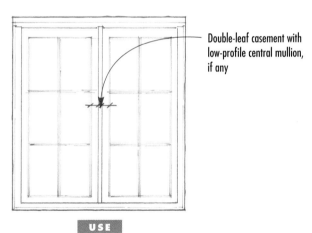

Double-leaf casement with low-profile central mullion, if any

USE

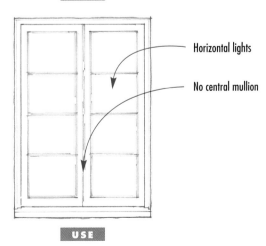

Horizontal lights

No central mullion

USE

5.42 **Dormer Details**

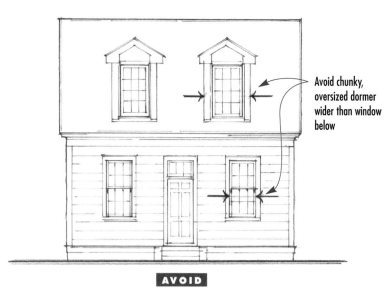

Avoid chunky, oversized dormer wider than window below

AVOID

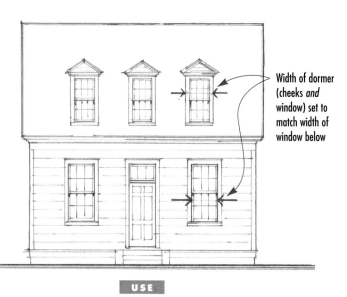

Width of dormer (cheeks *and* window) set to match width of window below

USE

5.43 **Dormer Windows**

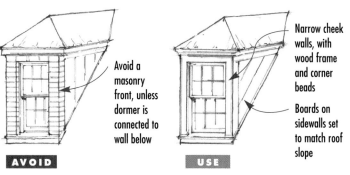

Avoid a masonry front, unless dormer is connected to wall below

AVOID

Narrow cheek walls, with wood frame and corner beads

Boards on sidewalls set to match roof slope

USE

DORMER WINDOWS

Dormer windows were traditionally used to let light into the attic and to create habitable space without the expense of adding an entire floor. Architecturally, they can be used to break up the mass of a large roof on bigger buildings. But a poorly designed dormer can drastically change the appearance of an otherwise nice house. Badly scaled or incorrectly detailed dormers are one of the number one disaster zones—and are visible for everyone to see.

Do You Need Dormers?

Because they so often go wrong, it's worth asking: does your building need dormers at all? Nowadays, dormer windows are among the trim details that builders put on the house in an attempt to "make it traditional"—not realizing that in so doing, they actually deny the effect they are after. If the dormer is just there for decoration, think about leaving it out.

And if your roof has become so large that it needs dormers to break up its bulk, think about the roof design again **(see Schematic Design, page 18, and Roofs, page 186)**.

If You Do, Keep Them Modest

If you are lighting an attic space that will be used for bedrooms, or for a "grow-space" such as a home office or den, then clearly dormer windows are invaluable in making the roof a usable space.

Traditional dormers are always modest in scale. The attic story of the traditional house was carefully designed never to overwhelm the elevation below. But in some suburban houses today, the dormer gets so large that it looks like another little house has landed on the roof. At that point, consider a formal gable, or look again at the scale of the rooms inside. Limit larger dormers to the rear elevation.

The width of the dormer—including the cheek walls—should never exceed the width of the sashes in the windows below. This means the sash itself is narrower than the regular windows. Adjust the height as well to keep the panes in proportion with those of the main house. If the attic is to be used as a bedroom, you will need to provide egress windows, ideally in the gable ends of the house or at the back.

5.44 **Dormers to Avoid**

Before detailing your dormers, first ask yourself if they are absolutely necessary to the composition. Dormers are expensive to get right, avoid gratuitous dormers. Save the budget for a nice door surround.

Avoid covering the roof almost entirely with dormers; a good rule of thumb is to make sure that the distance between the dormers is wider that the dormers themselves

AVOID

5.45 **Dormers to Use**

When using dormers, especially on the front of the house, relate the size to the windows below, and be careful not to let them cover the entire roof.

Use dormers sized in relation to the windows below

Limit the number of dormers on the roof so that they will look like objects rather than another story of the house

USE

5.46 Simple Dormers to Avoid

Avoid "Heavy Hat" roof set atop dormer

Avoid chunky corona eave

AVOID

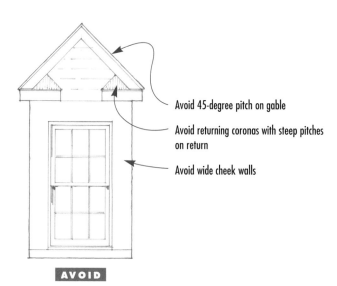

Avoid 45-degree pitch on gable

Avoid returning coronas with steep pitches on return

Avoid wide cheek walls

AVOID

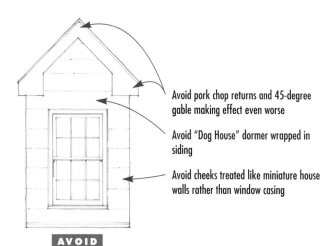

Avoid pork chop returns and 45-degree gable making effect even worse

Avoid "Dog House" dormer wrapped in siding

Avoid cheeks treated like miniature house walls rather than window casing

AVOID

DORMERS WITH SIMPLE EAVES

Once the dormer is sized and located on the roof, the next step is to take a closer look at the details. In general terms, the rules that govern the roof and eaves of the house itself will guide the design of the dormer. But, like every element on the house, dormers have their own set of rules that guides a successful design.

Dormer Rules of Thumb

Roof Pitch

The pitch of the dormer roof varies depending on material and style. Dormers do not have to match the roof slope, and their pitch is often set at $^5/_{12}$. The only slope to avoid is 45 degrees. **(See Roof Slopes, page 190.)**

Eave Details

Avoid steep-pitched corona eaves and "pork chop" returns (5.46 center). Rather than taking the time to box out the eave, wrap a cyma molding around the dormer (5.47). It costs the same and makes the dormer feel lighter.

Cheek Details

Think of the cheeks as a window casing rather than small walls. Avoid siding wrapping around the corners (5.46 bottom). A dormer should never look like a miniature house with a window.

Gable End Dormers/Eave Returns

The simplest treatment of a gable dormer is to use a detail with a cyma molding called the Poor Man's Cornice (5.47). Another option, on vernacular designs, is to run a fascia at the gable end (5.48 left). **(See The Poor Man's Cornice, page 204.)**

Hip Dormers

The most economical type of dormer to build has a hipped roof. Hips are easier to detail than pedimented gables, because the cornice is wrapped around the entire dormer without breaking.

5.47 **Simple Dormers to Use**

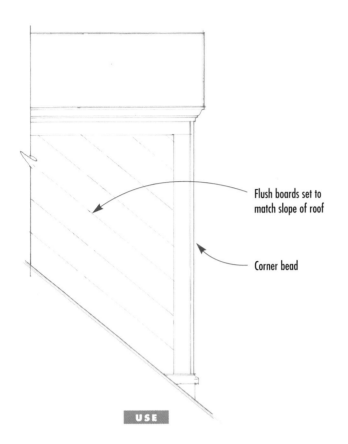

Flush boards

Poor Man's Cornice
with cyma only

Flush boards set to
match slope of roof

Corner bead

USE

USE

5.48 **Simple Dormer Variations**

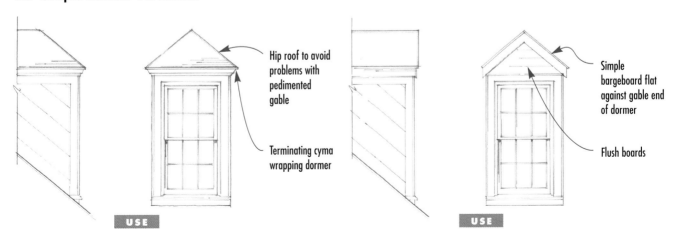

Hip roof to avoid
problems with
pedimented
gable

Terminating cyma
wrapping dormer

Simple
bargeboard flat
against gable end
of dormer

Flush boards

USE

USE

5.49 **More Dormers to Avoid**

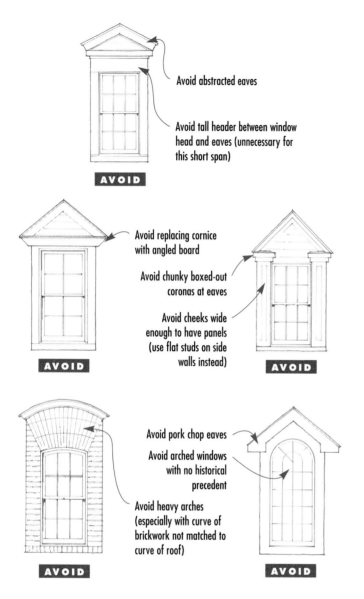

Avoid abstracted eaves

Avoid tall header between window head and eaves (unnecessary for this short span)

AVOID

Avoid replacing cornice with angled board

Avoid chunky boxed-out coronas at eaves

Avoid cheeks wide enough to have panels (use flat studs on side walls instead)

AVOID

AVOID

Avoid pork chop eaves

Avoid arched windows with no historical precedent

Avoid heavy arches (especially with curve of brickwork not matched to curve of roof)

AVOID

AVOID

CHECKLIST

Dormers

❑ Does the overall width of the dormer (window plus cheeks) match the width of the windows below?

❑ Do the cheeks look like a window casing (not like little walls)?

❑ Do the sideboards follow the house roof slope?

❑ Is the dormer roof sensibly sized?

❑ Have you avoided pork chops?

❑ If a full cornice is used, does it have all of the right parts?

DORMERS WITH FULL CORNICES

The level of detail you add at the dormers varies depending on your budget. Running a full cornice around the dormers can look beautiful. But if you are attempting this, it is important to get it right. There are very few half measures when it comes to cornices and eaves. As we say time and time again, if you can't build it correctly, don't build it: the house will look much better if the design is simplified to one that you can achieve. Refer to the previous two pages for designs that will fit any budget and look nice.

"Fancy" Dormers to Avoid

Don't forget the Orders **(see Learn the Vocabulary, page 13)**. The eaves of a dormer, even the simplified ones, are derived from the cornice of a classical temple. When a full cornice is used on a dormer, it needs to have the same elements that would be used in the Orders: a bedmold, corona, and cyma (5.50). Attempts to achieve this effect with an angled board or boxed-out steps will just look heavy-handed. 5.49 shows several unfortunate dormer variations you should avoid.

Arched Windows in Gable Dormers

Arched windows in gable dormers can be a nice addition to the house, but require care to get right. Look closely at historic precedent if you are going to attempt these designs. Apply the lessons discussed in the preceding pages to these dormers, especially regarding pork chop eaves and brick fronts (5.49).

Dormers to Use

Use the "Poor Man's" Cornice to resolve the gable end without an expensive trim detail. This can be used with a cornice that extends across the front of the dormer (5.50) or treated as eave returns. **(See The Poor Man's Cornice, page 204.)** Use a hip roof to eliminate the need for eave returns and detailing on the gable end (5.51 left).

5.50 **Dormers with Full Cornices**

This dormer, with a fully detailed cornice and pediment with properly raking cyma, is suitable for a formal classical roof. Attempt this level of detail only if you have the budget and the knowledge to execute it properly.

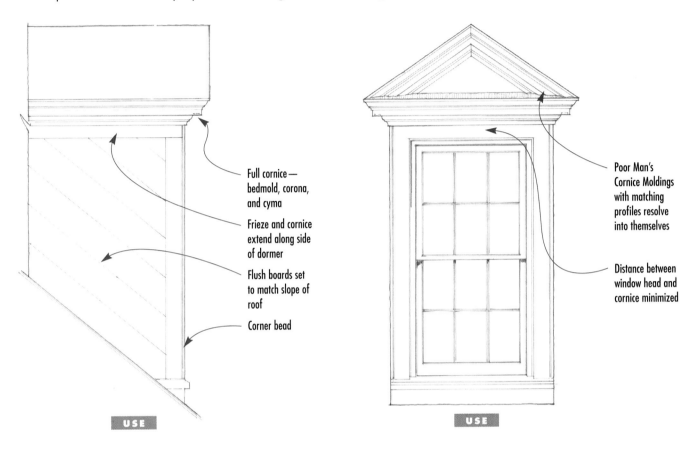

Full cornice—
bedmold, corona,
and cyma

Frieze and cornice
extend along side
of dormer

Flush boards set
to match slope of
roof

Corner bead

USE

Poor Man's
Cornice Moldings
with matching
profiles resolve
into themselves

Distance between
window head and
cornice minimized

USE

5.51 **Complex Dormer Variations**

Because the roof on the left is hipped, there is no need to construct a pediment; the correctly detailed cornice simply wraps the dormer. The dormer on the right has a correctly detailed pediment with a raking cyma; the lighter feel of the open pediment detail above the window would suit a smaller roof on a formal building.

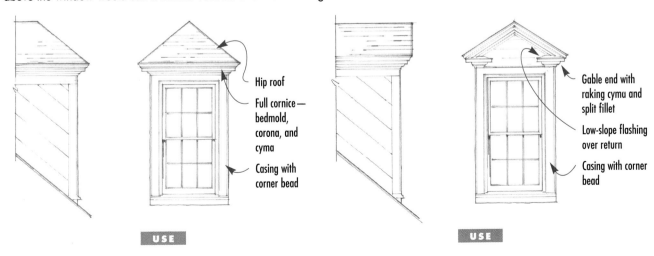

Hip roof

Full cornice—
bedmold,
corona, and
cyma

Casing with
corner bead

USE

Gable end with
raking cyma and
split fillet

Low-slope flashing
over return

Casing with corner
bead

USE

5.52 **Shed Dormers**

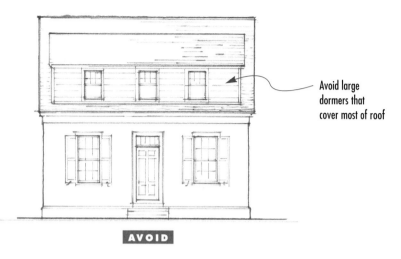

Avoid large dormers that cover most of roof

AVOID

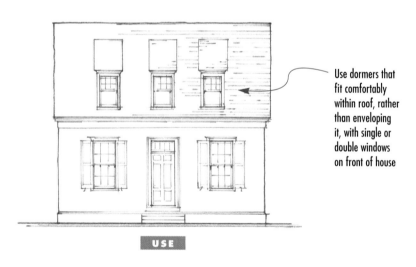

Use dormers that fit comfortably within roof, rather than enveloping it, with single or double windows on front of house

USE

5.53 **Sizing and Placing Shed Dormers**

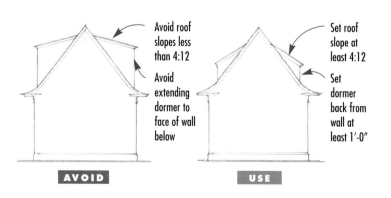

Avoid roof slopes less than 4:12

Avoid extending dormer to face of wall below

Set roof slope at least 4:12

Set dormer back from wall at least 1'-0"

AVOID   **USE**

SHED DORMERS

Shed dormers provide an opportunity to use grouped and paired windows in the roof, maximizing captured space without overwhelming the design. In some local vernacular styles such as Cape Cod, Craftsman bungalows, and Shingle Style, they were favored over hip or gable dormers even for single windows, as the framing and detailing of a shed dormer is somewhat simpler than the examples we looked at on the previous pages.

Keep the Dormer in Scale with the Roof

Make sure that the dormer doesn't overwhelm the roof: balance the desire to maximize space within the house with the appearance of the exterior. If your house is subject to ridgeline height restrictions, shed dormers are an effective way to get more finished space in the house. But be sure to leave some roof on the building. If the dormer envelops too much roof, the composition of the building will be out of balance.

Long shed dormers should be reserved for the back of the house, where they are not visible from the street. Figure 5.52 (top) illustrates a dormer that has taken over the entire roof. On the front of the house, keep the dormers small and in scale with the composition of the house (5.52 bottom).

To keep the dormer reasonably sized, set it back at least 12″ from the face of the wall below, and set a minimum roof pitch of 4:12 (5.53).

Grouped or Paired Windows

By their nature, grouped or paired windows are going to be too wide to look good with a hip or gable treatment. They are particularly well suited, therefore, to shed dormers, either in a continuous run of sashes or with shingles in between. Figure 5.55 shows some typical examples.

Sometimes, it does not work in the floor plan to fill the length of the shed dormer with windows, because of a conflict with a closet or bathroom. In these cases, use decorative shingles on the wall between windows to break up the solid dormer walls.

When using grouped or paired windows, make sure that the light configurations work **(see Grouped and Paired Windows, page 91).**

5.54 **Shed Dormers to Use**

In this well-detailed shed dormer for a shingle building, the cheeks are treated as a casing rather than as walls and the simple cyma details at the roof are based on historical precedent.

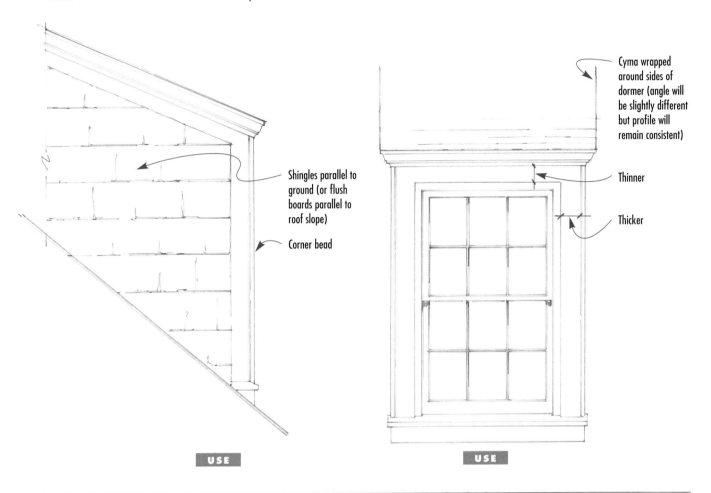

Cyma wrapped around sides of dormer (angle will be slightly different but profile will remain consistent)

Shingles parallel to ground (or flush boards parallel to roof slope)

Corner bead

Thinner

Thicker

USE

USE

5.55 **Shed Dormer Variations**

When combining windows in a shed dormer, make sure the proportions of lights are equal between sashes.
It is not necessary to fill the entire dormer with windows.

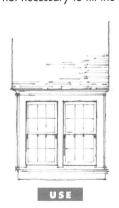

USE

Paired windows in shed dormers

USE

Grouped windows in shed dormers

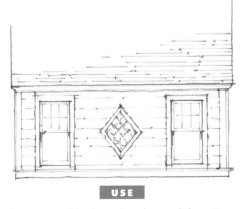

USE

Decorative shingles to break up solid portions of dormer

5.56 Bay Windows to Avoid

Incorrectly designed bays, whether floating or grounded, look like carbuncles stuck on the side of the house.

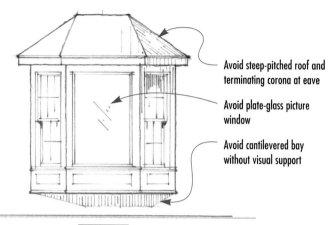

Avoid steep-pitched roof and terminating corona at eave

Avoid plate-glass picture window

Avoid cantilevered bay without visual support

AVOID

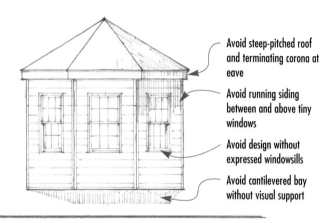

Avoid steep-pitched roof and terminating corona at eave

Avoid running siding between and above tiny windows

Avoid design without expressed windowsills

Avoid cantilevered bay without visual support

AVOID

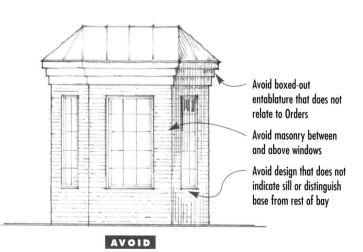

Avoid boxed-out entablature that does not relate to Orders

Avoid masonry between and above windows

Avoid design that does not indicate sill or distinguish base from rest of bay

AVOID

BAY WINDOWS

Projecting windows are an excellent way to bring more light and space into a room, as well as to provide space for seating. They can take a number of forms—curving *bow windows,* which were widely used during the Georgian period, and canted or straight-sided *bay windows.*

Today we are more likely to use bay windows. But while they are popular for good reason, they can often appear chunky and over-scaled by comparison to the rest of the house. This is the result of several design and detailing mistakes.

Roof Slope

Avoid a steep roof slope on bay windows. There is no need to shed a large amount of water from this relatively small area, so use a lower pitch, 4:12 to 5:12. (A very shallow, nearly flat pitch also works well with a lead or copper roof.) The lower slope engages the bay into the wall rather than making it look stuck on like the "carbuncles" shown in 5.56.

Visual Support

Always provide visual support for the bay, either by taking it to the ground with a foundation or by returning it to the wall as an oriel window (5.57). If the bay is cantilevered out of the house, it will look like a "clip-on" feature rather than a permanent element.

Cornice Design

Never terminate the cornice with the corona. Use either a full entablature or a reduced version of one to finish the bay. Break up the entablature into architrave, frieze and cornice.

Size the entablature to fit the height of the bay, not the house. The interior ceiling of the bay does not need to align with the ceiling in the room. It is often preferable to drop a beam on the inside so that the crown of the room continues in front of the bay rather than wrapping through the bay. This allows the bay to feel like a nook in the house, rather than a full extension of the room, and helps keep the entablature from getting too tall outside and looking out of scale with other building elements.

5.57 Bay Windows to Use

Finish a bay with a correctly detailed entablature, its height set according to the size of the bay. Don't try to align the ceiling of the bay with the ceiling of the room. Either extend the bay to the ground or transfer the mass back to the wall with brackets.

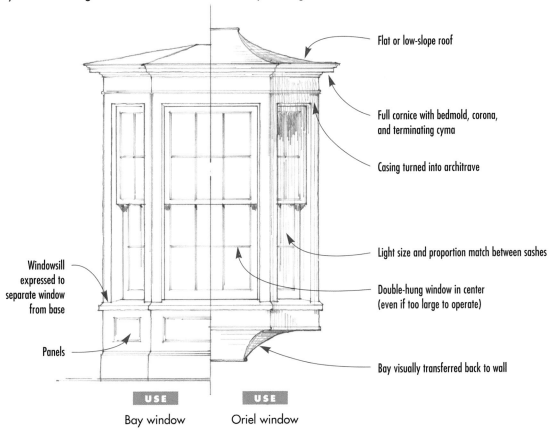

Flat or low-slope roof

Full cornice with bedmold, corona, and terminating cyma

Casing turned into architrave

Light size and proportion match between sashes

Double-hung window in center (even if too large to operate)

Bay visually transferred back to wall

Windowsill expressed to separate window from base

Panels

USE
Bay window

USE
Oriel window

Window Details

The division of lights between the windows in all the bays in an elevation needs to be the same, in size *and* proportion. A large central window may be too heavy to operate. Instead of placing a picture window in this location, use a fixed sash that is detailed to look like an operable sash window (5.57).

Angle of the Bay

The projection, width, and angle of the bay depend on your specific application. Typically, set your bay so it intersects perpendicular to the wall. The angle of the bay is rarely greater than 45 degrees (5.58).

5.58 Bay Window Variations

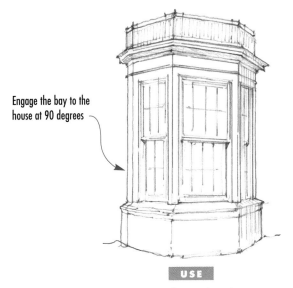

Engage the bay to the house at 90 degrees

USE
Bay window with railings

5.59 **Box Bays to Avoid**

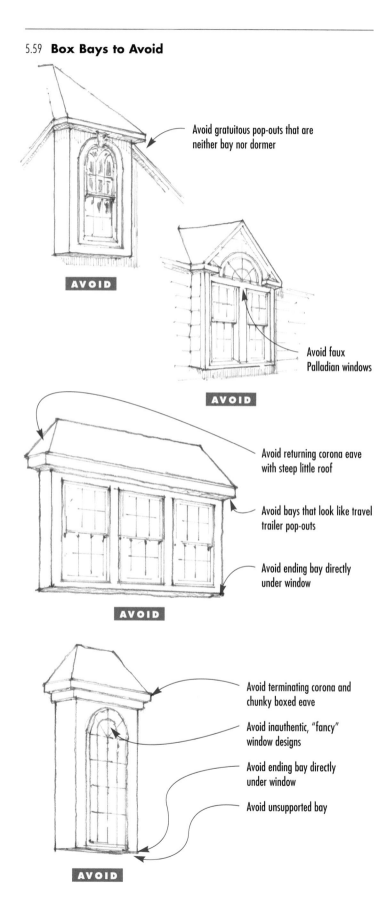

Avoid gratuitous pop-outs that are neither bay nor dormer

AVOID

Avoid faux Palladian windows

AVOID

Avoid returning corona eave with steep little roof

Avoid bays that look like travel trailer pop-outs

Avoid ending bay directly under window

AVOID

Avoid terminating corona and chunky boxed eave

Avoid inauthentic, "fancy" window designs

Avoid ending bay directly under window

Avoid unsupported bay

AVOID

BOX BAYS

Instead of a full bay or oriel window, in some cases it is nice to add a simple box bay to enhance the composition or provide an amenity in plan, such as a nook or a window seat. Before adding any projection to your building, make sure to take a step back and look at the big picture. Projections can add just the right touch, but if you are not careful they can become gratuitous clutter in the composition.

The style of your building will determine where and how box bays are located and detailed. Be especially careful when breaking the eave line with the bay. To keep your house from looking like a McMansion, limit the number of gables and projections in your roof. **(See Roofs, page 186.)**

Selecting Windows
The bay will be an accent on your building, which attracts attention. Don't let a faux Palladian window or pork chop eave be the thing that people notice. Carefully select the windows and detail the eaves.

Getting It Right
Box bays should not look like the pop-out sides of a travel trailer. They should look like permanent elements of the house. Always project the bay a minimum of 8″ and support it with brackets so it is not cantilevered.

A steep roof pitch on a box bay will make it appear stuck on. Use a pitch between 2:12 and 4:12.

If the bay projects more than 1′–0″, use flat panels on the sides to break down its scale. If the bay is deep enough add a side window, making sure that the height and width of the window lights match the front windows **(see Grouped and Paired Windows, page 91).**

5.60 Box Bays to Use

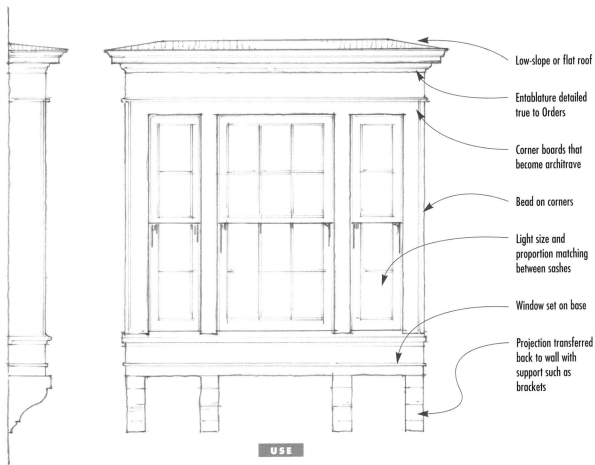

Low-slope or flat roof

Entablature detailed
true to Orders

Corner boards that
become architrave

Bead on corners

Light size and
proportion matching
between sashes

Window set on base

Projection transferred
back to wall with
support such as
brackets

USE

5.61 Box Bay Variations to Use

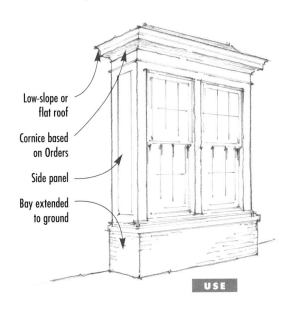

Low-slope or
flat roof

Cornice based
on Orders

Side panel

Bay extended
to ground

USE

CHECKLIST

Projecting Windows

❑ Does the bay have visual support (not cantilevered)?
❑ Is the feature window really necessary to the composition
(or it is gratuitous)?
❑ Does each window in the bay have the same light size and
proportions?
❑ Is the roof sized to the bay rather than
the house (with flatter slope)?
❑ Does the cornice have a bedmold, corona and cyma?

IMITATION ▷   MATERIALS·ELEMENTS·CONSTRUCTION   ◁ AUTHENTIC

Chapter 6

EXTERIOR DOORS

Exterior doors are an important area in the house—both in terms of hierarchy and in terms of use. A beautiful door is something that can be enjoyed by everyone coming in and out of the house every day. But too often, the details of doors go wrong. This chapter explains the rules for good door design and how to get them right.

EXTERIOR DOORS

THE FRONT DOOR IS HIERARCHICALLY the most important element of a building, the point through which we enter and leave, and therefore something we notice every day. The design of the front door and entrance should recognize this importance. In Chapter 7, we'll explore in depth the entry surround and portico. In this chapter, we look specifically at the door itself.

Styles of Doors

The character, design, and details of the front door vary according to style. Georgian houses usually had 6- or 8-panel doors. Craftsman or Arts & Crafts houses might combine long thin panels with small areas of glazing at the top of the door or use board and batten doors, while Dutch doors, with a pair of leaves split at the lock rail, became a signature element of Dutch Colonial architecture.

Most houses today have a front door that is ordered out of a catalog. As with all manufactured items, selecting the right door means knowing how to navigate the catalog and avoid the bad designs. The first step is to understand the basics of door construction.

Regardless of the configuration of panels or profile of moldings, the construction of a door remains constant (6.1). Doors are built up of a series of stiles (vertical members) and rails (horizontal members). The spaces between the stiles and rails are filled with either panels or glazing.

With doors, as with so many elements of a traditional building, less is more. Details in catalogs often attempt to mimic expensive details. To avoid the bad imitations, first you need to recognize the good designs.

Nothing should be more beautiful than the front door to a new house. A plain door, painted a suitable historic color and enriched by some good-quality architectural hardware (a door knocker and house number, for example), can be achieved very easily— if you know what to look for and ask for when ordering.

6.1 Door Construction

The basic construction of the door has remained unchanged for centuries. It is composed of stiles, rails, and panels.

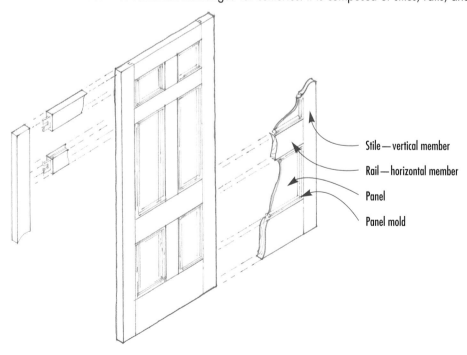

Stile—vertical member

Rail—horizontal member

Panel

Panel mold

6.2 **Types of Paneled Doors**

6-panel

4-panel
(often interior only)

2-panel

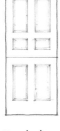

Dutch door

Ledged and braced
(Z-braced)

Arts & Crafts

6.3 **Exterior Door Definitions**

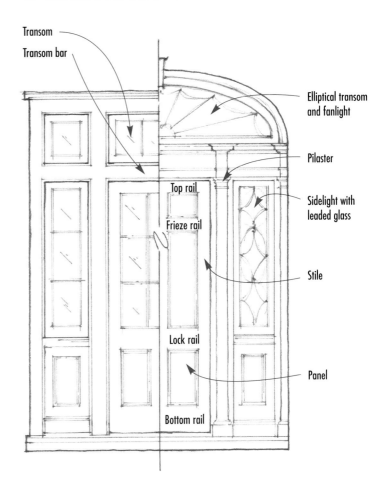

Transom

Transom bar

Elliptical transom
and fanlight

Pilaster

Top rail

Frieze rail

Sidelight with
leaded glass

Stile

Lock rail

Panel

Bottom rail

6.4 **Types of Glazed Doors**

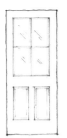

4 lights
with 2 panels

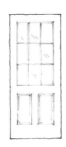

9 lights
with 2 panels

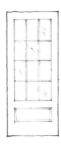

12 lights
with 1 panel

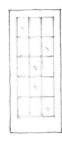

15 lights

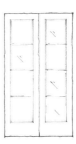

Double 4-light
French doors

6.5 Paneled Doors to Avoid

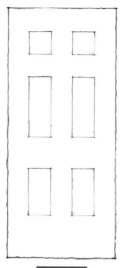

AVOID — Moldings larger than stiles and rails

AVOID — Panels smaller than stiles and rails

6.6 Panel Profiles to Avoid

Avoid moldings that deny the structural common sense of a traditional framed door.

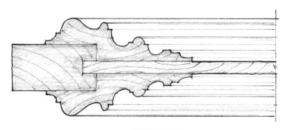

AVOID

Overly sculpted moldings that overwhelm stiles and rails

AVOID

Thin pressed-in profiles

WOOD PANELED DOORS

Paneled doors are the most common type for both interior and exterior. The door is made of a framework of rails and stiles, jointed together to provide structural stability and to prevent the door from sagging on its hinges over the years. The wood sections are sized from simple standard pieces, with the lock rail and bottom rail larger than the others.

Panels fill the voids between stiles and rails. Because of exposure to weather, the joint between panel and frame will often move over time. To disguise this, and provide ornamentation, a panel-mold was inserted at the junction. The panels themselves were sometimes worked to form "raised and fielded" doors. The history of these changing molding profiles reflects architectural fashions, but the basic construction of the door has hardly changed in 400 years.

A door's infill panels are most often wood, but in a dark hallway the upper frieze panels may be glazed instead. This is the *only* way in which glass should be incorporated into a paneled door, never in a fake "fanlight" or some such inauthentic detail.

Paneled Doors to Avoid

Figure 6.5 shows two doors commonly available from door manufacturers. In each of these examples the basic stile, rail, and panel form has been lost. Remember, stiles and rails are modeled after structural members; even though many new doors are not made of wood, the design will appear awkward and unbalanced if it is not based on the principles of wood construction.

Paneled Doors to Use

It is important to distinguish the different elements of the door. Figure 6.7 shows a typical 6-paneled door. The stiles and rails form a frame for the panels; the connection between panel and frame is concealed with a panel molding.

Figure 6.8 illustrates several types of panel details in section. Compare them to Figure 6.6 and note the differences in construction. Avoid doors that have overpowering moldings or barely defined pressed-in moldings. Use moldings that relate to the construction of the door.

6.7 **Paneled Doors to Use**

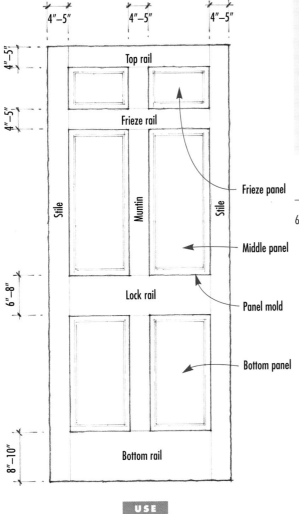

4"–5"   4"–5"   4"–5"

4"–5"

4"–5"

6"–8"

8"–10"

Top rail

Frieze rail

Stile

Muntin

Stile

Lock rail

Bottom rail

Frieze panel

Middle panel

Panel mold

Bottom panel

USE

Setting Out a Paneled Door

- The top rail, frieze rail, and stiles are often set at the same dimension.
- In more refined doors, the top rail and stiles will be $1/2''$–$1''$ larger than the frieze rail and muntin.
- Depending on the type of hardware and lockset used on the door, the lock rail may be set larger than the bottom rail. (Mortised locksets require more height than rim latches or tubular locksets.)

6.8 **Panel Profiles to Use**

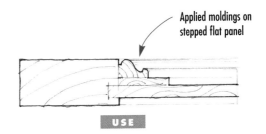

Bolection molding

USE

Bead flush in panel

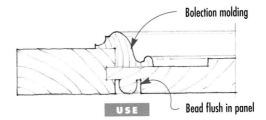

Applied moldings on stepped flat panel

USE

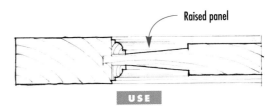

Raised panel

USE

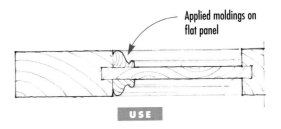

Applied moldings on flat panel

USE

6.9 **Types of Glazed Doors**

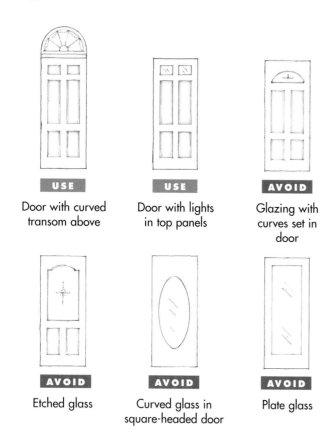

USE
Door with curved
transom above

USE
Door with lights
in top panels

AVOID
Glazing with
curves set in
door

AVOID
Etched glass

AVOID
Curved glass in
square-headed door

AVOID
Plate glass

6.10 **Glazed Doors to Use**

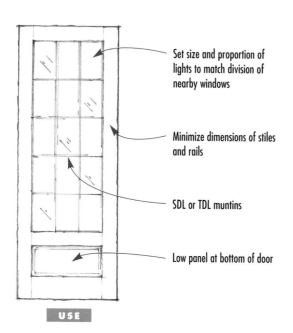

Set size and proportion of
lights to match division of
nearby windows

Minimize dimensions of stiles
and rails

SDL or TDL muntins

Low panel at bottom of door

USE

GLAZED DOORS

Glazed doors are used to light interior rooms, either where windows cannot be used (such as in a small hallway) or where the designer wants to achieve a greater connection between inside and outside—French doors off a living room or bedroom, for example.

Avoid Curved Panes in a Square-Framed Door

When using a paneled door and attempting to get light into a room, it is best to add a transom light above the door or to glaze the rectangular panels in the door. What should *never* appear in a traditional building is any form of curved "fanlight" or glazed panel within a square-headed door. Despite their extreme popularity in so-called "historical" building catalogs, these doors were never used in the past. Always tend toward simpler forms, which will give a much greater sense of authenticity to your traditional building.

Avoid Plate Glass and Etched Glass

Plate glass should be avoided in traditional work. As we discussed in Chapter 4 **(see Glazing Bars and Lights, page 90)**, large panes of glass could not be manufactured or transported until relatively late in the nineteenth century. Glazing bars are often omitted in an attempt to maximize a view, but in reality, they help to frame a view and, more importantly, to give the house scale. Always avoid etched glass in doors, sidelights, and transoms. Etched glass attempts to mimic traditional leaded glass but does so in a way that appears thin and unsubstantial.

Incorporate a Small Wood Panel

Glazed doors always look better if you use a small panel at the base (6.10). This allows you to use smaller stiles and rails without compromising the structural integrity of the door **(see Wood Paneled Doors, page 130)**. Visually, too, this detail looks far more authentic than running the glazing to the bottom rail itself. Glass was such an expensive material that traditional builders would never have used it in such a vulnerable location.

Divided Lights

The character of the glazed door will be defined by the type of glazing bars (muntins) used. It is very important to use either True Divided Light or Simulated Divided Light windows. Avoid snap-in or glued-on muntins, which will drastically impair the appearance of the house.

A common mistake is to set tall thin lights in the doors, ignoring the relationship to nearby windows. When setting the division of lights in the doors, remember to relate them to the surrounding windows and the composition of the house as a whole.

Transoms

Transoms are small windows above doors. They are either fixed or operable. When operable, they can be hinged on the top (an awning window) or the bottom (a hopper window). Transoms are the best way to bring light into an entry over a paneled door, and for this reason they are found in most traditional homes.

Avoid Horizontal Lights

Horizontal panes will make the transom appear squat (6.11). The detail can end up looking as though a heavy lintel has squashed the door, especially when the transom is over a glazed door with contrasting vertical lights. With the exception of Greek Revival buildings (where it is typical to have horizontal transoms and long, thin sidelights), it would be better to have no transom at all than to have thin horizontal lights.

6.11 Transoms to Avoid

AVOID

Etched glass in long
horizontal transoms

AVOID

Thin horizontal lights,
especially above a glazed door

6.12 Transoms to Use

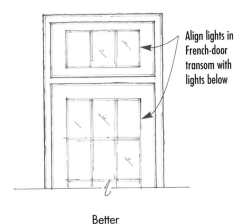

Align lights in
French-door
transom with
lights below

Better

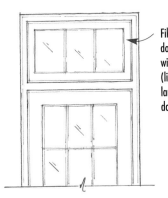

Fill French-
door transom
with glazing
(lights will be
larger than
door lights)

Best

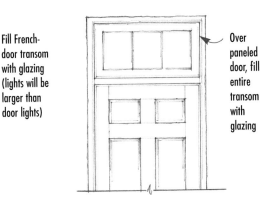

Over
paneled
door, fill
entire
transom
with
glazing

Best

6.13 **Doors with Sidelights to Avoid**

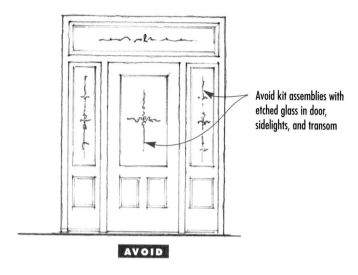

Avoid kit assemblies with etched glass in door, sidelights, and transom

AVOID

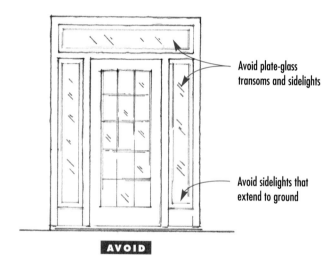

Avoid plate-glass transoms and sidelights

Avoid sidelights that extend to ground

AVOID

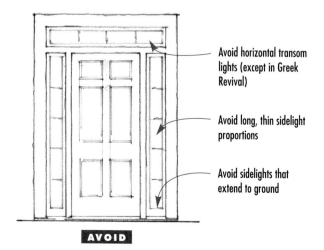

Avoid horizontal transom lights (except in Greek Revival)

Avoid long, thin sidelight proportions

Avoid sidelights that extend to ground

AVOID

DOORS WITH SIDELIGHTS AND TRANSOMS

In many houses it is not possible to light an entry hall with a full sash window adjacent to the door. Sidelights are a good way to make an elegant entrance hall in a relatively narrow space.

Avoid Cheap Door Kits

Despite the many examples available from the "historical" window manufacturers, most door kits are very poorly detailed. It is much better to buy the door and sashes off the shelf but have the framework and any paneled areas made up by a millworker.

Avoid Etched Glass, Plate Glass, and Too Much Glazing

Etched glass—an extremely popular feature on this sort of door—is completely without historical precedent (6.13 top). The etching is an attempt to reference traditional lead glazing. Don't use it— there is no substitute for the real thing (6.15 bottom left).

Avoid plate-glass transoms and sidelights (6.13 center). Make sure you always use a low panel below the sidelights.

Getting It Right

There are endless variations of door and sidelight designs. Successful combinations share a few common features. The door itself is usually paneled. The sidelights stop at the height of the lock rail, with panels below.

The transom can either carry across the entire assembly or be divided by the vertical members on either side of the door. The frame can be simple, without detail (6.14), or contain pilasters and an entablature (6.15 right).

The best way to design a transom and sidelights is to study examples of historical precedent in the style of your building, and to make sure that they are detailed with proper use of the classical Orders. Read Chapter 3 to design your pilasters and entablatures.

6.14 **Doors with Sidelights to Use**

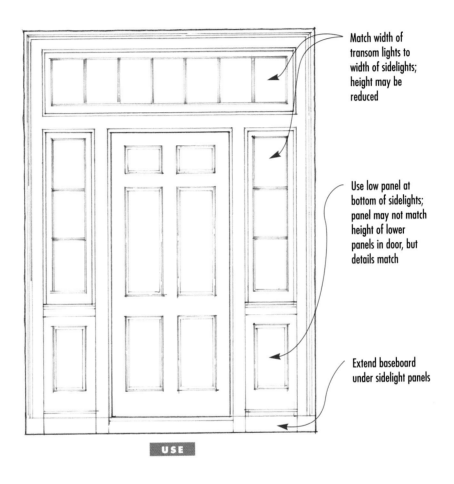

Match width of transom lights to width of sidelights; height may be reduced

Use low panel at bottom of sidelights; panel may not match height of lower panels in door, but details match

Extend baseboard under sidelight panels

USE

6.15 **Sidelight Variations**

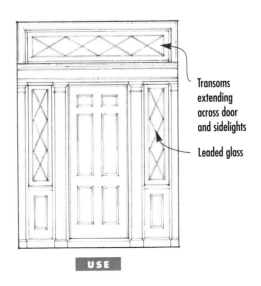

Transoms extending across door and sidelights

Leaded glass

USE

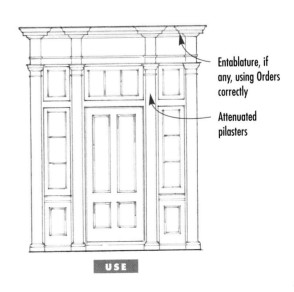

Entablature, if any, using Orders correctly

Attenuated pilasters

USE

6.16 **Doors with Sidelights and Elliptical Transoms to Avoid**

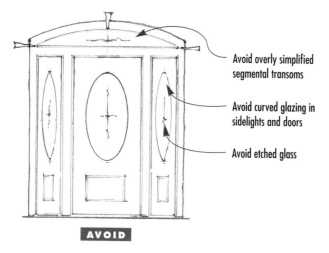

Avoid overly simplified segmental transoms

Avoid curved glazing in sidelights and doors

Avoid etched glass

AVOID

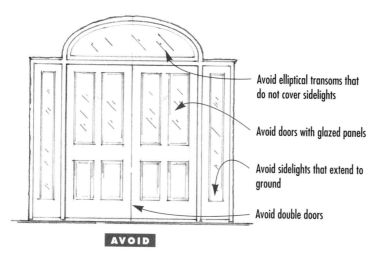

Avoid elliptical transoms that do not cover sidelights

Avoid doors with glazed panels

Avoid sidelights that extend to ground

Avoid double doors

AVOID

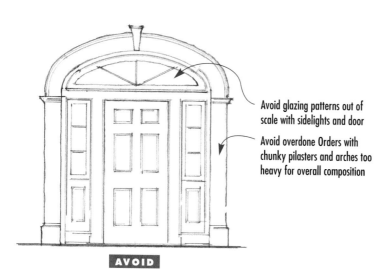

Avoid glazing patterns out of scale with sidelights and door

Avoid overdone Orders with chunky pilasters and arches too heavy for overall composition

AVOID

DOORS WITH SIDELIGHTS AND ELLIPTICAL TRANSOMS

In the Federal period, an elliptical transom over the door and sidelight assembly became particularly popular throughout the United States. In the late eighteenth and early nineteenth centuries, these doors were often detailed in extremely elaborate fashion with pilasters, entablatures, long stretched brackets around the doorframe, and leaded glazing at the sidelights and transom.

Glazing

For authenticity, use designs that are closely based on historic precedent. The "fancier" the catalog, the worse the designs get. Never use sidelights and doors with oval windows and etched glass (6.16 top). Never place sidelights outside the arch (6.16 center); the ellipse should always contain the entire assembly of door and sidelights. Avoid giant panes or plate glass and double doors, which were almost never used in traditional designs.

Avoid a Chunky Surround

Be careful that the millwork surrounding the assembly does not overpower the design (6.16 bottom). This is an issue of scale. Although the combination of sidelights, door, and elliptical transom make the entry a large element, it is near to the eye and should have a delicate scale.

Elliptical Arches

The rules for laying out an ellipse are described in Chapter 3 **(see Elliptical Arches, page 78)**. Follow these carefully.

Variations to Use

First get the proportions right, then apply detail. As with the transoms illustrated on the previous page, the best way to design elliptical transoms is to study examples of historical precedent and apply it to your work. Refer to Chapter 3 to learn how to detail the pilaster caps and bases and the entablature.

6.17 **Doors with Sidelights and Elliptical Transoms to Use**

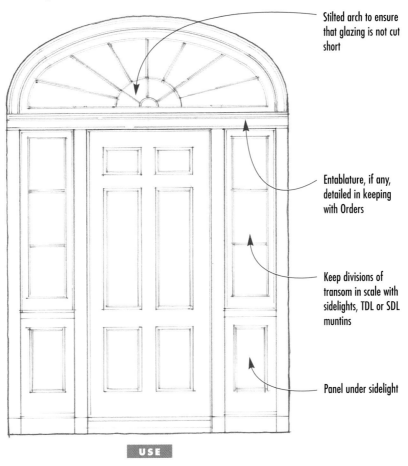

Stilted arch to ensure that glazing is not cut short

Entablature, if any, detailed in keeping with Orders

Keep divisions of transom in scale with sidelights, TDL or SDL muntins

Panel under sidelight

USE

6.18 **Sidelight and Elliptical Transom Variations**

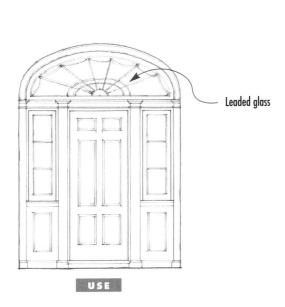

Leaded glass

USE

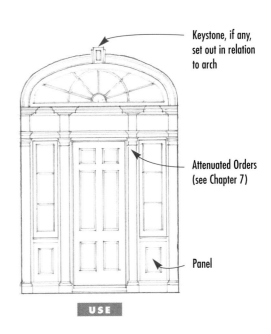

Keystone, if any, set out in relation to arch

Attenuated Orders (see Chapter 7)

Panel

USE

6.19 **Double Garage Doors to Avoid**

Long horizontal doors that serve more than one bay of garage

AVOID

Plain doors without panels to break up scale of door

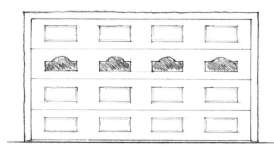

AVOID

"Fancy" details such as glazing with complex curves

6.20 **Single Garage Doors to Avoid**

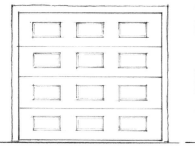 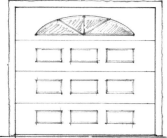

AVOID   **AVOID**

Miniature pressed-in panels and large stiles   Overly simplified glazing

GARAGE DOORS

Responding to the practical requirements of today's world, many households have two and sometimes as many as three or four cars. Not only do our homes have to accommodate more vehicles, the vehicles are often substantially larger than the ones housed in the traditional precedents we look to for guidance.

Historically, carriage house doors were either out-swinging or sliding. They were never more than a single carriage bay wide, because enormous doors would have been difficult to operate. Designs had Z or X bracing to keep the doors from sagging over time. Today the primary type of garage door is the up-and-over door. Although this type of door is convenient and practical to use, the results often have a negative visual impact.

Placing Your Garage
The location of the garage in the house can help to mitigate its impact on the design. Do everything you can to avoid designing a "snout house," a house where the garage takes up almost the entire street frontage. Push the garage to the side or back of the house. If the lot is large enough or if there is alley access, detach the garage.

Designs to Avoid
Regardless of the number of cars housed in the garage, do your best to use a single bay per vehicle. Avoid using giant garage doors two bays wide (6.19). The "double-wide" door merely over-emphasizes the horizontal nature of the garage. Avoid small pressed-in panels, glazing with complex curves, and details that would not be found on a swinging door (6.20).

Designs to Use
Make your door appear as vertical as possible. Apply sticking to make the door look like a pair of swinging doors (6.21). Use only vertical lights in simple forms. Consider using a single-pivot up-and-over door, (requires more headroom) or even traditional hinged doors (which can still be motor operated if required).

6.21 **Garage Doors to Use**

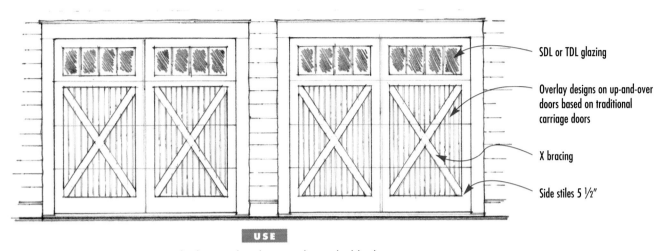

SDL or TDL glazing

Overlay designs on up-and-over doors based on traditional carriage doors

X bracing

Side stiles 5 ½"

USE

Two single doors rather than one large double door

6.22 **Garage Door Variations**

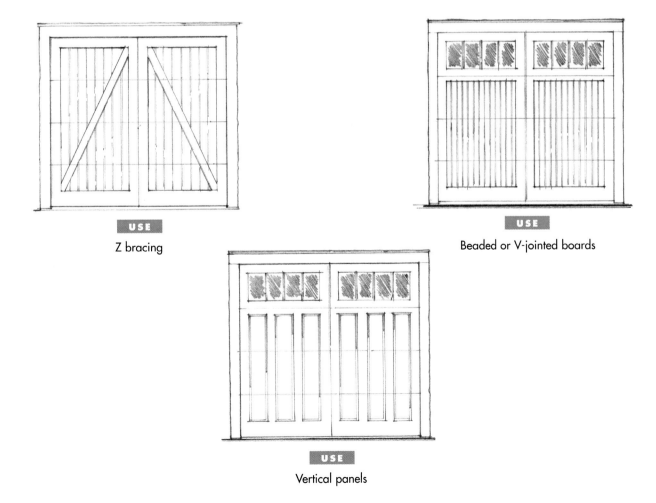

USE

Z bracing

USE

Beaded or V-jointed boards

USE

Vertical panels

~ C L A S S I C A L ~ FALSE LUXURY ~ FALSE ECONOMY ~

Chapter 7

ENTRANCES

The entrance to nearly all traditional buildings is a sophisticated piece of design. Builders knew to spend their time and money where it would be noticed. The details can be simple or more complex, depending on style, application and budget—but good entrance designs all share a common characteristic. They need to understand the classical Orders and apply them well and appropriately to the front door of the building. This chapter shows you how.

ENTRANCES

THE DESIGN OF AN ENTRANCE requires care and consideration. Other areas—compositional treatment, windows, or the roof and eaves—may play a larger role in defining the building's character, but the front door marks the point of arrival; hierarchically, it is the most important element in your design. Modern architects tend to play down the importance of the entrance, disguising it as just another panel of glass in a seamless façade. At the Villa Savoye, le Corbusier's 1928 landmark of International Modern style, the entrance is nowhere to be seen.

Finding the Front Door

Le Corbusier's design demonstrates a revolutionary brilliance, but by the middle of the century, ordinary people were starting to wonder what had gone wrong, as they struggled to find the way into their new post office, museum extension, hospital, or railway station. Innumerable modern buildings now require extensive signage just to direct people to the front door.

New houses today suffer from the opposite problem, yet, paradoxically, with a similar result. Often, they become so cluttered with architectural motifs that the entrance loses all significance. McMansions, although based on traditional forms, lack hierarchy because every element is designed to attract attention.

The entire composition of a traditional building, by contrast, works subtly to direct us to the entrance. Few people could mistake the entrance to a five-bay Georgian house or even a simple Craftsman bungalow. In these buildings, we are guided to the front door through the arrangement of openings, the balance of elements, and the hierarchy of the composition.

Using the Orders

While you read this chapter, keep the Canon of the Orders in mind and you will be well on the way to designing and installing a correctly detailed entrance.

Each type of door surround and covering has endless variations. In this chapter, we will introduce the basic types of door surrounds and identify the key relationships that are maintained in each design, regardless of how simple or complex. Because it is impossible to illustrate every variation, the small selection that we show here is intended to be a point of departure.

Combine these lessons with study of historic precedent, looking closely at the alignments, arrangements, and profiles. Once you learn to recognize the basic types of surround and understand these key relationships, your design palette will have no limits.

7.1 Finding the Entrance

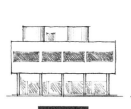

AVOID
In modern buildings, the entrance is often hidden.

AVOID
In McMansions, the entrance is celebrated, but so is every other element.

USE **USE**
In traditional buildings, the entrance is easily found, through a symmetrical arrangement or through subtle but clear compositional handling.

Chapter 7 (left margin)

7.2 **Types of Door Surrounds to Use**

Trabeated surround

Pedimented surround

Pedimented surround with arch

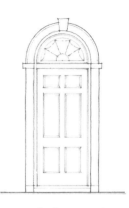

Arched surround

7.3 **Types of Entrances to Use**

Door surround

Projecting door surround

Portico

Door canopy

7.4 **The Orders**

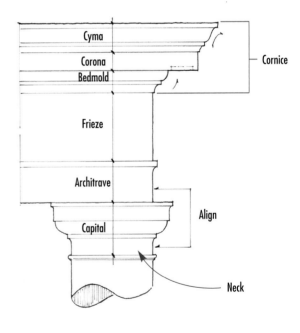

Cyma – Terminating molding (emphasis out)

Bedmold – Supporting molding (emphasis up)

7.5 **Attenuated Orders**

The Doric Order after Vignola (left) and an attenuated Doric Order (right).

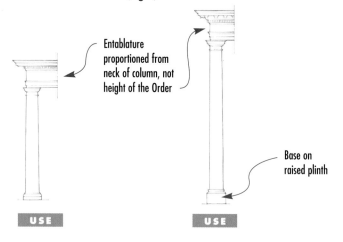

Entablature proportioned from neck of column, not height of the Order

Base on raised plinth

USE

USE

ATTENUATED ORDERS

The system of ratios for setting out the Orders, established in the Renaissance by architects such as Vignola and Palladio, were proportioned primarily for stone construction. When translated to wood, which has more tensile strength than stone and allows for far thinner structural members, these heavy proportions are structurally unnecessary and can end up looking chunky.

Taking this change of materials into account, many architectural styles (in particular, Colonial or Federal designs) employ *attenuated* or slenderized Orders at the entrance, where conventional proportions might be overpowering.

7.6 **Attenuating the Orders**

The Orders as prescribed by Vignola work for larger elements and masonry construction. A door surround will feel too heavy with Vignola's Orders directly applied; simply making the columns narrower will result in a top-heavy composition. Attenuate the Order correctly by elongating the columns, then set the height of the entablature in relation to the diameter, *not* the height, of the column.

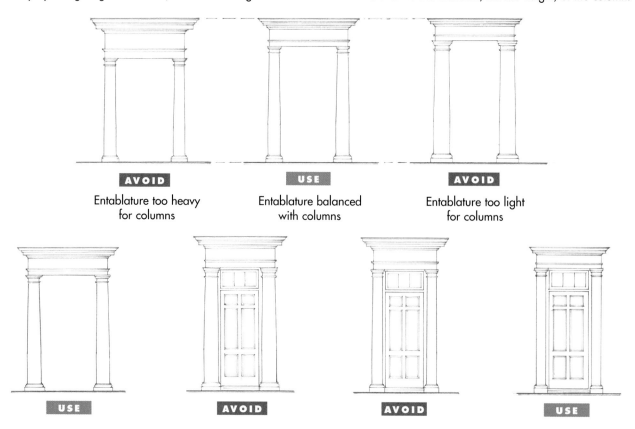

AVOID
Entablature too heavy for columns

USE
Entablature balanced with columns

AVOID
Entablature too light for columns

USE

AVOID

AVOID

USE

Maintain the relationship between the diameter of the pilaster and the height of the entablature (usually 1:2). Do not worry about the relationship between the height of the pilaster and the height of the entablature.

How to Attenuate the Orders

To attenuate the Orders, stretch the height of the columns. In effect, this means reducing the diameter of the columns compared to the normal dimensions for stone construction. Then proportion the entablature to the neck of the column, not to its height. The neck/entablature relationship is the critical one and keeps things proportioned correctly. Likewise with the base and plinth. Figure 7.7 shows you how.

Details

To acknowledge the taller proportions, the neck of the column is dropped slightly (never more than one diameter below the architrave), and the plinth is raised. The taller and thinner attenuated Orders often have additional detail and ornament, but use it carefully; any ornament used should directly relate to historical precedent and not be gratuitously applied.

7.7 **Setting out a Door Surround**

Attenuating the Orders in practice.

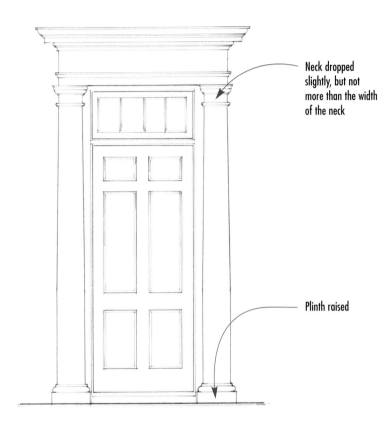

Neck dropped slightly, but not more than the width of the neck

Plinth raised

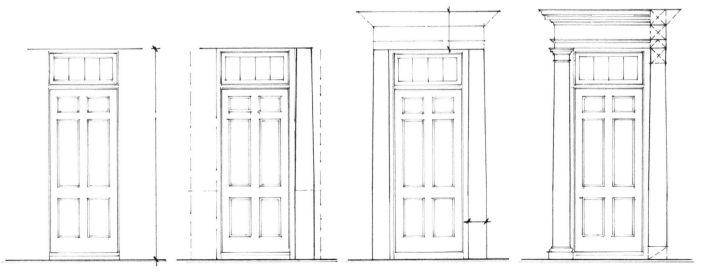

1. Determine the height of the door and transom.

2. Dot in the Vignola Orders. If they are too heavy, reduce the diameter of the column by 1/5.

3. Set the height of the entablature in relation to the attenuated diameter.

4. Divide the entablature and columns according to the rules of the Order being used.

SEVEN COMMON MISTAKES

7.8 MISTAKE 1: The Entablature

Avoid extra steps and overused cyma moldings. Relate the moldings to the basic entablature. Always use a cornice, frieze, and architrave (in that order).

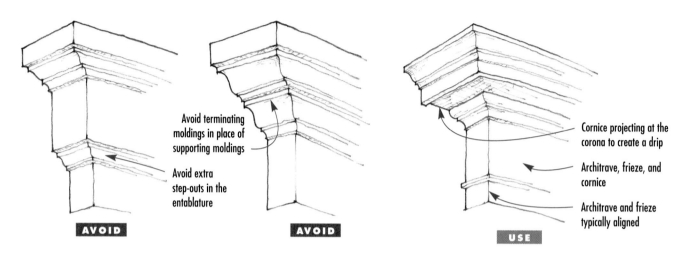

Avoid terminating moldings in place of supporting moldings

Avoid extra step-outs in the entablature

AVOID

AVOID

Cornice projecting at the corona to create a drip

Architrave, frieze, and cornice

Architrave and frieze typically aligned

USE

7.9 MISTAKE 2: The Cornice

Avoid terminating the cornice with a corona (the flat board). Use a cyma (crown molding) or terminating molding. Never use the cyma anywhere but at the top of the cornice, and never repeat the same molding twice.

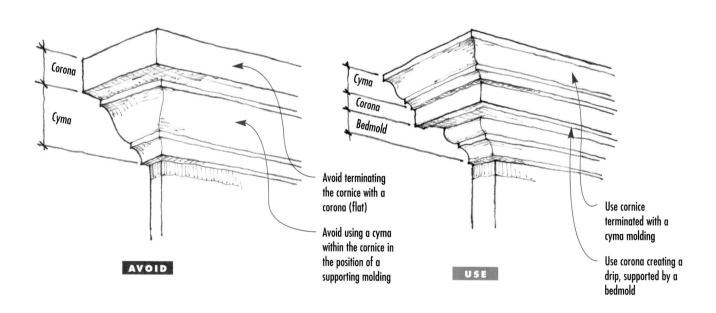

Corona

Cyma

Cyma

Corona

Bedmold

Avoid terminating the cornice with a corona (flat)

Avoid using a cyma within the cornice in the position of a supporting molding

AVOID

Use cornice terminated with a cyma molding

Use corona creating a drip, supported by a bedmold

USE

7.10 **MISTAKE 3: Alignments**

Avoid cantilevered entablatures. Line the entablature up with the face and side of the pilaster or column.

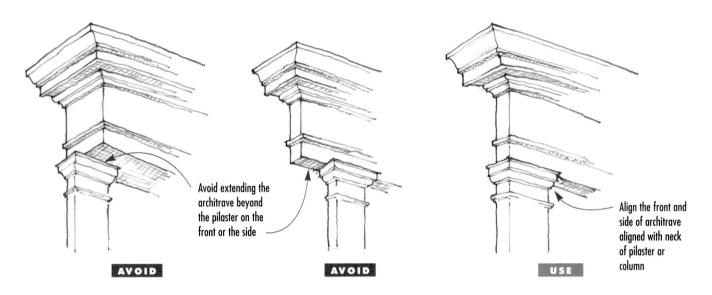

Avoid extending the architrave beyond the pilaster on the front or the side

AVOID

AVOID

Align the front and side of architrave aligned with neck of pilaster or column

USE

7.11 **MISTAKE 4: Post and Pilaster Design**

Avoid cyma or elongated capitals and bases; relate the capitals correctly to the basic capital and base.

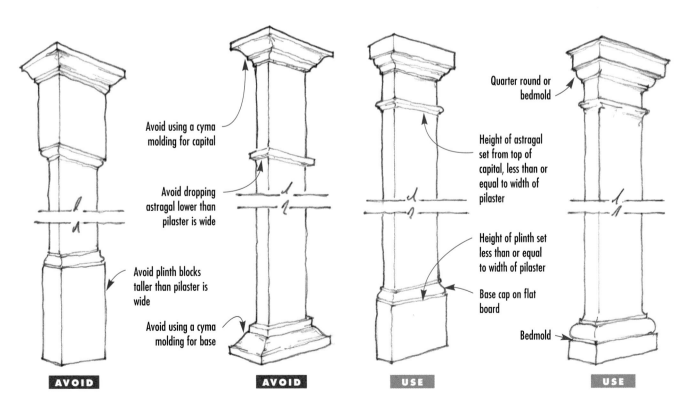

Avoid using a cyma molding for capital

Avoid dropping astragal lower than pilaster is wide

Avoid plinth blocks taller than pilaster is wide

Avoid using a cyma molding for base

Quarter round or bedmold

Height of astragal set from top of capital, less than or equal to width of pilaster

Height of plinth set less than or equal to width of pilaster

Base cap on flat board

Bedmold

AVOID

AVOID

USE

USE

7.12 **MISTAKE 5: Pediments**

Avoid any alternatives to the correct pediment design, and always use a raking cyma. If you can't afford a pediment, leave it off.

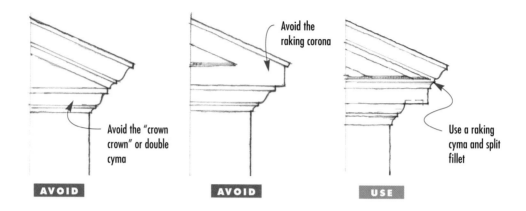

Avoid the raking corona

Avoid the "crown crown" or double cyma

Use a raking cyma and split fillet

AVOID   AVOID   USE

7.13 **MISTAKE 6: Arches**

Avoid the no-center arch.

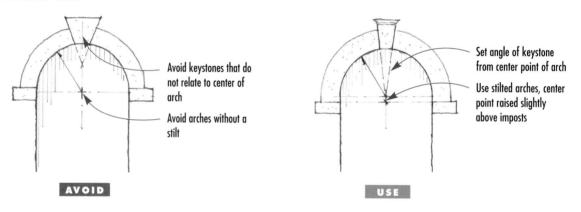

Avoid keystones that do not relate to center of arch

Avoid arches without a stilt

Set angle of keystone from center point of arch

Use stilted arches, center point raised slightly above imposts

AVOID   USE

7.14 **MISTAKE 7: Transoms and Ornament**

The transom should always have vertical lights, not horizontal, otherwise it will appear squashed. Never use gratuitous ornament stuck on to the frieze of the entablature.

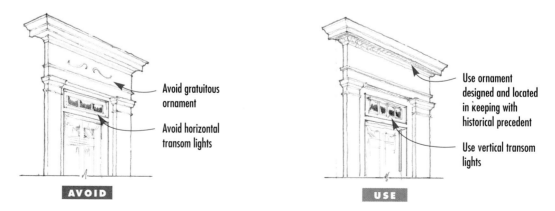

Avoid gratuitous ornament

Avoid horizontal transom lights

Use ornament designed and located in keeping with historical precedent

Use vertical transom lights

AVOID   USE

Mistakes to Avoid When Building Entrances

To be successful, door surrounds, porticoes, and canopies must stay true to the principles of the Orders. Many applications are a simplification of the full-blown classical Orders. But even in these cases, it is crucial not to forget the basic elements of the Orders and their relationship to each other. These are the details that make a difference between a house feeling authentic and one that feels "not quite right."

The preceding pages and the checklist at right illustrate common mistakes that occur again and again in the design of entrances. The rules of thumb introduced in this section can be applied to most architectural styles and types of entrance. They are principles that we see throughout the traditional building; learn them once and apply them everywhere.

Whenever you are designing an entrance, use the checklist to avoid mistakes 1-7. In so doing, you will save yourself from some of the most common disaster areas in traditional construction.

CHECKLIST

Seven Common Mistakes to Avoid

1. The Entablature: Avoid Extra Steps and Overused Cyma Moldings

❑ Are the elements that make up the entablature based on the essential components of the Orders?

❑ Do you have an architrave, frieze and cornice?

❑ Have you avoided extra step-outs that are not based on the Orders?

❑ Do terminating moldings appear only at the top of the composition?

2. Cornices: Avoid the Terminating Corona

❑ Does the cornice have a bedmold, corona, and cyma (in that order)?

❑ Is the cyma on top of the corona?

❑ Does the corona have a drip?

3. Alignments: Avoid Cantilevered Entablatures

❑ Does the face of the architrave align with the neck of the column/pilaster, both front and side?

4. Post and Pilaster Design: Avoid Abstract Caps and Bases

❑ Do the capital and base relate to the basic capital and base of a column?

❑ Have you avoided cyma moldings?

❑ Have you avoided overly elongated capitals and bases?

5. Pediments: Avoid Creative Alternatives to the Raking Cyma

❑ Have you used a raking cyma that is correctly detailed?

❑ Have you avoided the raking corona?

❑ Have you avoided the "crown crown"?

6. Arches: Avoid the "No Point Arch"

❑ Is the construction of the arch based on the essential principles of arch design? (See chapter 3.)

❑ Is the arch stilted (the center raised 2″ or so above the impost)?

❑ Do all of the joints of the keystone and voussoirs point to the center of the arch?

7. Transoms and Ornament: Avoid Horizontal Transoms and Gratuitous Ornaments

❑ Does the transom have vertical lights?

❑ Is ornament based on historical precedent? If not, leave it out.

7.15 Exterior Door Casings to Avoid

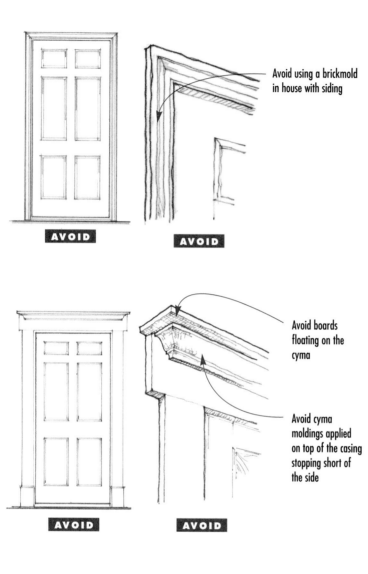

Avoid using a brickmold in house with siding

AVOID   **AVOID**

Avoid boards floating on the cyma

Avoid cyma moldings applied on top of the casing stopping short of the side

AVOID   **AVOID**

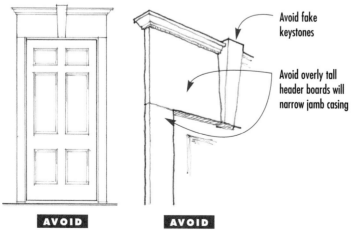

Avoid fake keystones

Avoid overly tall header boards will narrow jamb casing

AVOID   **AVOID**

EXTERIOR DOOR CASINGS

At side doors, or on a very simple house, it is not necessary to use a full-blown door surround with columns, pilasters, or even a bracketed canopy. Instead, use a simple exterior casing or architrave. This detail works both in masonry construction (where the architrave may be stone or stucco) and in wood. The key is to size your casing correctly, then to make sure its details are derived from the classical Orders.

Wood Casings to Avoid

Figure 7.15 shows three examples in which the intention is right, but the details and application are not.

Avoid using an interior door casing on an outside door. 3″ or 4″ will look too small when viewed against the exterior house. For a regular-sized door, your casing should be at least 5″ wide (6″ better). The wider the door, the wider the casing.

The middle example shows a door with "ears," where the top frame carries over a couple of inches beyond the side frame. This detail is found in traditional colonial architecture and can give interest and grace to a simple door surround, but you must ensure the cyma is correctly located and the reveal at the top of the door is not too deep.

In the third example, the top frame is too tall in relation to the side, and the keystone has no relation to the structure **(see Masonry Lintels, page 100)**.

Wood Casings to Use

The simplest exterior casing is an architrave that wraps around the opening just as with a window or interior door. A good ratio to use is to set the casing at $1/5$ the width of the opening. The backband and molding are often sized a little larger than for an interior door to allow the profile of the siding to resolve into the casing.

If you want to form "ears," keep the step minimal. Setting the header of the casing taller than the sides, typically one step larger, is also a common detail.

A simple alternative is a plain boarded frame. A drip cap protects the door surround from the weather and its slight shadow acts as a punctuation.

7.16 **Exterior Door Casings to Use**

Keep the exterior door casings simple. This illustration and those below show three possible options. For more information on door casings, see the details of interior door casings on page 226.

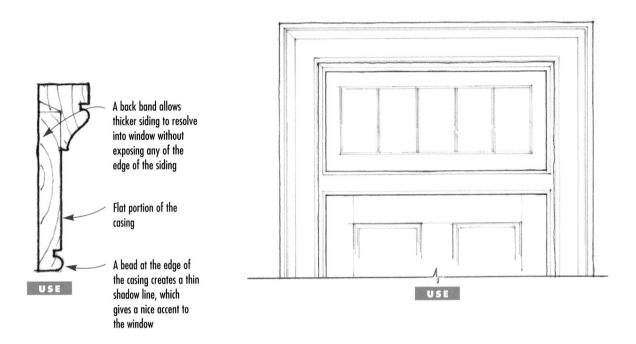

A back band allows thicker siding to resolve into window without exposing any of the edge of the siding

Flat portion of the casing

A bead at the edge of the casing creates a thin shadow line, which gives a nice accent to the window

USE

USE

7.17 **Exterior Door Casings Variations to Use**

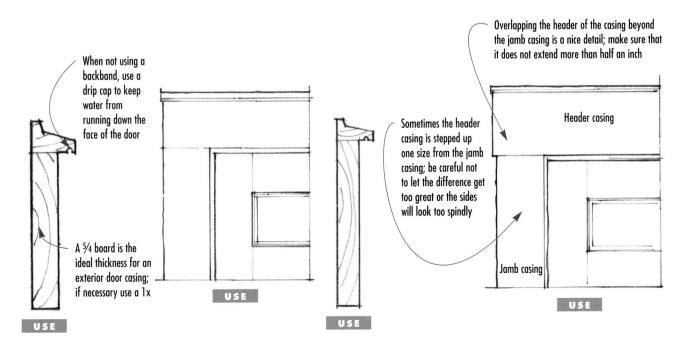

When not using a backband, use a drip cap to keep water from running down the face of the door

A 5/4 board is the ideal thickness for an exterior door casing; if necessary use a 1x

Overlapping the header of the casing beyond the jamb casing is a nice detail; make sure that it does not extend more than half an inch

Header casing

Sometimes the header casing is stepped up one size from the jamb casing; be careful not to let the difference get too great or the sides will look too spindly

Jamb casing

USE

USE

USE

7.18 **Trabeated Door Surrounds to Avoid**

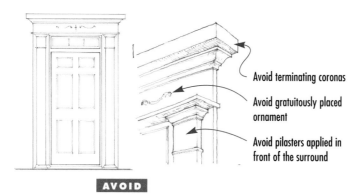

AVOID

Applied pilasters and terminating coronas

Avoid terminating coronas

Avoid gratuitously placed ornament

Avoid pilasters applied in front of the surround

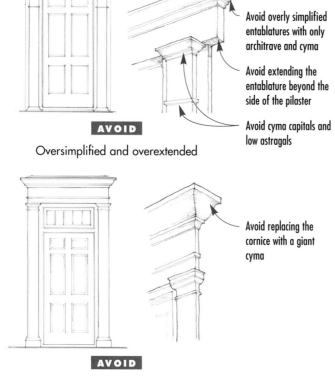

AVOID

Oversimplified and overextended

Avoid overly simplified entablatures with only architrave and cyma

Avoid extending the entablature beyond the side of the pilaster

Avoid cyma capitals and low astragals

AVOID

The cyma cornice

Avoid replacing the cornice with a giant cyma

CHECKLIST

Trabeated Door Surrounds

Check the relationship of parts:

❏ Does the pilaster align front and side with the architrave?
❏ Does the capital look like a capital?
❏ Is the cyma at the top of the cornice?

TRABEATED DOOR SURROUNDS

The trabeated (or post and beam) door surround is an arrangement of columns or pilasters supporting a horizontal entablature. Easy to construct from plain pieces of wood and stock moldings, this surround provides an excellent way to achieve a fine but economic entrance surround.

Details to Avoid

Before proceeding, review the Orders. You can easily avoid most mistakes with a basic understanding of the arrangement and relationship of parts.

Columns and pilasters need to support the entablature, rather than being applied in front (7.18 top). Avoid extending the entablature beyond the side of the pilaster (7.18 center).

Never replace the cornice with a giant cyma molding. A full entablature needs a full cornice: bedmold, corona, and cyma. If the trim details of a full cornice aren't in the budget, use a regular door casing or simple board configuration with ears **(see Exterior Door Casings, page 150).**

Details to Use

Align the entablature with the pilasters on the front and sides (7.19). Use an entablature with a full cornice that terminates with a cyma molding **(see Seven Common Mistakes, page 146).**

Compare the perspective in 7.18 with that in 7.20. Examine the alignments and order of parts. Note the differences. In 7.20, the capital looks like a capital. It is not just a cyma molding **(see Piers and Posts, page 62).**

7.19 **Trabeated Door Surrounds to Use**

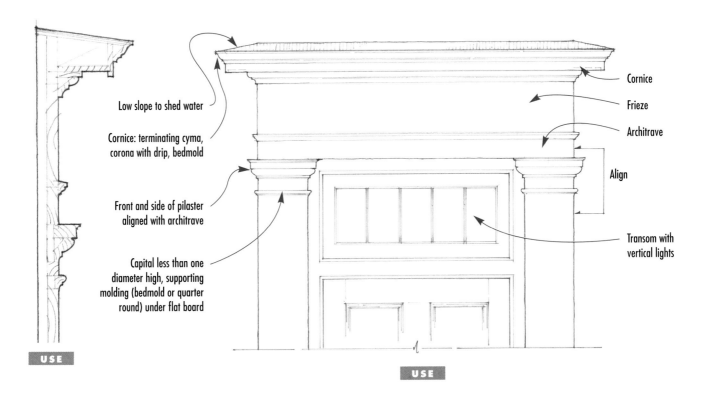

Low slope to shed water

Cornice: terminating cyma, corona with drip, bedmold

Front and side of pilaster aligned with architrave

Capital less than one diameter high, supporting molding (bedmold or quarter round) under flat board

Cornice

Frieze

Architrave

Align

Transom with vertical lights

USE

USE

7.20 **Trabeated Door Surround Variations**

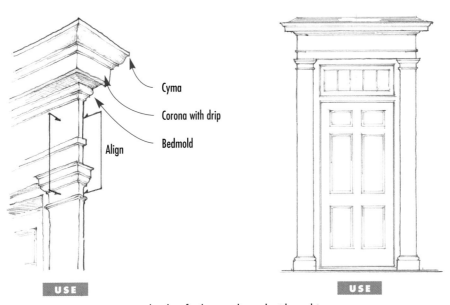

Cyma

Corona with drip

Bedmold

Align

USE

USE

Front and side of pilaster aligned with architrave

7.21 **Pedimented Door Surrounds to Avoid**

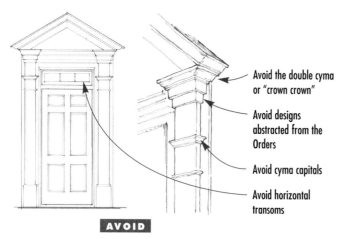

Avoid the double cyma or "crown crown"

Avoid designs abstracted from the Orders

Avoid cyma capitals

Avoid horizontal transoms

AVOID

The "crown crown"

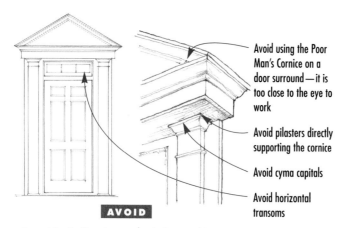

Avoid using the Poor Man's Cornice on a door surround—it is too close to the eye to work

Avoid pilasters directly supporting the cornice

Avoid cyma capitals

Avoid horizontal transoms

AVOID

Poor Man's Cornice and missing architrave

CHECKLIST

Pedimented Door Surrounds

❑ Are all of the elements of the entablature in place?
❑ Have you sized the pilasters and entablatures correctly?
❑ Have you used a raking cyma?
❑ Have you avoided the "crown crown"?

PEDIMENTED SURROUNDS

A richer architectural effect can be achieved with a pedimented door surround. By adding a triangular pediment, you effectively turn the entry door into a small temple-front. But if you are going to go to the extra effort to add a pediment, you *must* get the details right.

Use the Raking Cyma

In particular, the Pediment must have a raking cyma **(see Pediments, page 75)**. This molding is an expensive detail because it requires two differently profiled moldings, which requires making two custom knives to get things to meet right at the external corner. If you can't afford it, stick to the trabeated surround (without a pediment) in the previous section.

Avoid the "Crown Crown"

Carefully compare the perspective drawn in 7.21 (top) with the one in 7.23. Avoiding mistakes means recognizing the difference in these two illustrations. Figure 7.21 is too far removed from the Orders. Before trying to detail the pediment, make sure that the entablature has the right pieces. **(See Seven Common Mistakes, page 146.)** When detailing the pediment, follow instructions in Setting Out Pediments, page 82. The double cyma, or "crown crown," will never look right. And while a Poor Man's Cornice is fine for the roof eaves, this close to the eye it does not work. There are no half measures for the pediments on door surrounds.

Getting the Pedimented Surround Right

If you are using an attenuated order, set the entablature height in proportion to the neck of the pilaster, not its height. Use a full entablature with a raking cyma and split fillet. Do not carry a horizontal cyma across the front of the surround **(see Setting Out Pediments, page 82)**. Align the pilasters, front and side. Use moldings for the capital that relate to the true Orders.

7.22 **Pedimented Door Surrounds to Use**

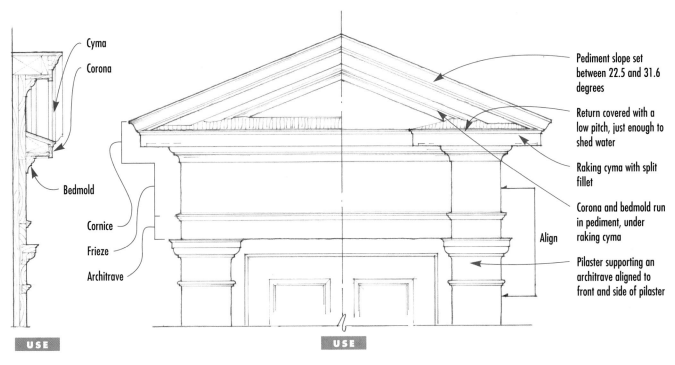

Cyma

Corona

Bedmold

Cornice

Frieze

Architrave

USE

Pediment slope set between 22.5 and 31.6 degrees

Return covered with a low pitch, just enough to shed water

Raking cyma with split fillet

Corona and bedmold run in pediment, under raking cyma

Align

Pilaster supporting an architrave aligned to front and side of pilaster

USE

7.23 **Pedimented Door Surround Variations**

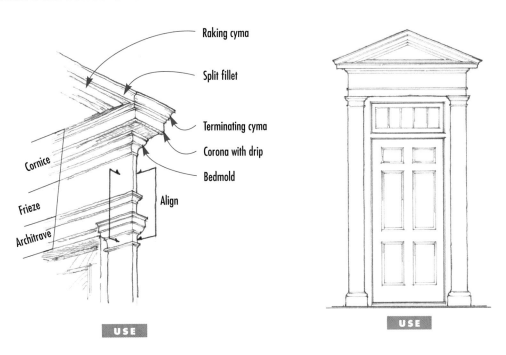

Raking cyma

Split fillet

Terminating cyma

Corona with drip

Bedmold

Cornice

Frieze

Architrave

Align

USE

USE

7.24 **Pedimented Door Surrounds with Arches to Avoid**

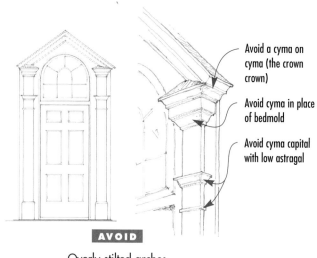

Avoid a cyma on cyma (the crown crown)

Avoid cyma in place of bedmold

Avoid cyma capital with low astragal

AVOID

Overly stilted arches

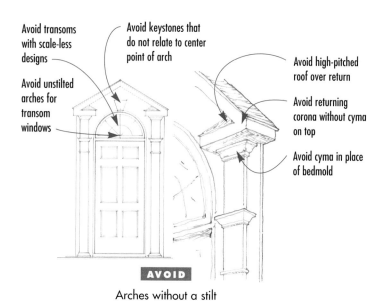

Avoid transoms with scale-less designs

Avoid keystones that do not relate to center point of arch

Avoid high-pitched roof over return

Avoid unstilted arches for transom windows

Avoid returning corona without cyma on top

Avoid cyma in place of bedmold

AVOID

Arches without a stilt

CHECKLIST

Pedimented Door Surrounds with Arches

❑ Is the arch stilted, by 2″, not more?

❑ Does the entablature have a bedmold, corona, and cyma?

❑ Do the capital and bases of the pilasters match the designs of a column?

PEDIMENTED SURROUNDS WITH ARCHES

One variation on the classic pedimented surround is to insert a fanlight within the triangular pediment. To do this, the entablature of the basic pediment is "broken." Instead of running all the way across as before, the entablature self-returns above the columns or pilasters to make space for an arched fanlight.

Most of the common mistakes that occur with this type of surround can be avoided by understanding the Orders and the mistakes that have been described in the preceding pages on trabeated and pedimented surrounds. But in addition to getting the Orders right, you must pay attention to the design of the fanlight.

Stilt the Arch

Stilt the arch, that is, raise its centerline two inches or so above the head of the door frame. This allows the glazing to resolve as a true half round within the fanlight framing. But avoid extending the arch beyond a half circle as shown in 7.24 (top). **(See Semicircular Arches, page 76.)** Relate the division of lights to the scale of the detail on the surround and the adjacent windows. Avoid large-scaled lights in the transom; they will conflict with the overall composition. Keep returns small and cover them with just enough flashing to keep the water out. Never make a mini roof as shown in 7.24.

Variations and Details

The level of detail will depend on your overall scheme and available budget.

If you have the know-how, you could consider enrichments such as fluting and ornamented moldings. If height is an issue, the fanlight can be elliptical rather than semi-circular (7.26 center). The lights in the transom are usually divided into five, and sometimes six, panes. Usually, they terminate in a semicircle just above the center point of the arch. The divisions can be simple straight bars, connected with swags, or even rounded on the ends to look like petals from a flower.

7.25 **Pedimented Door Surrounds with Arches to Use**

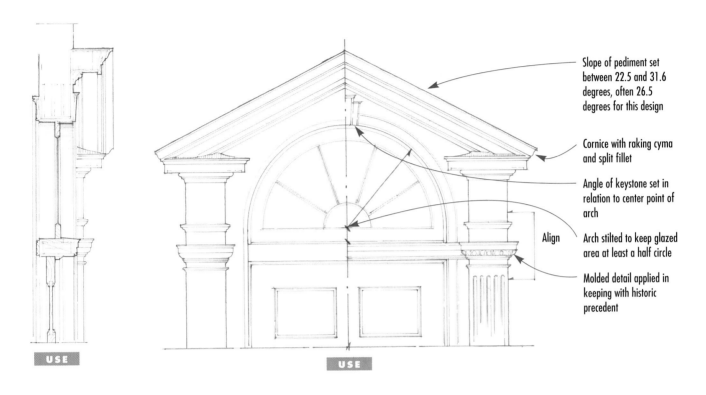

Slope of pediment set between 22.5 and 31.6 degrees, often 26.5 degrees for this design

Cornice with raking cyma and split fillet

Angle of keystone set in relation to center point of arch

Arch stilted to keep glazed area at least a half circle

Molded detail applied in keeping with historic precedent

Align

USE

USE

7.26 **Pedimented Door Surround with Arch Variations**

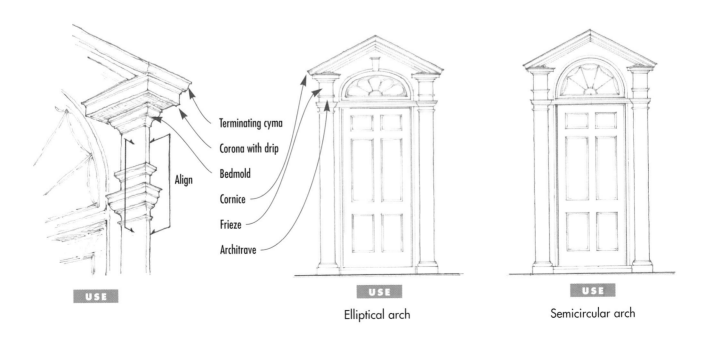

Terminating cyma

Corona with drip

Bedmold

Cornice

Frieze

Architrave

Align

USE

USE

Elliptical arch

USE

Semicircular arch

7.27 Arched Surrounds to Avoid

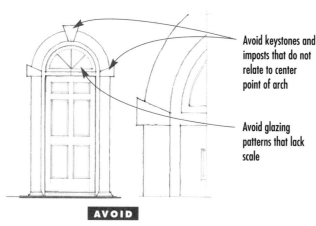

AVOID

No-point imposts and keystones

Avoid keystones and imposts that do not relate to center point of arch

Avoid glazing patterns that lack scale

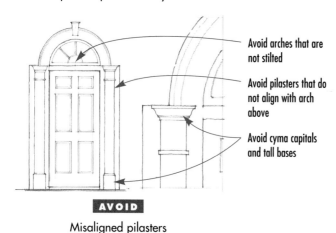

AVOID

Misaligned pilasters

Avoid arches that are not stilted

Avoid pilasters that do not align with arch above

Avoid cyma capitals and tall bases

CHECKLIST

Arched Door Surrounds

❑ Do the sides of the keystone point to the center of the arch?

❑ Is the arch stilted?

❑ Are the imposts rectangular?

❑ Do the edges of the pilasters align with the arch that they are supporting?

❑ Does the division of lights in the transom agree with the scale of adjacent windows?

ARCHED DOOR SURROUNDS

Arched surrounds are common in Georgian houses, especially in attached townhouses or row houses where architectural beauty is achieved by repeating simple, well-proportioned and detailed classical elements. Before designing an arched surround, review the guidelines for setting out an arch detailed in Chapter 4 **(see Arches and Arcades, page 80).** You can avoid most mistakes by following these instructions.

Arched Surrounds to Avoid

Figure 7.27 (top) has three things wrong. The first is that the keystones and imposts do not relate to the construction of the arch. Second, the configuration of lights is out of scale with the details of the opening. Third, the pilasters have a cyma for a base. Not only is this molding the wrong profile, it is too small to be practical at this location and will quickly be damaged in everyday use.

Figure 7.27 (bottom) attempts more detail, and would be close to getting it right, but important alignments have been missed. The pilasters have slid out from under the arch. Either the arch should be wider or the pilasters moved closer together. The keystone appears to be floating in the arch. And the details of the pilasters are still incorrect **(see Piers and Posts, page 62).**

Arched Surrounds to Use

In arched surrounds, the pilaster usually supports the arch directly. If the design is simplified and pilasters are not used, an *impost* is added to mark the transition between arch and casing. The crucial elements to maintain regardless of level of detail and variation are: alignment of pilaster and casing; stilt of the arch; rectangular, not triangular, imposts; a keystone set from the center point of the arch; and transom lights in scale with the opening.

Two variations are illustrated in 7.29. Both maintain the rules outlined above, yet they feel completely different.

7.28 **Arched Surrounds to Use**

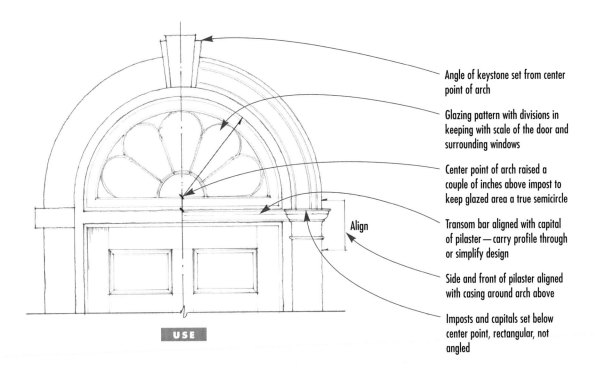

Angle of keystone set from center point of arch

Glazing pattern with divisions in keeping with scale of the door and surrounding windows

Center point of arch raised a couple of inches above impost to keep glazed area a true semicircle

Transom bar aligned with capital of pilaster—carry profile through or simplify design

Side and front of pilaster aligned with casing around arch above

Imposts and capitals set below center point, rectangular, not angled

Align

USE

7.29 **Arched Surround Variations**

USE

USE

7.30 **Projecting Surrounds to Avoid**

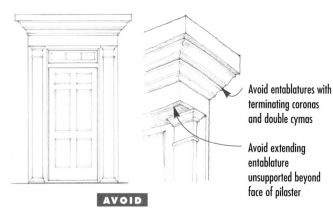

AVOID

Incorrect entablature with incorrect alignment

Avoid entablatures with terminating coronas and double cymas

Avoid extending entablature unsupported beyond face of pilaster

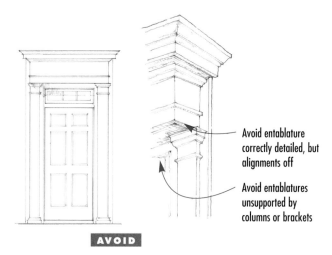

AVOID

Correct entablature with incorrect alignment

Avoid entablature correctly detailed, but alignments off

Avoid entablatures unsupported by columns or brackets

CHECKLIST

Projecting Door Surrounds

❏ Is the projected entablature supported with either brackets or columns?

❏ Are the Orders employed correctly?

❏ Are the brackets based on accurate historic precedent?

PROJECTING OR BRACKETED SURROUNDS

The examples we have looked at so far support the entablature on two posts—pilasters or engaged columns. An alternative detail is to omit the columns and instead support the entablature on a pair of supporting brackets. This allows some protection against the weather, albeit less than a fully projecting canopy.

Details to Avoid

If you are going to omit the columns from a projecting surround, you must use brackets instead. The entablature needs to be supported. As always, the first step is to make sure that the entablature is arranged correctly. Figure 7.30 (top) illustrates a surround that is both incorrectly detailed and projects without support. Figure 7.30 (bottom) shows a properly designed entablature, but in this case the alignment of pilaster to face of architrave is incorrect. It looks as though someone forgot to install the columns, leaving the surround feeling top-heavy and unstable.

Details to Use

Since a bracketed surround usually projects only a few inches, projecting the entire entablature can in some cases feel too heavy. A way to mitigate this effect is to limit the projection to the cornice. The frieze and architrave (which is effectively the door casing) still need to be expressed, but remain in the same plane as the pilasters (7.31).

We have said several times in this book that columns should never directly support the cornice **(see Installing Columns, page 52)**. Although this is true, you can bend this rule in the case of projecting surrounds, as long as the basic relationships of the Orders are maintained (7.32).

The design of the bracket can be as simple or as ornate as your budget allows. Take care when selecting brackets from catalogs. As with most elements, navigating through the badly designed products can be time-consuming and difficult. Avoid applied ornament or profiles that are not directly based on traditional precedent. Remember, the simplest is often the best.

7.31 **Projecting Surrounds to Use**

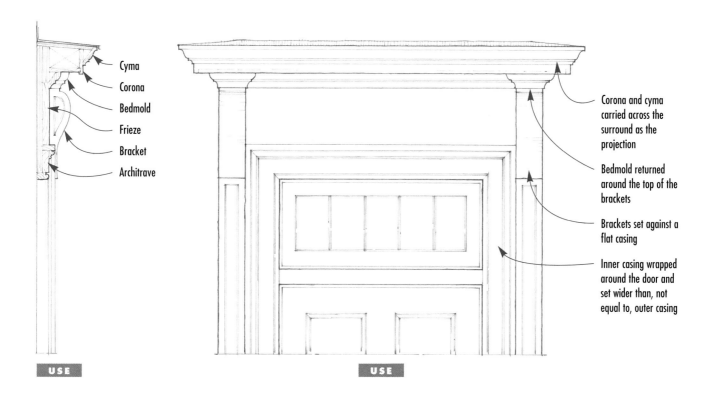

Cyma
Corona
Bedmold
Frieze
Bracket
Architrave

USE

Corona and cyma carried across the surround as the projection

Bedmold returned around the top of the brackets

Brackets set against a flat casing

Inner casing wrapped around the door and set wider than, not equal to, outer casing

USE

7.32 **Projecting Surround Variations**

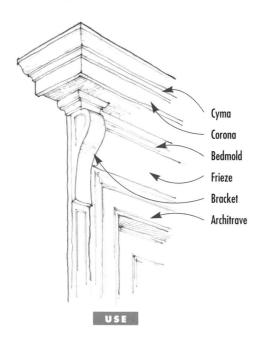

Cyma
Corona
Bedmold
Frieze
Bracket
Architrave

USE

USE

7.33 Trabeated Porticos to Avoid

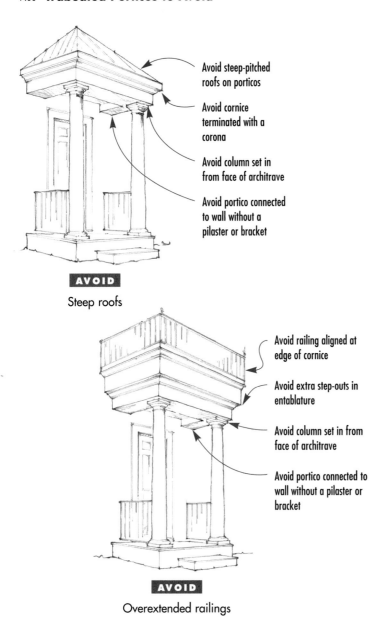

Avoid steep-pitched roofs on porticos

Avoid cornice terminated with a corona

Avoid column set in from face of architrave

Avoid portico connected to wall without a pilaster or bracket

AVOID

Steep roofs

Avoid railing aligned at edge of cornice

Avoid extra step-outs in entablature

Avoid column set in from face of architrave

Avoid portico connected to wall without a pilaster or bracket

AVOID

Overextended railings

CHECKLIST

Trabeated Porticos

❑ Is the pitch of the roof low?

❑ Is the railing aligned with the face of the architrave?

❑ Are you using the Orders correctly—especially the entablature?

❑ Is the neck of the column aligned with the face of the architrave, front and side?

❑ Is there a pilaster where the portico meets the wall?

TRABEATED PORTICOS

Porticos, like door surrounds, are closely related to the classical Orders. While surrounds are engaged—that is, attached to the wall—porticos project from the face of the building to provide better cover from the elements and more of a transition between the exterior and interior.

The same rules apply to porticos as surrounds. The first step is to use the Orders correctly. Use an entablature with an architrave, frieze, and cornice. Use a cornice with a bedmold, corona, and cyma. Align the neck of the column with the face of the architrave, both on the front and on the side. Any design that does not follow these basic rules will be incorrect.

Roof Pitch

The pitch of the roof over the portico should *not* match the slope of the roof on the house (7.33 top). A steep pitch will make the portico appear stuck on rather than a seamless part of the design. Set the slope at either 3:12 or 4:12, not more (7.34).

Railings Above the Portico

Often a railing is placed above a trabeated portico as an informal version of a parapet. Set the height and alignments of the railing according to the rules of setting out a parapet **(see Attics and Parapets, page 70)**. Set the height to $^1/_3$ the height of the column. If the deck is accessible and railings need to be set to meet code, **refer to Window and Door Railings, page 182**, for ways to meet code while mitigating the visual impact of a too-high railing.

Align the railing with the architrave. Never set the railing at the edge of the cornice (7.33 bottom).

Variations to Use

The possible variations of the trabeated portico are endless, as long as the basic relationship of parts remains constant. Figure 7.35 shows one variation: paired attenuated columns supporting an entablature with a railing with lilted (raised) corners.

7.34 **Trabeated Porticos to Use**

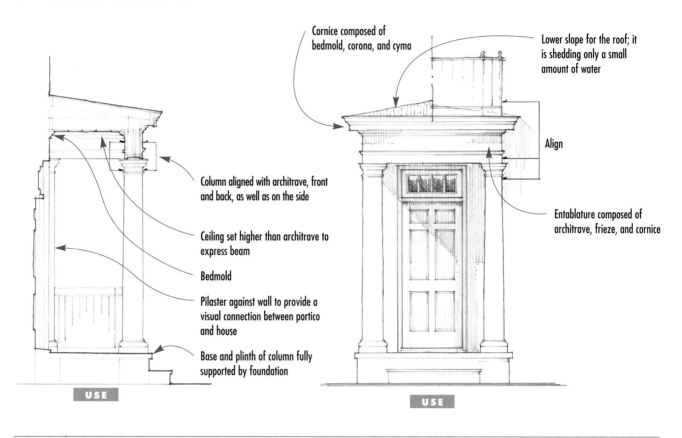

Cornice composed of
bedmold, corona, and cyma

Lower slope for the roof; it
is shedding only a small
amount of water

Align

Column aligned with architrave, front
and back, as well as on the side

Ceiling set higher than architrave to
express beam

Bedmold

Pilaster against wall to provide a
visual connection between portico
and house

Base and plinth of column fully
supported by foundation

Entablature composed of
architrave, frieze, and cornice

USE

USE

7.35 **Trabeated Portico Variations**

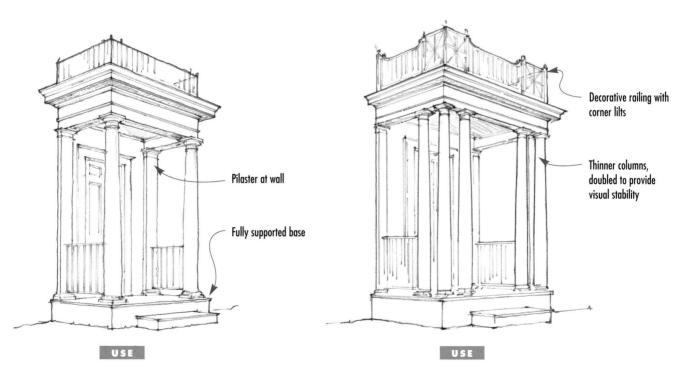

Pilaster at wall

Fully supported base

Decorative railing with
corner lilts

Thinner columns,
doubled to provide
visual stability

USE

USE

7.36 **Pedimented Porticos to Avoid**

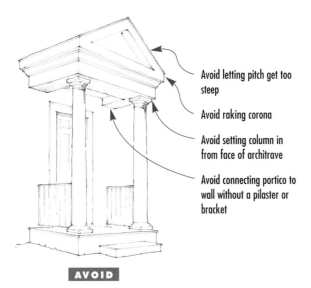

Avoid letting pitch get too steep

Avoid raking corona

Avoid setting column in from face of architrave

Avoid connecting portico to wall without a pilaster or bracket

AVOID

Incorrect relationships with the correct span

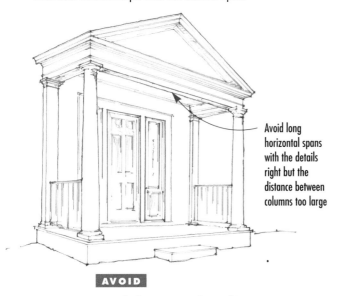

Avoid long horizontal spans with the details right but the distance between columns too large

AVOID

Incorrect span with the correct relationships

CHECKLIST

Pedimented Porticos

❑ Is the pitch of the pediment between 21.5 and 31.6 degrees?

❑ Have you used a raking cyma?

❑ Is the span reasonable for the height and size of columns?

❑ Is the neck of the column aligned with the face of the architrave, front and side?

❑ Is there a pilaster where the portico meets the wall?

PEDIMENTED PORTICOS

Adding a pediment to a portico provides an additional level of enrichment. With its temple-front form, this type of portico is a fully developed essay in classical design. But, as we discussed with pedimented surrounds, there are no half measures for getting the details right. If it is not in the budget to build a raking cyma, stick to the trabeated porticos.

Four Steps to Use

First, set the elements of the entablature based on the basic principles of a classical Order: architrave, frieze, and cornice. **(See Learn the Vocabulary, page 13.)** Second, align the columns with the face of the architrave. Third, don't forget a pilaster where the portico meets the wall. Fourth, set the slope of the roof and raking cyma following the instructions in Setting Out Pediments, page 82. Don't let the roof get steeper than 31.6 degrees.

Figure 7.36 (top) illustrates a portico that does not conform to any of the four steps outlined above. The result is a portico that appears heavy and chunky. The steep slope with raking corona, the misalignment of the columns, and the omission of the pilaster combine to make a portico that looks inauthentic, as if it were stuck onto the house.

Mistakes to Avoid

Even if the alignments and relationship of parts are detailed correctly, things can still go wrong. Figure 7.36 (bottom) illustrates a portico that follows all of the steps above, but sets the columns too far apart. The result is a span that feels uncomfortable. This design can be fixed in two ways: either add two more columns along the front to break down the span (7.38 right) or reduce the width of the portico **(see Intercolumniation, page 64)**.

Side Railings

Depending on the height of your floor level over grade, you may need side railings to meet code. Often, the regulations demand that these be taller than many traditional examples. You can learn more about how to maintain a good railing design while meeting codes in Chapter 8.

7.37 **Pedimented Porticos to Use**

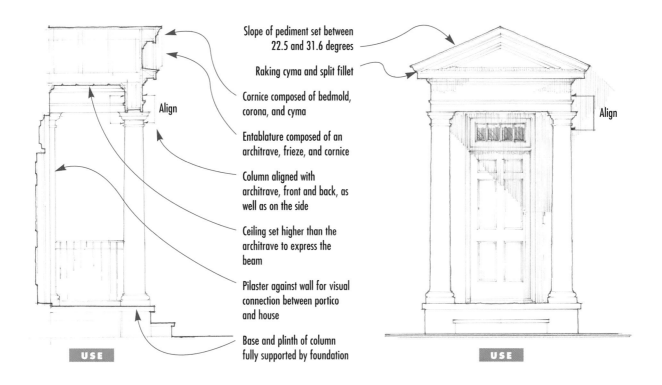

Slope of pediment set between 22.5 and 31.6 degrees

Raking cyma and split fillet

Cornice composed of bedmold, corona, and cyma

Entablature composed of an architrave, frieze, and cornice

Column aligned with architrave, front and back, as well as on the side

Ceiling set higher than the architrave to express the beam

Pilaster against wall for visual connection between portico and house

Base and plinth of column fully supported by foundation

Align

USE

Align

USE

7.38 **Pedimented Portico Variations**

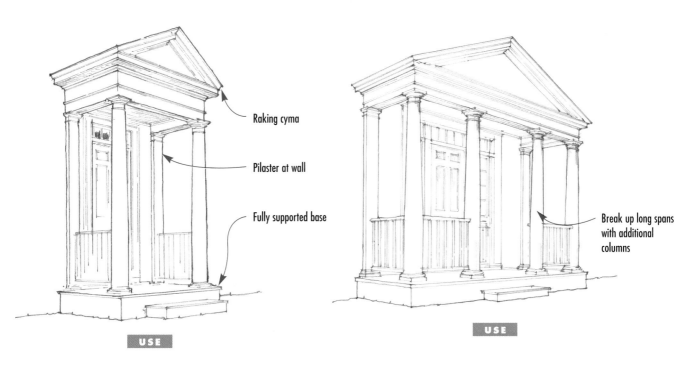

Raking cyma

Pilaster at wall

Fully supported base

Break up long spans with additional columns

USE

USE

7.39 **Pedimented Porticos with Arches to Avoid**

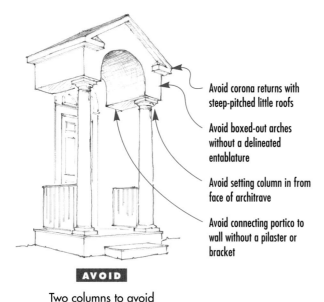

Avoid corona returns with steep-pitched little roofs

Avoid boxed-out arches without a delineated entablature

Avoid setting column in from face of architrave

Avoid connecting portico to wall without a pilaster or bracket

AVOID

Two columns to avoid

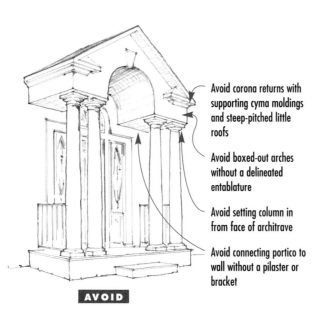

Avoid corona returns with supporting cyma moldings and steep-pitched little roofs

Avoid boxed-out arches without a delineated entablature

Avoid setting column in from face of architrave

Avoid connecting portico to wall without a pilaster or bracket

AVOID

Four columns to avoid

CHECKLIST

Pedimented Porticos with Arches

❑ Has the entablature been expressed?

❑ Does the arch start above the entablature?

❑ Does the entablature wrap around the inside of the arch?

PEDIMENTED PORTICOS WITH ARCHES

Arches can be incorporated in a pedimented portico to lighten the composition. This type of design can be very beautiful when executed perfectly and a disaster when the details are incorrect. Take care: getting this type of portico right is expensive. As always, less is more. If the budget or your knowlege doesn't allow you to get the details right, simplify the design to something that you *can* get right. It will look better than cutting corners or making mistakes.

Examples to Avoid

Most mistakes arise from a misunderstanding of where to spring the arch. In proper classical design, arches are carried above the entablature, or at least above the architrave. They don't spring directly from the capital of the column, as shown in 7.39. The columns end up appearing visually weak and unable to support the load of the arch above.

If the arch is to be used correctly, it needs to be articulated. The diagrams in 7.39 show the arches formed as simple boxes without entablatures. Both are wrong. The boxed framing, combined with the column misalignments, means that the columns have no visual relationship with the roof.

Examples to Use

Whether you use two or four columns, the basic premise remains constant. Columns should support a full entablature. The arch (slightly stilted) springs from a point just above the cornice. The face of the arch aligns with the face of the architrave and the neck of the column. The arch can either be segmental, more common with two columns (7.41 left) or elliptical (7.41 right). Refer to the instructions in chapter 4 **(see Arches and Arcades, page 80)** when setting out the arches.

Don't forget the interior elevation of the entablature. Make sure that the entablature wraps around the inside of the portico and returns above the door. When four columns are used, express the beam that connects the center columns to the wall by raising the ceiling above the sidelights.

7.40 **Pedimented Porticos with Arches to Use**

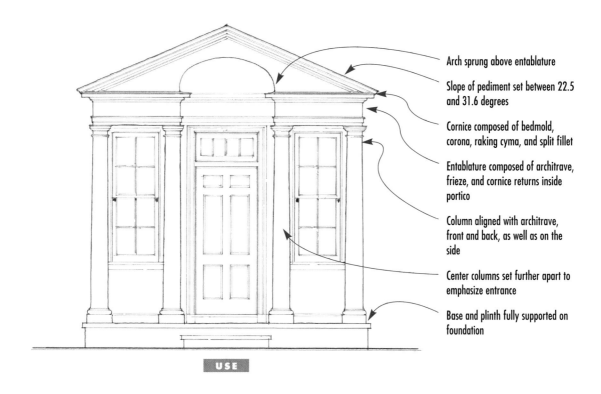

Arch sprung above entablature

Slope of pediment set between 22.5 and 31.6 degrees

Cornice composed of bedmold, corona, raking cyma, and split fillet

Entablature composed of architrave, frieze, and cornice returns inside portico

Column aligned with architrave, front and back, as well as on the side

Center columns set further apart to emphasize entrance

Base and plinth fully supported on foundation

USE

7.41 **Pedimented Portico with Arch Variations**

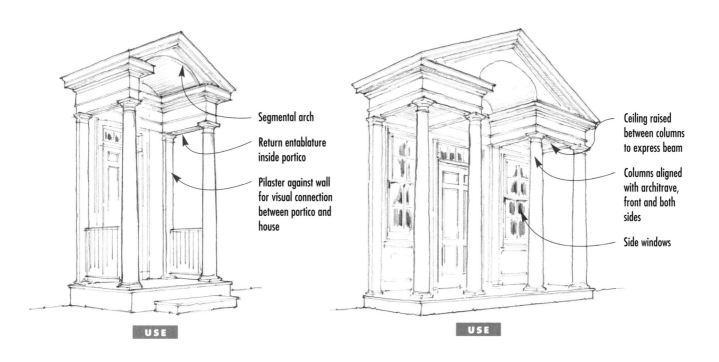

Segmental arch

Return entablature inside portico

Pilaster against wall for visual connection between portico and house

Ceiling raised between columns to express beam

Columns aligned with architrave, front and both sides

Side windows

USE

USE

7.42 **Door Canopies to Avoid**

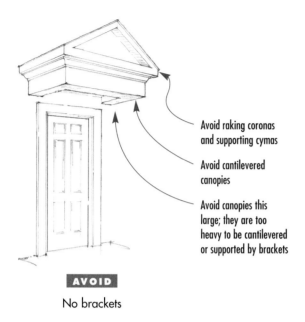

Avoid raking coronas and supporting cymas

Avoid cantilevered canopies

Avoid canopies this large; they are too heavy to be cantilevered or supported by brackets

AVOID

No brackets

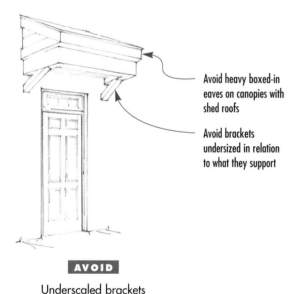

Avoid heavy boxed-in eaves on canopies with shed roofs

Avoid brackets undersized in relation to what they support

AVOID

Underscaled brackets

CHECKLIST

Door Canopies

❑ Are brackets supporting the canopy?
❑ Are these brackets balanced in size to support the canopy?
❑ Is the scale of the canopy right for brackets, not columns?
❑ Are brackets based on historic precedent?

DOOR CANOPIES

Door canopies are the middle ground between surrounds and porticos. Unlike projecting surrounds, where brackets or corbels take the place of engaged columns and support a shallow projection, canopies provide genuine protection from the elements in an application where a full-blown portico would be too formal. They can be particularly useful at service entrances to kitchens, mudrooms, and side doors.

Figure 7.42 shows two typical mistakes. Not only are these canopies chunky and poorly detailed, but the brackets appear weak and unable to do the job. Still worse is the canopy with no bracket at all. With rare exception, this cantilevered detail is not found in traditional work, and your canopy should *always* have visual support. **(See Design with Common Sense: Practicality Check, page 9.)**

Brackets

Good brackets are the key to a successful canopy. We can borrow from many different historic models. The choice of design will depend on the style of the building and the specific application.

More formal canopies (7.43) use a tighter, more architectural bracket relating to the *modillions* found in the classical Orders. **(See Kicks and Modillions, page 208.)** Make sure that the brackets don't get too insubstantial—they need to be thick enough to visually support the load they are carrying.

Less formal applications (7.44) can use a more rustic bracket. At its simplest, this could be a plain, square piece of wood making the transition between canopy and wall. It can be enhanced by expressing the millwork joints and with the addition of profiles as shown.

7.43 **Door Canopies to Use—Closed Eaves**

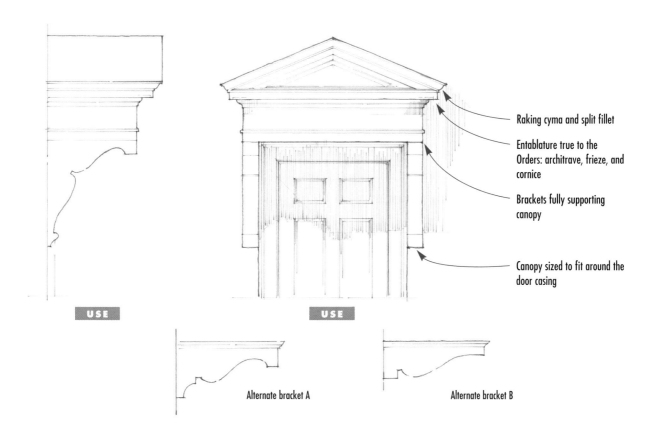

Raking cyma and split fillet

Entablature true to the Orders: architrave, frieze, and cornice

Brackets fully supporting canopy

Canopy sized to fit around the door casing

USE

USE

Alternate bracket A

Alternate bracket B

7.44 **Door Canopies to Use—Open Eaves**

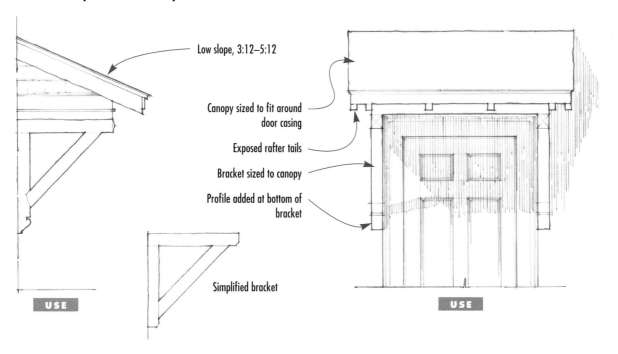

Low slope, 3:12–5:12

Canopy sized to fit around door casing

Exposed rafter tails

Bracket sized to canopy

Profile added at bottom of bracket

Simplified bracket

USE

USE

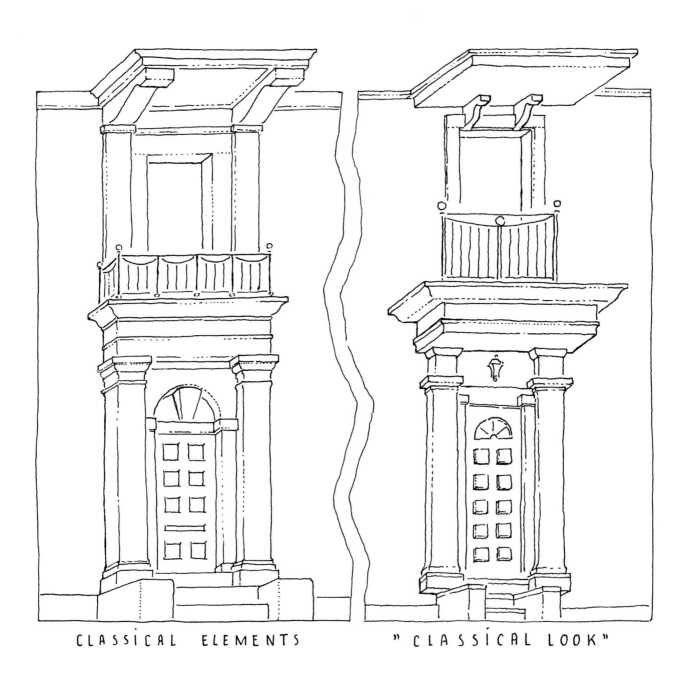

CLASSICAL ELEMENTS   " CLASSICAL LOOK "

Chapter 8

PORCHES, BALCONIES, AND RAILINGS

In many traditional American houses, the porch is the single most "architectural" piece of the building. Designing columns and entablatures, and handling double-height applications correctly, can seem daunting—not least because so many so-called "traditional" buildings seem to get it wrong. In fact, the rules are relatively simple—as long as you think ahead and design carefully with the Orders in mind.

PORCHES

PORCHES, BALCONIES, AND RAILINGS

PORCHES have been a popular architectural feature since the eighteenth century. Some of the finest early examples can be found in Charleston, South Carolina, where the double-height porches, located along one side of the house to catch the breeze, are called piazzas. Interestingly, this is the Italian word for square, which reinforces the porch's public/private nature.

Around the middle of the twentieth century, as architectural styles changed, air conditioning became common, and suburban America turned away from the street and toward the television as the prime focus of social activity, porches began to fade as a standard of the American home. Thankfully, planners and house builders have since realized what we were losing—not only architecturally, but also in terms of the social fabric of a town—and porches are reappearing.

Porch Styles

Architecturally, porches are as varied as the houses that they adorn. Georgian porches tended to use a classical vocabulary of columns, pilasters, and turned baluster railings. Victorian designs often used simpler chamfered posts, but with elaborate pierced-wood ornaments, turnings, or both. Arts and Crafts applications did without much of the fussy Victorian decoration, relying on an expression of simple wood craftsmanship for effect. Whatever the style, it is important to get the details right. Before reading this chapter, it is worth reviewing Chapter 3, The Orders, and Chapter 7, Entrances, as many of the rules in those pages should apply to your porch.

Balconies and Railings

Balconies, in iron, wood, or stone, give texture to your house as well as providing outdoor space at upper floors. A change of material and color (a painted iron balcony on a brick or wood building, for example) can give richness to an otherwise simple structure. These textural qualities are enhanced still further by the potential for planting.

Railings are required by most building codes when there is a drop of over 18 inches. On balconies and porches alike, the design of these railings will help determine if the building looks authentic. A simple building can be enhanced by adding carefully selected iron or stonework, or spoiled by poorly designed, out of scale elements. Balconies and railings are icing on your cake! Treat them with care, and make sure that they complement everything else you have achieved in the design.

8.1 Porches, Balconies, and Railings

Porches create outdoor "rooms" between the public space of the street and the private space of the interior.

Balconies add outdoor space to a building's upper floors.

8.2 Types of Porches

Double-height porch:
Charleston Single House

Double galleries wrapping the entire house:
Low Country and French Colonial

One-story porch: American Four Square

Integrated porch: Classical Villa

8.3 Porch Details

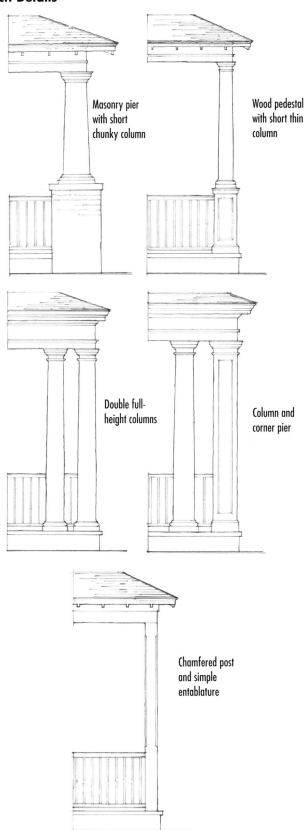

Masonry pier with short chunky column

Wood pedestal with short thin column

Double full-height columns

Column and corner pier

Chamfered post and simple entablature

8.4 Column Alignments to Avoid

Once the foundation is poured and the rough framing completed, the alignments are set; the finish carpenter may have no option but to install the columns incorrectly, either at the base or the neck.

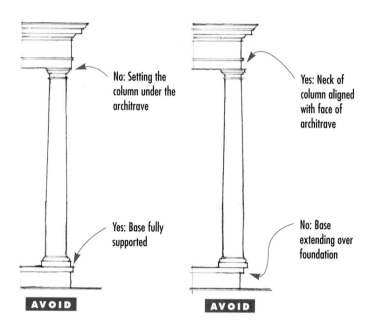

No: Setting the column under the architrave

Yes: Base fully supported

AVOID

Yes: Neck of column aligned with face of architrave

No: Base extending over foundation

AVOID

8.5 Column Alignments to Use

By thinking ahead, you can make it easy to install correctly aligned columns where the neck aligns with the face of the architrave and the base is fully supported.

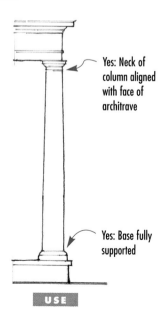

Yes: Neck of column aligned with face of architrave

Yes: Base fully supported

USE

PORCH PLANNING

Getting your porch right is easy, but only if you think about it before construction begins. Good planning requires an architectural drawing that clearly dimensions both the foundation and the framing of the entablature. This drawing needs to be part of the minimum requirements of even the smallest sets of construction documents.

Column Alignment

Misaligned columns are probably the most common mistake made in new traditional construction. The correct relationship is to align the neck of the column with the face of the architrave, while the base is completely supported on the deck. The important thing to remember is that the neck of a column is thinner than the base. The problems usually occur on site because the entasis (tapering) of the column is not taken into account during framing. Unfortunately, it is quite easy to forget this when framing up the building. The foundation goes in first. Then the rough framer constructs the roof. By the time the trim carpenter arrives to set the columns and handrails, the outcome is determined. All he can do is fill in the blanks. He can't fix flawed alignments (8.4).

Think Ahead

Use the centerline of the column as a reference point, positioned in relation to the face of the house. To align the neck of the column correctly, and support the base, the foundation will extend further away from the house than the architrave. Architectural plans should clearly note these dimensions, both on the foundation plan and framing plans. The set of drawings needs to include a dimension locating each element back to the wall. The contractor will not be able to get this right on site if he is not given the information ahead of time.

8.6 Setting Out the Porch

When setting out your porch, set all the dimensions to the centerline of the column; show dimension from the house to the centerline and the centerline to the outer extension at each crucial point.

Include the following dimensions in every set of drawings:

1. House to centerline of column
2. Center line of column to exterior face of foundation
3. Center line of column to exterior face of column at base
4. Center line of column to neck of column
5. Center line of column to face of architrave

NOTE: If the alignment is correct, the face of the architrave will not align with the face of the foundation.

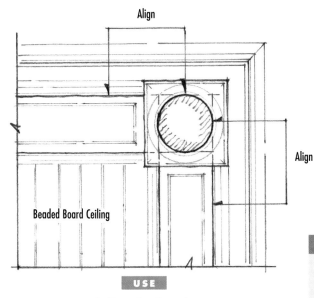

Align

Beaded Board Ceiling

Align

USE

Reflected ceiling plan

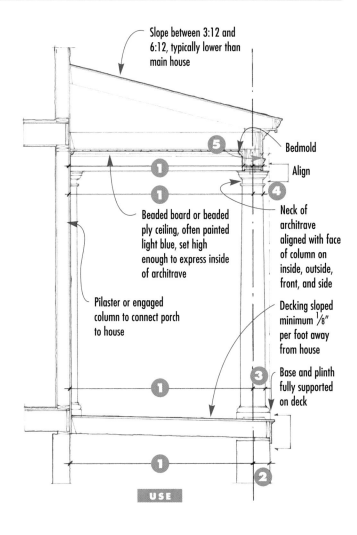

Slope between 3:12 and 6:12, typically lower than main house

Bedmold

Align

Beaded board or beaded ply ceiling, often painted light blue, set high enough to express inside of architrave

Neck of architrave aligned with face of column on inside, outside, front, and side

Pilaster or engaged column to connect porch to house

Decking sloped minimum $\frac{1}{8}''$ per foot away from house

Base and plinth fully supported on deck

USE

NEED TO KNOW

Porch Tips

- A minimum depth of 8'-0" is good for everyday use. If the porch gets too narrow, it will be hard to use comfortably when furnished.
- Use a pilaster or engaged column at the wall to visually engage the porch to the house.
- Express the beam on the inside of the porch.
- Align the inside face of the architrave with the neck of the column.
- Use a bedmold for the crown inside the porch (8.5).
- Use beaded board or V-joint boards on the ceiling of the porch (or substitute beaded board plywood). Often the porch ceiling is painted light blue.
- Dimension to rough framing—so framers know what to do.

8.7 **Architrave Framing Details**

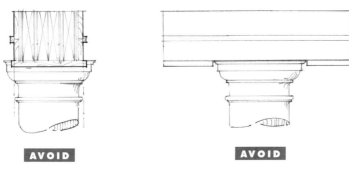

AVOID   AVOID

Rough framing too large, resulting in misalignments when trim and columns are installed

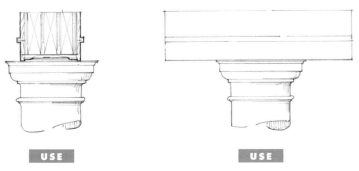

USE   USE

Enough space to finish beam off above column

8.8 **Column Support**

Without proper support, the column may start to push up the edge of the decking.

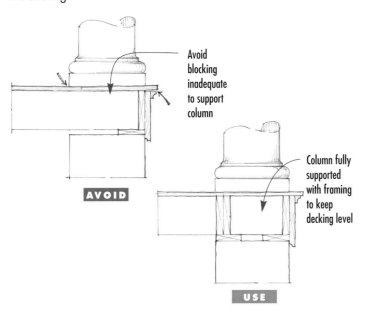

Avoid blocking inadequate to support column

AVOID

Column fully supported with framing to keep decking level

USE

PORCH DETAILS

Finishing the Beam

Don't forget to allow for the finish carpentry. The rough framing of the beam needs to be set at a dimension that allows the finish face of the architrave to align with the neck of the column. It also needs to be high enough to allow room to install finish trim between the rough framing and the top of the column. Columns should not be directly supporting rough framing (8.7).

Supporting the Columns

Make sure that the column is supported front and back with framing. Columns that are not fully supported can lift up and warp the edge of the decking (8.8).

Double Porches

On two-story porches, align the center lines of the columns from floor to floor (8.9), regardless of the size and type of column. Larger columns or piers always support smaller columns or posts. **(See Superimposition, page 66.)**

The size of the entablature should relate to the dimensions of the column, not to the overall height of the building. **(See Attenuated Orders, page 144, and Setting the Eave Height, page 200.)**

Engaging the Building

Where the porch engages to the house, the two areas of concern occur at the architrave and at the cornice.

Always support the architrave at the wall with a pilaster or engaged column, but take care with details. Pilasters typically project $1/5$–$1/4$ the diameter of the column with a width set to match the neck of the column. Engaged columns typically project $5/8$–$3/4$ the diameter of the adjacent columns **(see Pilasters and Engaged Columns, page 60)**. Do not use engaged half columns; they do not look substantial enough to support the porch. Do not set a full column next to the wall; it is unnecessary and will trap water at the base (8.10).

Porches can engage the cornice in several ways. One-story porches are engaged to the house as an additional mass. Either the architrave resolves into the house and the eave returns around the corner (8.11) or both fully resolve into the house.

Two-story porches can be more complicated. If the porch has its own roof it will engage like a one-story porch. But if the porch is included under the roof of the main house, special attention must be given to the alignments of the column from base to neck, to make sure that the eaves are aligned correctly with the building's foundation.

8.9 **Double Porch Variations**

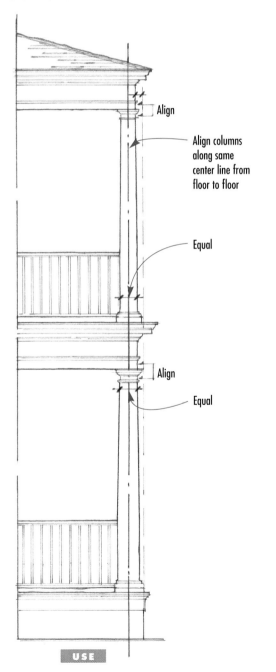

Align

Align columns
along same
center line from
floor to floor

Equal

Align

Equal

USE

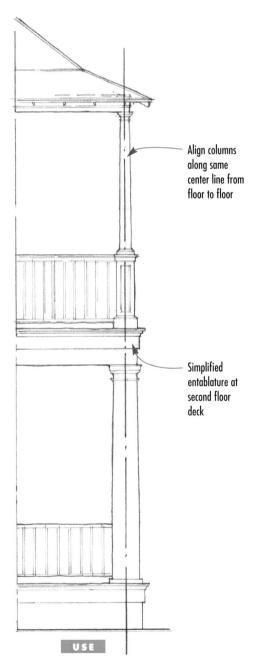

Align columns
along same
center line from
floor to floor

Simplified
entablature at
second floor
deck

USE

8.10 **Engaging the Porch to the Building at the Architrave**

To support the architrave where the porch meets the building, always use a pilaster or an engaged column, which throws enough shadow to visually provide support.

No support at wall

Engaged half column (too insubstantial; will look as though it is being swallowed by wall)

Full column adjacent to wall (unnecessary; will create a place for water to collect)

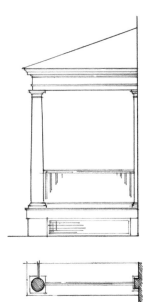

Pilaster projecting $^1/_5$–$^1/_4$ of column diameter, width matched to diameter at neck of column

Engaged column projecting $^5/_8$–$^3/_4$ of diameter from wall

8.11 Engaging the Porch to the Building at the Cornice

A one-story porch engages to the building as an additional mass; the treatment of a two-story porch depends on whether or not it has its own roof.

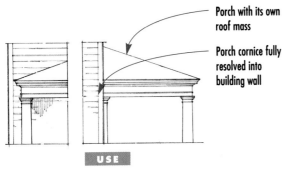

Porch with its own roof mass

Porch cornice fully resolved into building wall

USE

One-story porch with fully engaged cornice

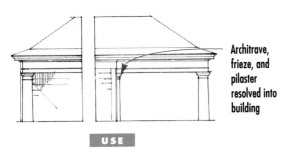

Porch with its own roof mass

Cornice wraps around corner of building

USE

One-story porch with cornice wrapping around corner

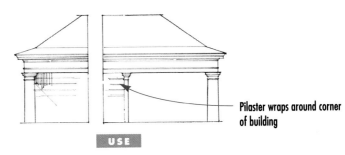

Pilaster wraps around corner of building

USE

Two-story porch fully incorporated in roof

Architrave, frieze, and pilaster resolved into building

USE

Two-story porch with cornice matching roof, architrave and frieze stepped back

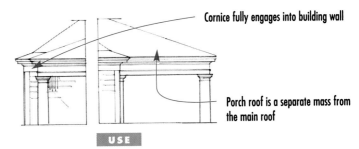

Cornice fully engages into building wall

Porch roof is a separate mass from the main roof

USE

Two-story porch with its own roof

8.12 **Wood Railing Details to Use**

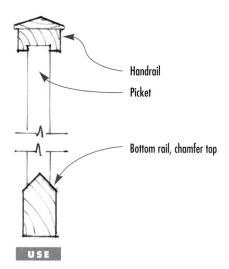

Handrail

Picket

Bottom rail, chamfer top

USE

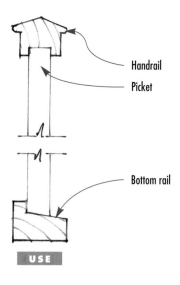

Handrail

Picket

Bottom rail

USE

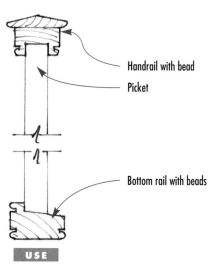

Handrail with bead

Picket

Bottom rail with beads

USE

RAILINGS

Railings made of wood or iron are both a practical requirement and an opportunity to give a layer of texture to a house. The key to making them look right is to find creative methods of meeting contemporary building codes.

Wood Railings

There are many different design options for the traditional house. Choose according to the style of your house and the overall degree of ornamentation you want to achieve. At the simplest end of the spectrum, we have square pickets and a simple handrail. For a more interesting effect, you can set the pickets diagonally to cast greater shadow and increase the apparent section.

There are relatively few mistakes to make with wood railing design. The biggest concern for the traditional builder should be material. Never use white plastic. Although PVC might seem to be a labor-saving option, it doesn't look right and cannot be maintained.

Railing Height

It is easier to design wood railings to meet contemporary building codes than it is with iron or stone, but in some applications the required height does interfere with the best design. Figure 8.13 illustrates two options for reducing the apparent height by adding a secondary iron railing, either directly above or set back behind the primary railing.

More Elaborate Railings

Turned balusters are also used on wood railings. These can be relatively thin, or on more expensive projects they can be formed from larger sections to relate more closely to classical models. Turned urns and other ornaments can be used to enrich the handrail. Handrails, likewise, can have a simple profile or more weight and detail for more ornate projects. Regardless of the profile, always slope or curve the top of the rail to cast water. For a richer effect, gooseneck the handrail at perimeter posts as shown in 8.14.

8.13 Railing Extensions to Use

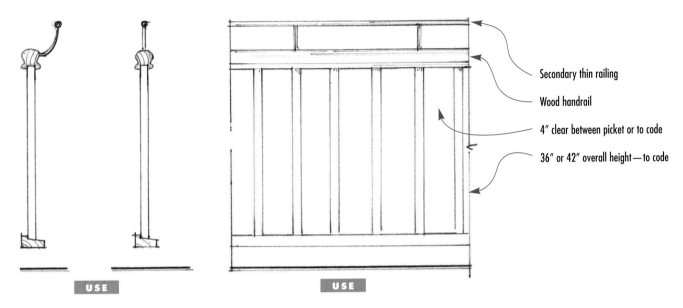

Secondary thin railing

Wood handrail

4" clear between picket or to code

36" or 42" overall height — to code

USE

USE

8.14 Railing and Newel Variations

USE

Newel with chamfered corners, ball finial, and turned pickets

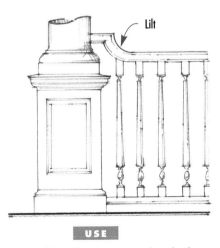

Lilt

USE

Pedestal kept low by raising handrail height over column base

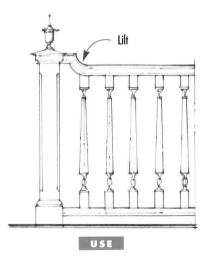

Lilt

USE

Newel with chamfered corners, urn finial, and lilted handrail

8.15 Balconies on Windows

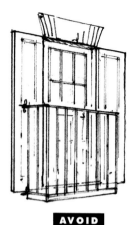
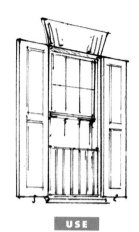

AVOID

Avoid a railing ½ height of opening or more and a railing extended beyond opening, especially when window has shutters.

USE

Use a railing ⅓ height of opening or less, installed within jamb.

8.16 Balconies on Doors

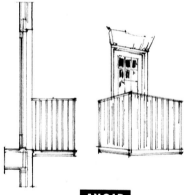

Avoid projecting balcony more than a few inches without brackets and tall pickets without horizontal divisions.

AVOID

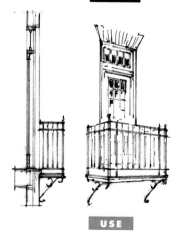

Use brackets to visually transfer load back to wall, horizontal divisions to break down verticality, and minimal projection from wall (ideally 18" or 24").

USE

WINDOW AND DOOR RAILINGS

Railings are usually installed on windows for aesthetic reasons rather than to meet a code. Only when windows extend to the floor does it become a code requirement to have some sort of window guard. Where child safety is a concern (and where law requires guards), you can install temporary guards that can be removed later without compromising the original design.

Window Railings for Aesthetics

Keep the height of the railing less than half the height of the opening. Otherwise, it will overpower the window.

Never overlay a railing in front of a window and its shutters (8.15 left). Remember what we discussed in Chapter 1: Everything should look as though it could work **(see Design with Common Sense: Practicality Check, page 9)**. The placement of this railing means the shutters can never be closed.

Instead, install the railing inside the window jambs. This will help to keep it in scale with the opening and ensure that the shutters remain visually operable (8.15 right).

Window Railings for Code

Watch the height of the railing. If the window is low enough to require a railing it is usually tall enough to accept it aesthetically, but it is important to be aware of the height. Check your local code requirements. If local code permits, measure the railing from the finished floor level, rather than from the windowsill.

Balconies on Doors

The new code requirements—for a railing height of 36" (or even 42" for multi-family dwellings)—are much higher than many traditional examples. A regular 6'-8" door can be completely overwhelmed by the railing of the balcony onto which it opens (8.16 top). The balcony will appear massive and the door too small. But there are a few tricks to help keep your composition balanced.

Railing Design and Depth

If the balcony is iron, add extra horizontal divisions in the railing to help break down its verticality. With a secondary top rail added, the vertical pickets will terminate a few inches lower than the required height. A raised bottom rail will also help with this effect. Now, rather than 36", the pickets can be as little as 30" high.

Keep the balcony shallow—ideally, 2'-6". Balconies are accessories, often just for standing or for a single chair; unlike porches, they can get too deep (8.16 bottom).

Transoms and Brackets

Add a transom with vertical lights above the door to give it as much height as possible. This helps to maintain the correct visual balance between the height of the balcony and the opening.

If your balcony projects from the building, always use brackets to support it. This achieves two ends: First, it provides visual support, avoiding the "open drawer" effect of unsupported balconies, and second, it gives more verticality to the composition.

Figure 8.17 (left) illustrates a deep balcony without horizontal divisions, a transom, or brackets. The result is an out-of-scale balcony that completely overwhelms the door. Figure 8.17 (right) shows a balcony that is balanced with the door because of the transom, depth of projection, added horizontal rails, and brackets.

Adjust the Appearance of Height

Another option to consider is increasing the height of the platform that supports the railings. This reduces the actual railing height while maintaining the correct overall height for code compliance (8.17 bottom).

Iron Railing Details

Cast- and wrought-iron pieces readily available from several catalogs can be combined to build simple yet beautiful iron railings (8.18). When using ironwork, be careful not to let it get too chunky or heavy. Traditional ironwork is often slender and light in its design. Study and copy historic precedent to find designs that fit the style of your house.

8.17 Balconies on Doors—More Views

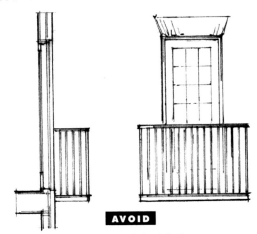

AVOID

Low openings with high balconies

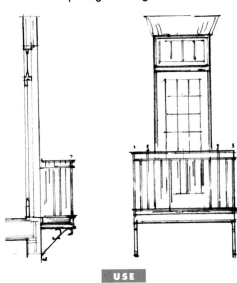

USE

Raised platform framing to reduce picket height; brackets, transoms, and taller doors to balance balcony

8.18 Iron Balcony Designs

AVOID

Chunky ironwork

USE

Finials and prefabricated pieces to enhance design

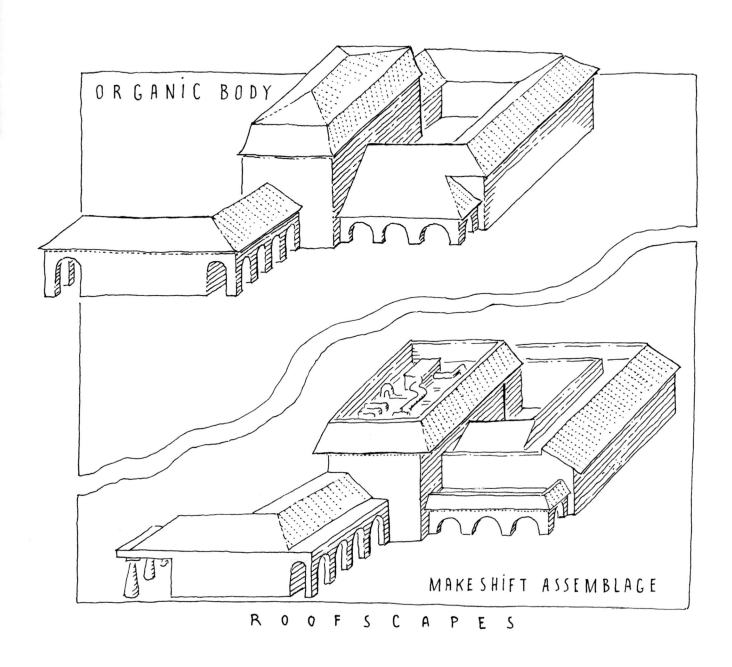

ORGANIC BODY

MAKESHIFT ASSEMBLAGE

ROOFSCAPES

Chapter 9

R O O F S

The roof protects a house from the elements, throwing water or snow away from the walls and offering a deep shadow from the sun while also visually defining the massing of the house. The old adage is true: Keep your foundations and your roof in good repair and your house will stand for years.

ROOFS

ROOFS

The pitched roof is one of the key distinguishing features of a traditional building. It provides protection to the house by keeping water and snow away from the walls while visually defining the massing of the house. With the exception of very arid climates, which developed flat roof architecture, almost all traditional architecture the world over uses pitched roofs. As we will see, the pitch of the roof is closely linked to climatic concerns and the constraints of indigenous roofing materials.

In the twentieth century, this simple response to climate and material was turned on its head. Architects used flat roofs for aesthetic ends, not least because they knew that by abandoning pitched roofs they would make their buildings look unlike anything we had seen before. The result has been a century of poorly detailed, leaking structures.

Detailing the Roof

For the traditional house builder today, detailing the roof and eaves correctly is one way to achieve authenticity in the design on both a macro and a micro scale. From a distance, the roof provides the determining silhouette of the building **(see Massing, page 22)**. Up close, the treatment of the eaves, gutters, and cornice will have a significant effect on whether the building succeeds or fails as a convincing work of traditional architecture. We will look at these aspects in more detail in Chapter 10, Cornices and Eaves.

In the past, builders understood the protective requirements of the roof because they could not rely on modern plastic sheathings or damp-proofing to keep the building dry. That work had to be performed by the detailing of the roof and eaves, which were accordingly made as substantial as possible. Keep this in mind when planning the massing of the roof.

In Chapter 2, we discussed the importance of the roof plan in relation to the overall massing of the building. Although it is at the top of the house, it is one of the first things that you need to think about. When laying out a unified composition of the house, keep it simple and keep it consistent (9.1). Avoid gratuitous projections. Many otherwise perfectly designed houses look wrong because the roof is fussy or over-designed. As you read this chapter, think about two general principles for designing your roof: keep the massing simple but the details generous.

Traditionally—for economy—roofs would seek the lowest pitch practical, given the climate and the materials. Although modern systems of construction have made this concern less relevant, achieving an authentic traditional building requires remembering and applying the traditional principles of roof design.

9.1 **Roofs & Massing**

Complicated massing and multiple gables do not add interest to the house; the only thing they add is unnecessary cost. Use volumes that are easy to cover with a simple roof profile, and add interest to the design with details such as the door surround or cornice.

AVOID   USE

9.2 **Roof Types**

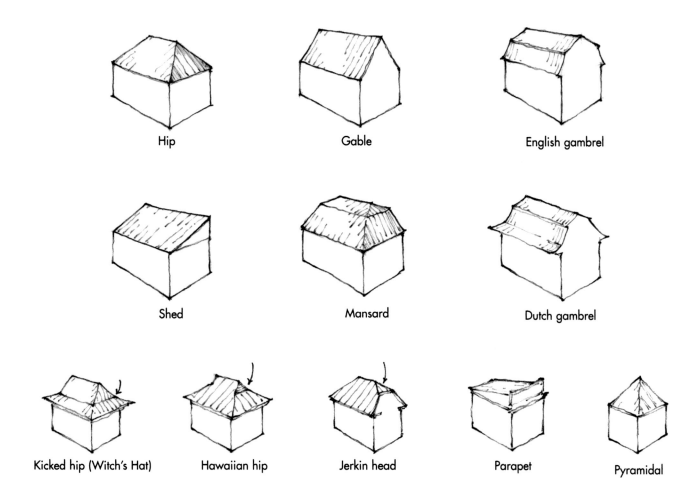

Hip   Gable   English gambrel

Shed   Mansard   Dutch gambrel

Kicked hip (Witch's Hat)   Hawaiian hip   Jerkin head   Parapet   Pyramidal

9.3 **Elements of the Roof**

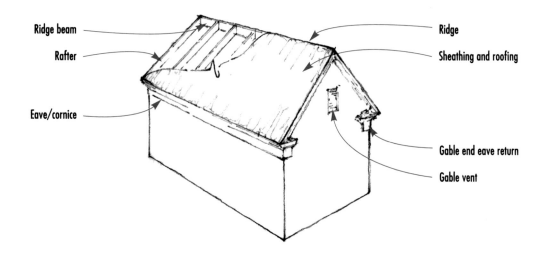

Ridge beam

Rafter

Eave/cornice

Ridge

Sheathing and roofing

Gable end eave return

Gable vent

9.4 Roof Materials and Climate

Slate

Northern climates with rain and snow

Metal

Southern humid climates with heavy rainfall

Barrel tile

Southern Mediterranean low-pitched roofs, best in climates without heavy rainfall

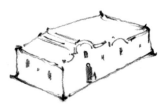

Adobe clay

Hot arid climates with little rain and a lot of sun

MATERIALS AND MASSING

Design for Climate and Material

Colder climates with rain and snow require a steep pitch; warmer climates allow for a shallower pitch. Thatch roofs require a steep pitch, while lead roofs require very little pitch at all. Therefore, you may see steep roofs in the tropics, where there was a tradition of thatch (for example, Thai long houses), and flat lead-covered roofs on buildings in northern Europe. Hip roofs are most appropriate for southern climates, allowing for broad eaves on four sides, sheltering the house from the more vertical angle of the sun and diverting rainfall evenly.

Barrel tile or Mediterranean tile roofs are shallow because the tiles are traditionally held in place by mortar tension and would slide off steeper roofs. Therefore, they offer little protection from driving rains. Arid climates may have flat roofs with no eaves, finding protection from the sun in the use of pergolas and deep reveals.

Think about the Roof Plan First

Today, many so-called traditional buildings give the impression that the whole floor plan was designed with no thought given to massing, and the roof was stuck on afterwards. Sunrooms, garages, and single-story extensions swell from the main structure without rhyme or reason. The result can be chaotic.

Always plan from the roof down. Avoid multiple gables, enormous and complex hips, and "leftover" flat-top areas where mismatched masses don't quite meet. Common sense dictates that enclosing the building under one roof structure uses materials most economically. Where more space is required, simple wings can be added under secondary roofs (9.5).

Ridge Length and Slope in Plan

When using a hip roof, avoid the "mini ridge," which results from a floor plan that is almost square. In this case, either use a gable roof or rework the plan to have a clear ridge (9.6). When designing the roof in plan, it is easy to lose sight of the slope. To avoid mistakes, always use 45-degree angles. This will ensure that roofs with different widths will have different ridge heights, not different slopes (9.7).

9.5 Roof Massing in Plan

Don't ignore the roof plan when designing the floor plan. Think of the building as a series of volumes harmoniously combined together.

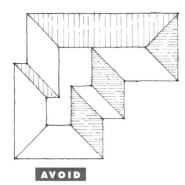

AVOID

Floor plan that results in complicated massing and portions of flat roof

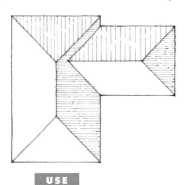

USE

Floor plan that takes roof massing into account from the beginning

9.6 Ridge Length

If the ridge of a hip roof is too short, it will make the roof appear too heavy on the building. If the plan is too deep for a substantial ridge, use a gable roof or reproportion the plan to create a longer ridge

AVOID

Hip roof with extremely short ridges

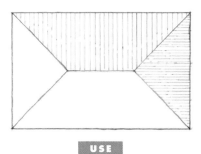

USE

Ridge of hip roof set equal to or greater than length of sloping portion

9.7 Roof Pitch in Plan

When drawing a roof in plan, always use 45-degree angles at the corners to make sure that the slope remains constant. With any other angle, the sides of the building will have different roof slopes.

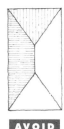

AVOID

Changing slope of roof within a volume

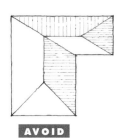

AVOID

Keeping ridge height if footprint gets narrower

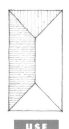

USE

Same slope throughout a roof volume

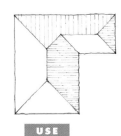

USE

Ridge lowered as necessary

9.8 **Traditional Roof Slopes**

Traditional roof slopes historically were set as a ratio of the relationship between span and king post. The most common ratios were 1:5, 2:5, and 3:5.

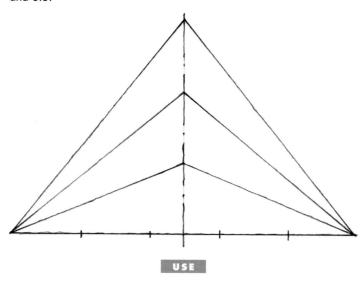

USE

9.9 **Slopes of Different Roof Types**

Each roof type has characteristics that change the way it is viewed in three dimensions. If all the pitches are the same, the gable and pediment appear far too steep. Set different types of roof at different pitches.

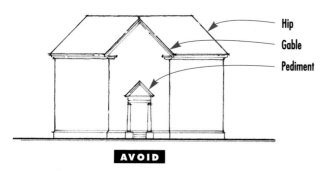

Hip

Gable

Pediment

AVOID

Different roof types set at the same pitch

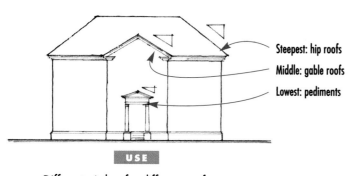

Steepest: hip roofs

Middle: gable roofs

Lowest: pediments

USE

Different pitches for different roof types

ROOF SLOPES

In the 18th and 19th centuries, trusses were described as a ratio of span to king post (the height of the roof) This was most often calculated in fifths of the span, leading to a prevalence of roofs that are $^{1}/_{5}$, $^{2}/_{5}$, and $^{3}/_{5}$—even in buildings where the king post was not employed or after it fell out of use. These pitches, 21.5, 38.5, and 50 degrees—or 4.75:12, 9.5:12, and 12:10—are still commonly used in today's system of framing.

Combining Roof Types

Many traditional buildings incorporate different types of roofs within a single composition.

The three most common types of roofs used in combination are hips, gables, and pediments **(see Roof Types, page 187)**. Don't use the same pitch for each roof. Each type has its own characteristics and needs a different slope (9.8 and 9.9).

The Hip

Hip roofs have the steepest slope of all of the roof types. These roofs are always sloping away from view and are never seen in true elevation. Because of this, a hip roof will always visually appear lower than its actual height. It needs to be set at a higher pitch to balance the height of adjoining gable ends.

The Gable

Unlike a hip roof, the gable is seen in true elevation and its actual height is visible. Set the pitch lower to accommodate this. When you set a gable against a hip roof, lower its pitch to keep it from appearing steeper than the hipped portion. A formal classical pedimented gable (9.9) often has a pitch of 26.5 degrees.

The Pediment

The pediment has the lowest slope of the three types. It is a formal motif relating to the Orders. The most common pitch is 22.5 degrees, but as pediments get wider or narrower, the pitch increases or decreases slightly—typically, from 21 to 26.5 degrees. **(See Pediments, page 75.)**

Combining Similar Types of Roofs

Similar roof types can have similar or different slopes depending on the size and orientation of the masses that are being covered. If the two parts of the building are roughly equal in size, set the slopes to match.

Side wings can overpower the main house if the slope gets too high. Set the side wings to match the main house if the pitch is 7:12 or lower. Set the side wings lower than the main house for any pitch over 7:12. Avoid setting the side wings higher than the main house (9.10).

NEED TO KNOW

Avoid: 45-Degree Roofs

One pitch in particular should be avoided for all gable roofs: a 45-degree slope. When you're designing with a computer or even with a triangle, it seems rather simple to use this angle for your roof, but the result will look static. Hip roofs may be 45 degrees, but they usually look better if the slope is set even a few degrees higher or lower.

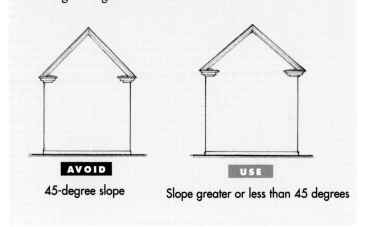

AVOID
45-degree slope

USE
Slope greater or less than 45 degrees

9.10 Slopes of Similar Roof Types

Don't let the roof of the side wing overpower the composition; use roof slope to keep it secondary to the main house.

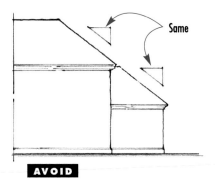

Same

AVOID

Avoid setting slope of the side wing to match main house if side wing roof will hit main house cornice.

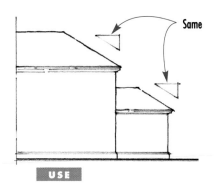

Same

USE

Set slope of side wing to match main house if it is low enough to remain secondary.

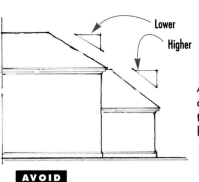

Lower
Higher

AVOID

Avoid setting slope of side wing higher than slope of main house.

Higher
Lower

USE

Lower slope of side wing to keep it from overpowering main house.

9.11 **Compound Roofs**

Compound roofs allow you to use a steep slope on a house with a wide plan, maximizing usable space while keeping the overall height of the building low.

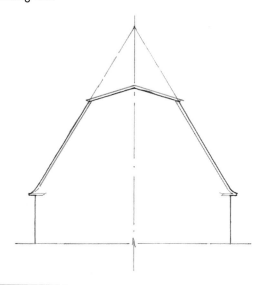

9.12 **Types of Compound Roofs to Use**

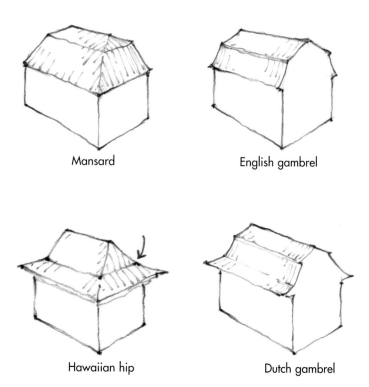

Mansard

English gambrel

Hawaiian hip

Dutch gambrel

COMPOUND ROOFS

Compound roofs employ more than one pitch in a single mass. The most common types of compound roofs are mansards, gambrels, and witches' hats. The benefit of a compound roof is that you are able to use a steep slope on a wide building to maximize usable space in the attic without creating a roof that overwhelms the building (9.11). Gambrels first appeared to lessen the overbearing look of a steep gable roof across a wide span. A mansard on a hip roof has the same effect.

Mansard Roofs

In mansard roofs, commonly found in French architecture, the lower portion of the roof is very steep, almost vertical, and is often treated as a sloping attic story. For this reason, dormers in mansard roofs are considered an extension of the wall below and should align with the windows below **(see Dormer Windows, page 114)**. Most common mistakes in mansard roofs occur at the eaves. Avoid roofs that look like hats pulled down over the house. The roof should sit on the wall plate. Extend eaves with a radius or kick, rather than a flat projection (9.14).

Gambrel Roofs

There are two types of gambrel roofs: Dutch and English.

Dutch gambrel roofs are common throughout the Northeast, especially in coastal summer homes. Gambrel roofs pull back from the wall of the house more than mansards and read as a roof, rather than an extension of the wall. Dormers in Dutch gambrel roofs are objects, and do not need to align with the windows below. The eaves of Dutch gambrel roofs are often radiused and are deeply extended.

In the English gambrel, the lower roof is generally steeper than in the Dutch. Good examples are found in Williamsburg, Virginia, and as well as throughout the mid-south and Connecticut. As with the mansard roof, the dormers typically align with the windows below. The crown of the dormer always works into the chine—the line where the roof slopes intersect—either by continuing the pitch of the upper roof as a shed, or projecting horizontally from this point to wrap around the top of the dormer, which could be flat or pedimented.

The chine itself is an important element of a gambrel roof. It is often painted to match the trim on the house and provides a contrasting highlight to break up what otherwise could be a large roof mass. Don't forget the chine.

9.13 **Mansard Roofs**

AVOID

Mansard roof that looks like a hat pulled down over the building

USE

Mansard roof with an eave condition that relates to the building

NEED TO KNOW

Designing a Gambrel Roof

1. Set the slopes. The diagrams labeled "USE" illustrate typical slope combinations for English and Dutch gambrel roofs.

2. Set the lower roof off of the plate and achieve a deep eave projection with a kicked or radiused eave. **(See Kicks and Modillions, page 209.)**

3. Set the relationship of the lower to the upper roof. The lower roof should always be longer than the upper roof; if the upper roof is too large, it will overwhelm the building. A ratio of approximately 3:5 works well.

4. Make sure the massing of the roof in some way relates to a circle, intersecting either at the chine or at the ridge. If the geometry does not fit in a circle, it will feel awkward.

9.14 **Setting out a Gambrel Roof**

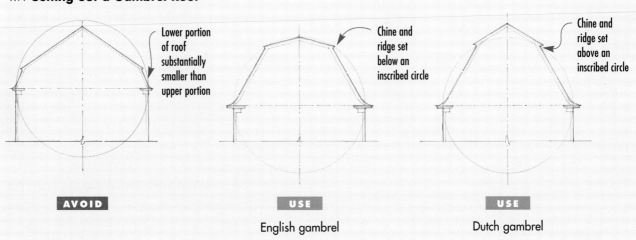

Lower portion of roof substantially smaller than upper portion

Chine and ridge set below an inscribed circle

Chine and ridge set above an inscribed circle

AVOID

USE

English gambrel

USE

Dutch gambrel

9.15 **Gable Vents**

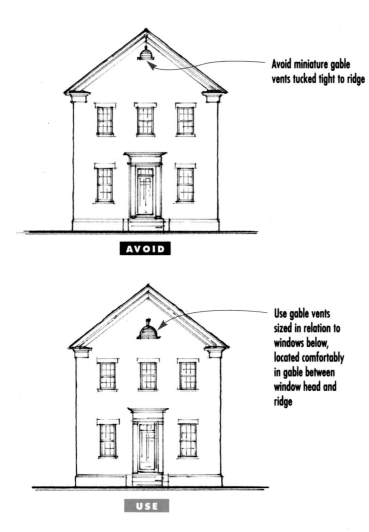

Avoid miniature gable vents tucked tight to ridge

AVOID

Use gable vents sized in relation to windows below, located comfortably in gable between window head and ridge

USE

9.16 **Gable Vent Details**

Keep your details true to the Orders: Keystones must relate to the center of the arch.

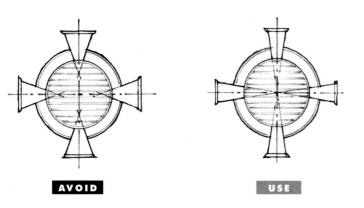

AVOID   **USE**

VENTING

Modern construction methods, with tightly sealed framing, insulation and double-glazed windows, create houses that are more airtight than historic structures. Ventilation to the roof is now required by code as well as for good practice. A roof can be ventilated through active or passive means.

Active Roof Venting

Active roof venting systems employ a fan or ventilating assembly to circulate and cool air in the attic. These systems are being used today in increasing numbers as people come to appreciate the value of energy efficiency and sustainable building. With the humidity and heat in the attic reduced, the entire house will take less energy (and be less expensive) to cool during summer months. In this area of constantly evolving technology, the builder, designer, and homeowner must work together to determine the best system to meet the needs of each specific project.

Passive Roof Venting

Passive ventilating uses physics to circulate air through the attic. The detailing of the venting depends on the type of roof. Often a ridge vent is added to maximize the circulation of air. Avoid ridge vents. They tend to be highly visible at just the point where you would not expect to see a vent in an authentic traditional building.

Gable Roof Ventilation

Gable roofs are vented by a combination of eave vents and vents in the gable ends of the building. In most cases, the gable end vents are purchased from a lumberyard or millwork catalog. Watch out for four things when purchasing and installing the gable end vents: size of vent, architectural details on the vent, location in wall, and depth of projection.

Size

Avoid tiny vents. The gable end of a house is often quite large, and needs something to fill out the composition. But do not oversize the vent so that it overwhelms the composition. Typically, the width of the vent should match that of the windows below (9.15).

Detail

Simpler vents tend to be most appropriate for traditional architecture. When manufacturers get too ornate they often seem to get things badly wrong. If using details such as keystones, **refer to Arches, page 74**, to check that everything is in the right order. The keystones should terminate at the center of the vent (9.16).

Location

Gable vents are prominent and will be an important element in your design. Locate them carefully, and when using a shaped vent, never place it too close to the ridge, which will leave a large area of blank wall below.

Projection

Set the vent into the wall like a window; go as far as giving it a casing to ground it in the elevation so that it doesn't look glued on. Avoid installing the vent to project out from the plane of the wall, which will make it appear to float in the wall.

More Options

As an alternative for an outbuilding, consider a cupola at the ridge. Many examples are available from catalogs. The simple examples tend to be the best designs. Make sure the cupola is a suitable scale for the building. Cupolas that are too small can look like small pimples on the roof. Equally, on smaller roofs, don't let them dominate. Another option is to vent the roof through the chimney to make use of extra space next to a single flue.

Venting the Eaves

The most common detail for venting the eaves is to use a strip vent in the soffit (9.18 left). This detail will work, but it is not ideal; the long strip looks modern and has the effect of de-materializing the eave. If you have the budget, it is better to install small round vents between rafters throughout the building (9.18 right). This detail requires a little more effort, but the results are worth the trouble.

9.17 Venting Hip Roofs

Venting a hip roof can be difficult. Consider using a form of active venting. If venting a hip roof passively, choose the vent type carefully.

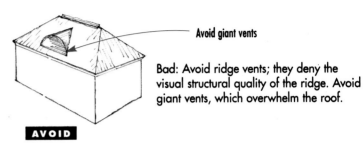

Avoid giant vents

AVOID

Bad: Avoid ridge vents; they deny the visual structural quality of the ridge. Avoid giant vents, which overwhelm the roof.

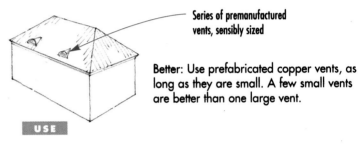

Series of premanufactured vents, sensibly sized

USE

Better: Use prefabricated copper vents, as long as they are small. A few small vents are better than one large vent.

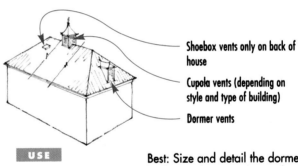

Shoebox vents only on back of house

Cupola vents (depending on style and type of building)

Dormer vents

USE

Best: Size and detail the dormer as if it had a window in it, but replace the window with a louvered vent.

9.18 Eave Vents

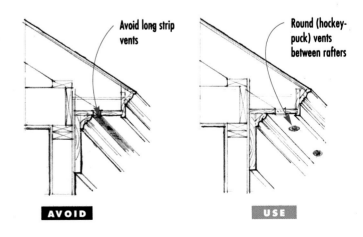

Avoid long strip vents

Round (hockey-puck) vents between rafters

AVOID   **USE**

CALL ME A "TRADITIONAL" BUILDING   I AM A TRADITIONAL BUILDING

Chapter 10

CORNICES AND EAVES

The eaves of a house are directly derived from the cornice of the classical Orders. While many traditional building elements today have become more ornamental than functional, the role of the eave has changed little since its origins in antiquity—its job is to keep water away from the face of the house.

CORNICES AND EAVES

CORNICES AND EAVES

THE PURPOSE OF THE EAVE is to keep water away from the building by means of the gutter and a drip (10.1). As we discussed in Chapter 9, traditional builders could not rely on modern weatherproofing materials to keep a building dry. Accordingly, they put great effort into creating an eave and cornice profile that did its job well.

Eave Design

Even the simplest eaves relate to the cornice of the Classical Orders. Made up of a cyma (often a gutter), corona (the drip), the bedmold, and a fascia, the eaves provide the termination of the wall and the transition to the roof.

Like so many aspects of traditional construction, the practical advantages have a positive aesthetic result too. A projecting eave casts a shadow line around the building at just the point, compositionally, where a strong horizontal is needed to counteract the vertical lines of the walls. If your eave is too shallow, the shadow will be lost and the junction will feel clipped and abrupt.

Types of Eaves

The type of eave used on a building depends on the architectural style and local climate. Houses in northern climates often have shallower eaves to allow maximum light through the windows. In southern climates, eaves are often deep to protect from the hot sun by casting cool shadow around the house. Eaves can be boxed in a more formal design or open in a more vernacular building (10.2). The projection of the eaves can be extended with kicks and radiuses (10.2). When a boxed eave is projected out with a kick or radius, modillions can be added to support the extended soffit (10.4). Gutters are used in many eave designs; the two most common profiles are ogee and half round (10.5).

Eave Details

Getting the eaves right is all about following rules—carefully and accurately. There are few half-measures. The right details don't necessarily require more money or materials, but they do require more thought. Get these details right and everything else will follow. Get them wrong, and even if you've worked hard to specify the right windows, doors, or materials, the end result will not feel right.

10.1 Cornices and Eaves

Cornices and eaves are derived from the Orders of classical architecture. They provide a visual termination to the wall and a visual transition into the roof above. Cornices and eaves keep rain away from the face of the wall and cast a shadow for protection from the sun.

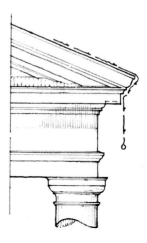

10.2 **Types of Eaves to Use**

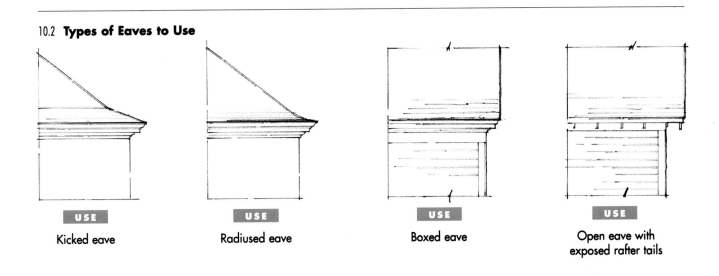

USE

Kicked eave

USE

Radiused eave

USE

Boxed eave

USE

Open eave with
exposed rafter tails

10.3 **Eave Definitions**

Drip flashing

Gutter

Cyma (crown)

Corona (fascia) with drip

Soffit with vent

Bedmold

Frieze (fascia)

10.4 **Modillions**

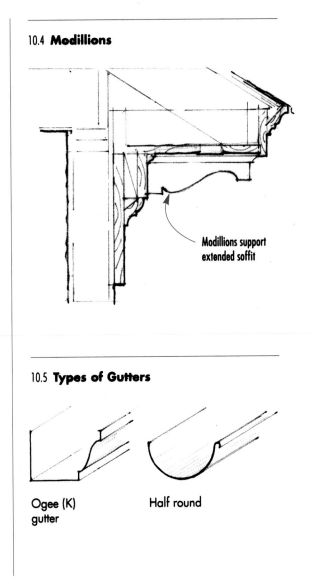

Modillions support
extended soffit

10.5 **Types of Gutters**

Ogee (K)
gutter

Half round

10.6 **Setting the Eave Height**

If the cornice gets too large, the roof will overpower the building; if it is too small, the roof will appear perched on the building. Superimposing a pedestal, column, and entablature (regardless of the Order) results in a cornice that is approximately ¹/₁₆ the height of the building.

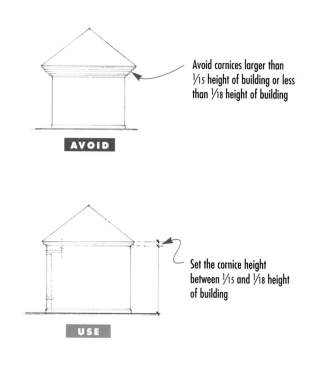

Avoid cornices larger than ¹/₁₅ height of building or less than ¹/₁₈ height of building

AVOID

Set the cornice height between ¹/₁₅ and ¹/₁₈ height of building

USE

10.7 **Eave Height and Building Height**

The height of the cornice is set in relation to the height of the building, so taller buildings have taller cornices.

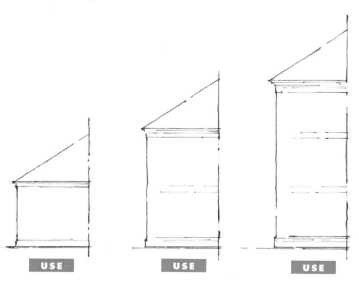

USE   **USE**   **USE**

EAVE AND CORNICE HEIGHT

The first step in designing the cornice or eave of a building is to determine its height. This dimension has a proportional relationship to the height of the building: the taller the building, the larger the cornice (10.7).

The size of the eaves determines how the roof sits on the building. If the eaves are too large, the roof will overpower the building below. If the eaves are too small, the roof will be too weak for the house (10.6).

In the classical Orders the ratio of cornice height to the height of the overall Order is typically 1:12.5, but this ratio creates a cornice that is too heavy for most houses. To balance the cornice with the house, a pedestal is added to the Order to calculate the height. The resulting ratio of cornice height to house height is approximately 1:16.

The height of the cornice will vary depending on materials and architectural style. Setting the cornice between 1:15 to 1:18 the height of the building typically achieves a good balance.

When a building has side wings or elements with lower heights, don't use a single cornice height throughout the building. Vary the size of the cornice in relation to the height of that individual part of the building. Lower wings have smaller cornices than the taller parts of the house (10.8).

Cornice Details

Once the height is determined, the next step is to detail the cornice. The divisions and relationships of the cornice vary by style and building material, so look at local historic precedent when determining your schematic design. Figure 10.9 illustrates three options to use as a point of departure for most designs. Frame buildings often have frieze boards within the cornice. This helps to lighten the proportions of the details while keeping the overall height within the 1:15 to 1:18 range.

The simplest type of cornice has a frieze board, bedmold, and corona. In this design the cyma can be made up with a half round gutter. Adding a cyma makes the cornice more formal. Masonry buildings often omit the frieze to give more weight to the cornice.

10.8 **Eave Heights within a Building**

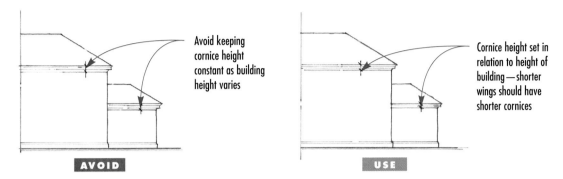

Avoid keeping cornice height constant as building height varies

AVOID

Cornice height set in relation to height of building — shorter wings should have shorter cornices

USE

NEED TO KNOW

Setting Out a Box Eave

1. **Height:** Determine the height of the cornice in relation to the height of the building ($^1/_{15}$-$^1/_{18}$ building height).

2. **Type:** Determine the type of eave to be in keeping with the style, scale and materials of the building. Decide whether a frieze board will be included in the cornice design. Wood buildings with siding often have lighter eaves with a frieze board included in the height of the cornice. Masonry buildings often do not have a frieze board (10.9 lower right).

3. **Vertical divisions:** The individual divisions vary for each eave. Watch out for a few common mistakes:
   • Don't let the corona get larger than the frieze
   • Don't use a miniature bedmold
   • Don't forget the drip
   • Don't use a cantilevered ogee gutter

4. **Set the projection:** Determined by the style and region. Northern eaves are often shallower to avoid ice damming and let maximum light into the house. Southern eaves are often deeper to cast a shadow around the house and provide protection from the hot sun. The projection of the eave is usually equal to the height of the cornice.

10.9

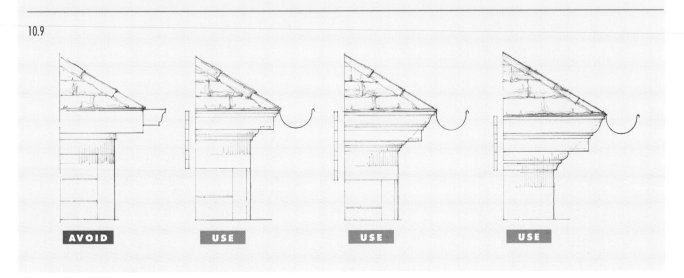

AVOID **USE** **USE** **USE**

10.10 **Box Eaves to Avoid**

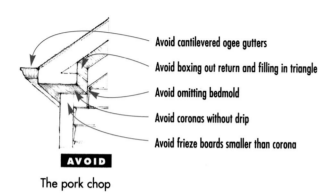

Avoid cantilevered ogee gutters

Avoid boxing out return and filling in triangle

Avoid omitting bedmold

Avoid coronas without drip

Avoid frieze boards smaller than corona

AVOID

The pork chop

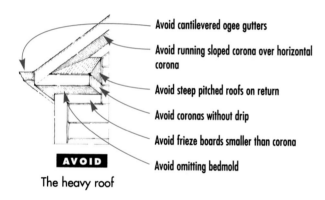

Avoid cantilevered ogee gutters

Avoid running sloped corona over horizontal corona

Avoid steep pitched roofs on return

Avoid coronas without drip

Avoid frieze boards smaller than corona

Avoid omitting bedmold

AVOID

The heavy roof

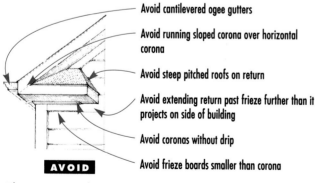

Avoid cantilevered ogee gutters

Avoid running sloped corona over horizontal corona

Avoid steep pitched roofs on return

Avoid extending return past frieze further than it projects on side of building

Avoid coronas without drip

Avoid frieze boards smaller than corona

AVOID

The exaggerated return

BOX EAVE RETURNS

Resolving the eave at the gable end of a building can be complicated. This is where the horizontal cornice turns to wrap the corner and meets the sloping profiles that transition the roof to the wall surface. It is at this point that several mistakes occur that greatly impact the appearance of the house.

Never Use the Pork Chop Return

The pork chop return, a boxed-out eave with no distinction between the horizontal and angled elements (10.10 top), is one of the most common details in contemporary house construction. *Never* use it. It does not belong in the traditional vocabulary. It is an over-simplification of the box eave that will be out of scale with the house.

Other Returns to Avoid

Figures 10.10 center and 10.10 bottom are one step above the pork chop eave. They are better because they differentiate between the horizontal and sloped elements, but they still make many mistakes.

The slope of the roof over the return should not match the slope of the main roof. Set it at the lowest slope possible to minimize its visibility. This will refine the look of the return.

Avoid ogee gutters, unless they are built into the cornice. Use a half round gutter instead. Avoid returns longer than the eave projection. Avoid friezes (bottom fascia) shorter than the corona (top fascia).

Box Eave Returns to Use

Figure 10.11 shows the same eave return correctly detailed. Be careful to maintain several key relationships. Resolve the sloping members into the horizontal members. Extend the corona at a distance less than or equal to the eave projection. Use a low roof slope over the return. Use a half round gutter. Make sure that the frieze is larger than the corona. Return all the elements of the cornice into the building. Don't cut it short.

Setting the Distance of the Return

The length of the return relates to the width of the gable, slope of the roof, and height of the building.

10.11 **Box Eave Returns to Use**

Designing a Box Eave Return

1. Cornice design: Set the height and division of the eave per instructions in Setting Out a Box Eave, page 201.

2. Length of the frieze: Either set the length of the frieze equal to the height of the cornice or set it equal to one diameter of an Order superimposed on the corner of the house.

3. Projection of the return and extent of the corona: Set the projection from the wall, and the distance that the corona extends beyond the frieze, less than or equal to the projection of the eave on the side of the building.

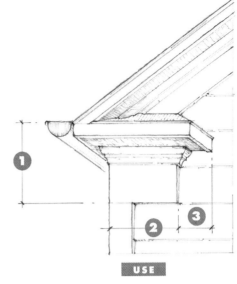

USE

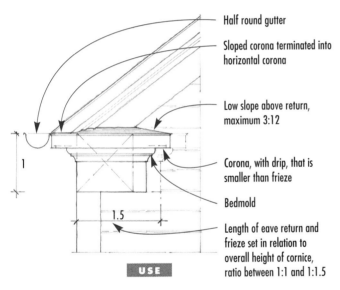

Half round gutter

Sloped corona terminated into horizontal corona

Low slope above return, maximum 3:12

Corona, with drip, that is smaller than frieze

Bedmold

Length of eave return and frieze set in relation to overall height of cornice, ratio between 1:1 and 1:1.5

1

1.5

USE

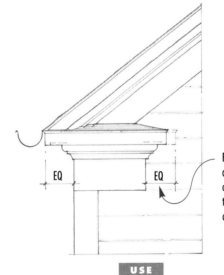

EQ   EQ

Projection of corona equal to or up to 50% less than projection of eave

USE

Beyond the general rules of thumb, you will have to trust your eye. Start by setting the length of the frieze in relation to the overall height of the cornice. At a minimum, set the frieze equal to the height of the cornice. At a maximum, set it 1.5 times the height of the cornice. The next step is setting the projection of the corona. The corona can either be equal to the projection of the eave or, in a case where the eave has an extended projection, the returning corona can be reduced up to 50 percent.

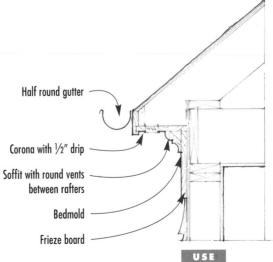

Half round gutter

Corona with ½" drip

Soffit with round vents between rafters

Bedmold

Frieze board

USE

10.12 **Eave Returns to Avoid**

Use either a proper cyma molding or a simple box eave, but not a faux cyma made of an angled board; such an abstracted mis-interpretation will never look right. A double molding will not resolve cleanly at the corner, and the "crown crown" effect will look too heavy running along the side of the building.

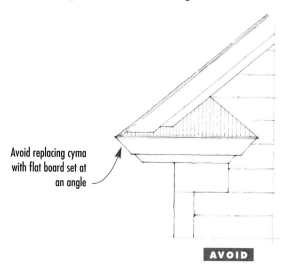

Avoid replacing cyma with flat board set at an angle

AVOID

Avoid a double cyma at gable end

AVOID

THE POOR MAN'S CORNICE

The gable end of a roof derives from the pediment of the classical Orders. In a formal classical building with a fully expressed order (either pilasters or columns), it is necessary to follow the rules for setting out the pedimented Order very closely **(see Setting Out Pediments, page 82)**.

The principal detail to get right is the raking cyma, which ensures that everything resolves correctly at the external corner. But this is an expensive detail because it requires two differently profiled moldings to be run. At the roof level, getting things exactly right is not such a pressing concern as it is at ground level, closer to our eye-line. So a modified, more modest solution developed: the "poor man's" cornice return.

Poor Man's Returns to Avoid

Figure 10.12 shows the basic concept gone wrong. Never use a flat board as a substitution for a profiled molding. If you can't afford a profiled eave, use a simple box eave as shown on the previous page. In 10.12 (bottom), the cornice is in the correct order on the return side of the building, but there are two problems with this detail. The first is the awkward connection that results where the two cyma profiles meet. Since the top cyma doesn't resolve into the horizontal cyma, there is no way to resolve this con-nection. The second occurs on the side of the building with the continuous cornice. This cyma is doubled up, creating a "crown crown," which makes the cornice appear too heavy for the house.

Poor Man's Returns to Use

Detailing the poor man's cornice is as simple as taking the exact cornice relationships and profiles, running them on the sloping gable, then completely resolving them into the horizontal cornice (10.13). Set the length of the return on the gable wall as shown in 10.11.

10.13 **The Poor Man's Cornice**

Setting Out the Poor Man's Cornice

1. Design the cornice as per Setting Out a Box Eave, page 201.

2. Detail the return as per Designing a Box Eave Return, page 203.

3. For the poor man's return, repeat the profiles of the cornice on the sloped portion of the roof. Resolve the sloped cornice into the horizontal cornice. (The sloping frieze may be smaller than the horizontal frieze.)

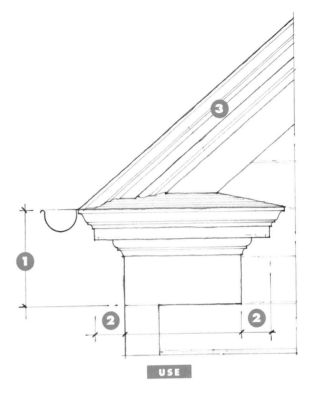

USE

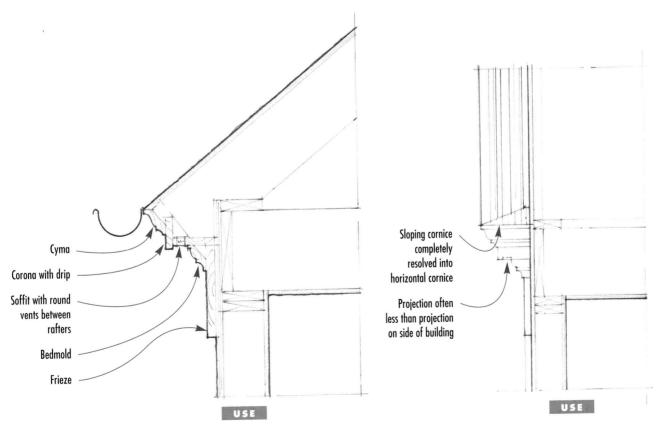

Cyma

Corona with drip

Soffit with round vents between rafters

Bedmold

Frieze

USE

Sloping cornice completely resolved into horizontal cornice

Projection often less than projection on side of building

USE

10.14 **Built-in Gutters**

Size the gutter in relation to the cornice so as not to overwhelm the composition. This detail requires active venting of the roof.

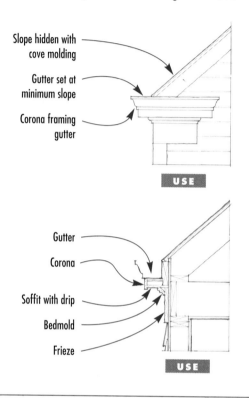

Slope hidden with cove molding

Gutter set at minimum slope

Corona framing gutter

USE

Gutter

Corona

Soffit with drip

Bedmold

Frieze

USE

10.15 **Profiled Bargeboard**

This design works in northern climates where minimal eave projections are preferable to deep projections. Don't project the bargeboard from the wall, which would turn it into a pork chop eave.

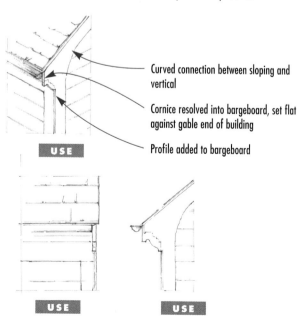

Curved connection between sloping and vertical

Cornice resolved into bargeboard, set flat against gable end of building

Profile added to bargeboard

USE

USE   USE

BOX EAVE VARIATIONS

Built-In Gutters

To achieve a clean, classical feel at your eaves, you can use a built-in ogee gutter whose profile acts as a terminating molding to your cornice.

The only way to use an ogee gutter is to support it with another molding. It should never be cantilevered. Ogee gutters are provided in stock sizes. Specify carefully to make sure the height and projection fit well within the design of the cornice.

It is difficult to get the proportions exact, but as long as the overall relationship of parts is visually right, the cornice will work (10.14). When using this detail, do not slope the gutter; set it level. The water will drain out on its own.

Eave Returns: A Simple Alternative

An economical alternate is to eliminate the projection at the gable end and resolve the entire cornice into a bargeboard, the fully exposed board at the gable end of the building. This detail is traditionally found in New England homes.

The cornice runs straight into a bargeboard, which is cut at a profile to enhance the design. The bargeboard typically transitions to the corner board with a gentle curve (10.15). The result, easy to achieve, adds elegance and grace and looks appropriate on a simple traditional building.

Although this design appears similar to the pork chop, the difference is that it is flat to the building, not projecting, at the gable end.

Brick Cornices

A simple approach to the cornice on a masonry building is to form it out of brick. The projection of the cornice is achieved by corbeling a few courses of bricks out from the face of the wall (10.16). Additional depth and detail is achieved by alternately recessed and projecting headers within a single course. This detail can achieve (for a minimum effort) a rich effect approximating the dentils found in the classical orders. Alternatively, turn the bricks 45 degrees to form a dog-tooth cornice (10.17).

10.16 Brick Eaves with Corbels

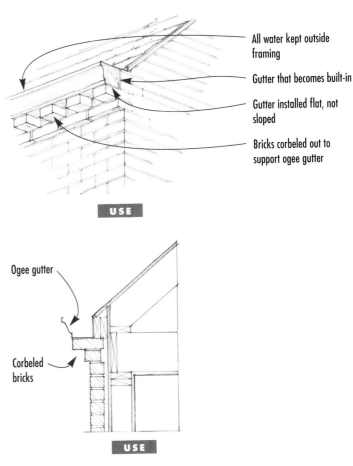

All water kept outside framing

Gutter that becomes built-in

Gutter installed flat, not sloped

Bricks corbeled out to support ogee gutter

USE

Ogee gutter

Corbeled bricks

USE

10.17 Brick Eaves with Dog-Tooth Dentils

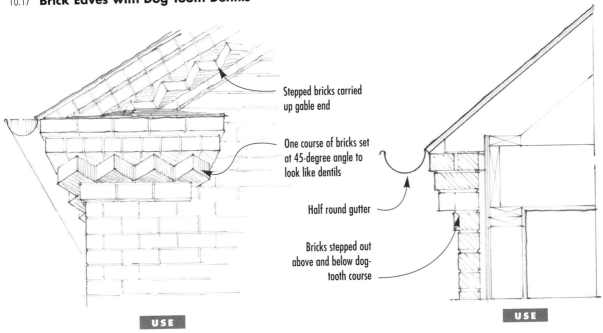

Stepped bricks carried up gable end

One course of bricks set at 45-degree angle to look like dentils

Half round gutter

Bricks stepped out above and below dog-tooth course

USE

USE

10.18 Roof Kick Angles

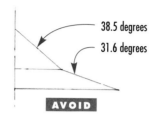

38.5 degrees
31.6 degrees

AVOID

Avoid changing slope
more than 18 degrees.

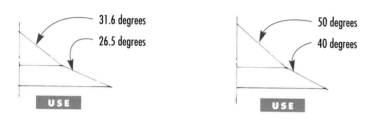

31.6 degrees
26.5 degrees

USE

50 degrees
40 degrees

USE

10.19 Roof Kick Section

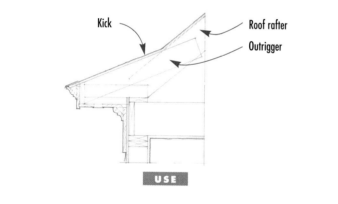

Kick

Roof rafter
Outrigger

USE

10.20 Radiused Eave Section

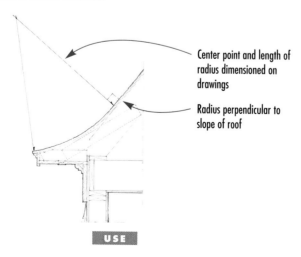

Center point and length of
radius dimensioned on
drawings

Radius perpendicular to
slope of roof

USE

KICKS AND MODILLIONS

Roof kicks are an effective way to extend a deep eave on a building with a steep roof slope, helping to cast shadow and to shed water further away from the house. A kick in the roof allows the cornice to project further from the house without dropping too low on the wall. It also allows for a softening of the line between the wall, cornice and roof, making the roof mass sit more elegantly on the building.

Framing a Roof Kick

Framing a roof with a kick is the same as framing a typical roof. If using conventional lumber, frame the main roof, then face nail the smaller members to each rafter at a lower angle to form the kick. If using pre-manufactured trusses, specify the angle and size of the kick, and it will be incorporated into the design at the factory.

The angles for the kick change depending on the roof pitch. The best combinations are shown in 10.18. A formal building with a closed box cornice tends to have a smaller kick. In the example shown, the kick exists more for visual reasons, to soften the junction of wall, cornice, and roof slope, than for practical purposes, to extend the projection of the eaves (10.19).

Vernacular buildings with open eaves often have larger kicks. The deeper the projection, the greater the shade, which is why this sort of roof mass is so typical in Southern and West Indian architecture. Note how the length of the kick is also increased. The distance the kick rises depends on the style of the house, but typically it remains on the lower third of the roof.

Radiused Eaves

The next level of refinement is to add a curve to the kick. This is called a radiused eave. Radiused eaves can be found throughout the American South and the West Indies, as well as in late nineteenth century Shingle Style houses in the Northeast—which themselves revived early Dutch Colonial models.

The point at which the radius starts relates to the distance the eave projects. Unlike a simple roof kick, a radiused eave can only extend so far before it begins to curve up. A greater depth can be achieved by increasing the length of the radius. The radius of the eave needs to originate from a point perpendicular to the roof slope. If you use any other starting point, the geometry won't work and the eave will have a kink. When detailing this in an architectural drawing, clearly mark the springing point in relation to the cornice and roof (10.20).

Using Modillions

Modillions are brackets in a cornice supporting a projecting corona. They relate closely to the classical Orders of architecture, and provide an additional layer of enrichment at the eave. Modillions tend to be used only on buildings that have a high level of detail.

Modillions were developed in antique classical buildings as the formal, architectural version of rafter tails or projecting joists that might have been found in earlier wooden temple structures. Their location implies a certain visual logic.

Setting Out

When laying out the modillions, start at the corners of your building. The outside face of the modillion should touch and form a square in the corner of the soffit (10.21). Don't allow the corners to be leftover space **(see Ionic and Corinthian Entablatures, pages 58-59)**.

10.21 **Modillions**

Brackets called modillions provide support to the deeper eave projection, as shown here in section and reflected ceiling plan.

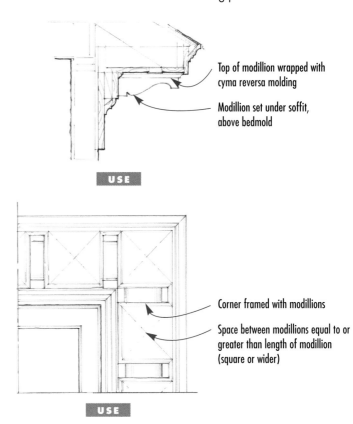

Top of modillion wrapped with cyma reversa molding

Modillion set under soffit, above bedmold

USE

Corner framed with modillions

Space between modillions equal to or greater than length of modillion (square or wider)

USE

10.22 **Roof Kicks & Radiused Eaves to Use**

Kicks and radii can be small or large on the roof, depending on style and regional variation. The general principles of geometry and construction apply regardless of size.

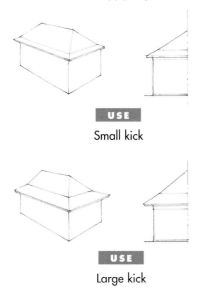

USE
Small kick

USE
Large kick

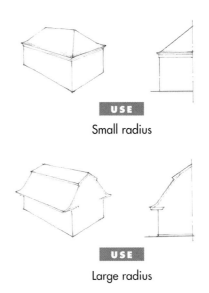

USE
Small radius

USE
Large radius

10.23 Open Eaves to Avoid

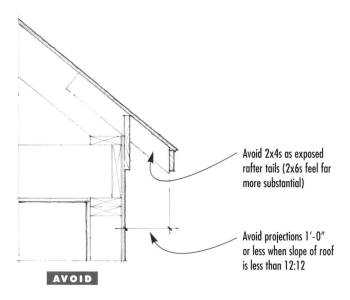

Avoid 2x4s as exposed rafter tails (2x6s feel far more substantial)

Avoid projections 1'-0" or less when slope of roof is less than 12:12

AVOID

10.24 Gable Brackets to Use

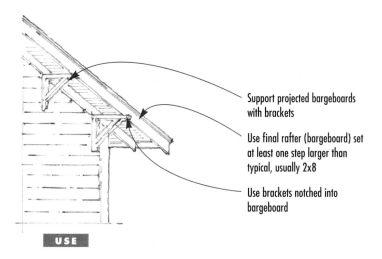

Support projected bargeboards with brackets

Use final rafter (bargeboard) set at least one step larger than typical, usually 2x8

Use brackets notched into bargeboard

USE

10.25 Bracket Details to Use

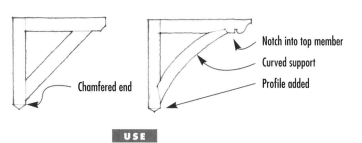

Chamfered end

Notch into top member
Curved support
Profile added

USE

OPEN EAVES

Vernacular and less formal buildings often have open eaves with exposed rafter tails. This is a common detail in Craftsman bungalows of the early 1900s as well as buildings inspired by the West Indies. Traditionally, exposed rafter tails were literally the roof rafters extending out of the house. Today, with manufactured trusses and alternative framing options, the rafter tails are usually made of boards scribed onto the rafter or the trusses.

Sizing Rafter Tails

On the main house, exposed rafter tails should be 2×6s. 2×4s should typically only be used on porches and outbuildings. 3-bys are even better to use, if it is in the budget.

Rafter Tail Projections

The overhang and projection of the eaves vary depending on architectural style, regional influences, and climate. In general set the overhang of the main house at 2' or more, smaller houses and outbuildings can be smaller (1'-0" or more). In the Deep South and Florida these projections are often increased still further. Depending on the design and thickness of the rafter tails, the eaves can be as deep as 3'. The slope of the roof also guides the length of the eave projection. Steeper roofs typically project less than shallow pitched roofs. For instance, if the roof is over 12:12, the projection away from the house might be only 1', for simple reasons of geometry.

Bargeboards at the Gable End

The bargeboard is always at least one step larger than the typical rafter tails. For example, if the typical exposed rafter is a 2×6, then the bargeboard should be a 2×8. If the bargeboard projects more than 12" from the face of the gable wall, use brackets up the roof slope to provide visual support (10.24). The design of the brackets can be as simple as 4×4s with chamfered ends, or more detailed with curved supports and profiled ends (10.25).

Details to Use

Figure 10.26 shows the simplest form of open eave. In this detail, the sheathing sits directly on top of the rafter tail. Ideally, the ply sheathing used in the exposed portion of the roof will be V-jointed or beaded with the joints running perpendicular to the rafters. One drawback to this detail is that if the roofer is not very careful, nails can poke through and be visible under the eaves.

If the budget allows, add an extra layer of plywood between the roof sheathing and rafter tails. This extra thickness will provide the depth necessary for the roofer's nails to dig into. Again, the sheathing should be either V-jointed or beaded boards.

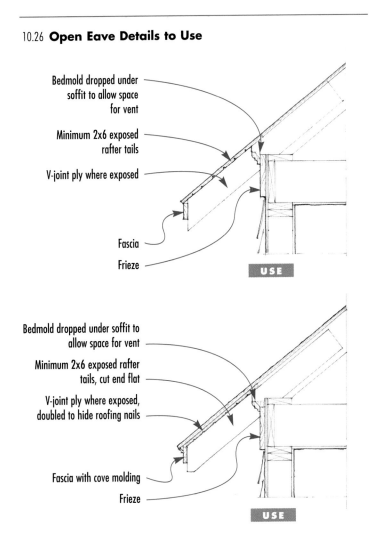

10.26 Open Eave Details to Use

Bedmold dropped under soffit to allow space for vent

Minimum 2x6 exposed rafter tails

V-joint ply where exposed

Fascia

Frieze

USE

Bedmold dropped under soffit to allow space for vent

Minimum 2x6 exposed rafter tails, cut end flat

V-joint ply where exposed, doubled to hide roofing nails

Fascia with cove molding

Frieze

USE

10.27 Rafter Tail Variations to Use

For a more refined design, saw cut the ends of each rafter tail with a bracketed profile. This technique relates back to old Mediterranean models.

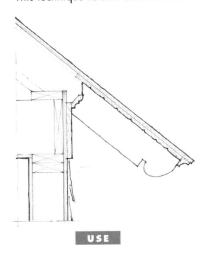

USE

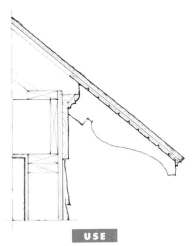

USE

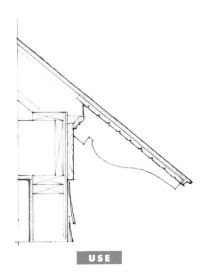

USE

CROWNED ROOF

CLUTTERED ROOF

Chapter 11

CHIMNEYS

Chimneys have been an endangered species in the last fifty years as our reliance on open fires has diminished. In the process, the visual appearance of many "traditional" buildings has been weakened by poorly sized and detailed chimneys. This chapter lays out the rules of thumb for getting your chimneys in good visual order. In traditional design, it is not always possible to reduce your design to the lowest common denominator.

CHIMNEYS

FOR MILLENNIA, THE HEARTH was quite literally the center of the home, with a fire—the single source of heat for keeping warm and cooking food—kept burning the year round. With fire as the focal point of the home, the masonry fireplace and chimney became a central element of all traditional architecture across the world. But the introduction of electricity and central heating rendered the fireplace and chimney redundant.

In the early part of the last century it became possible, for the first time, to banish open fires from domestic architecture. Until then, coal-burning stoves threw off soot and required considerable daily upkeep. Destruction by fire was a constant threat in every large city. Most descriptions of nineteenth-century cities speak vividly of air pollution from hundreds of thousands of coal and wood fires.

The desire to sweep all this away has had a dramatic effect on the basic appearance of most houses constructed in the Western world. For the first time since their introduction thousands of years before, we have begun to build houses without chimneys. It is very efficient, but in traditional architecture it just doesn't look right.

Home and Hearth

Thankfully people have never lost the desire for an open fire, even if it has become a matter of choice rather than of necessity. The fire is still an important element within a house. The fireplace provides the focus of a room even if it is rarely used. It is so important that all seating and furniture is usually arranged around it.

Unfortunately, the evolution of the fireplace and chimney has drifted far from traditional precedent. What was once a substantial masonry element has turned into a shack stuck onto the side of the house (11.1). In lower-budget projects, it may not be possible to support the expense of a masonry chimney. If this is the case, take care to include the gas fireplace in your building in a way that is sympathetic to traditional building design.

If you can afford a chimney, don't take shortcuts. Be generous with it. Chimneys are one of the central architectural motifs of the traditional home. When done right, their effect on a townscape is remarkable. A collage of roofs, punctuated with brick and stone chimneys, can help a town achieve a sense of authenticity and place.

11.1 **Chimneys Through Time**

An unfortunate progression from tepee to gas pimple.

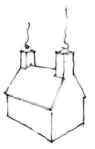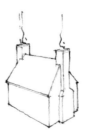

MODERN FIREPLACES

Gas Fireplaces

Gas fireplaces are a convenient option for many houses today. They are easy to use, clean, and economical to build. Gas fireplaces in themselves are not bad. It is the way they are designed into the house that creates an aesthetic problem.

If you use a gas fire, don't announce the fact on the outside of your building. Never use a cantilevered shack stuck to the side of your building (11.2). This may be the cheapest possible form of construction (avoiding the need to pour a foundation), but it will always look like just that—a cheap stick-on that has no logic or common sense.

Instead, bring the fireplace within the main wall of the house. Use the extra depth to form a chimney breast in the room, which makes space for window seats or bookshelves on either side (11.3)—both very attractive architectural features for the homeowner.

Freestanding Stoves

Freestanding stoves are a popular addition to a traditional house. Based in appearance on traditional wood-burning stoves, today's models use new technologies to provide cleaner, more even heating with wood, gas, or pellets made of sawdust and other waste materials.

Wood-burning stoves give the authentic feeling of a traditional home, and many today are designed to make this traditional means of heating much easier and more reliable to use. Gas stoves are the easiest to use; they provide heat at the touch of a button with no need to clean or to manage wood or pellets. If you choose a gas stove, look for models with logs that look real, not too plastic.

Pellet stoves, designed to look like traditional wood stoves, are an increasingly popular option for supplemental heating in a home. The pellets, made of sawdust, nutshells, and corn, turn waste materials into a clean and even source of heat. Pellets come in packages that are easy to handle and store, making these stoves a good option for homeowners who want the effect of a wood-burning stove without the trouble of handling wood.

11.2 Gas Fireplace Designs to Avoid

Avoid cantilevered gas shacks attached to the house; they will always look cheap and stuck on.

AVOID

11.3 Gas Fireplace Designs to Use in Plan

Pull the fireplace into the room and build it in with either bookshelves or window seats for an authentic appearance outside and an attractive selling point inside.

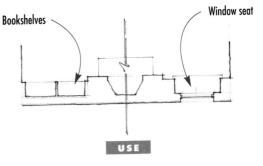

Bookshelves   Window seat

USE

11.4 Freestanding Stoves to Use

Wood-burning and pellet stoves are good alternatives to a traditional fireplace.

USE

11.5 **Masonry Chimneys to Avoid**

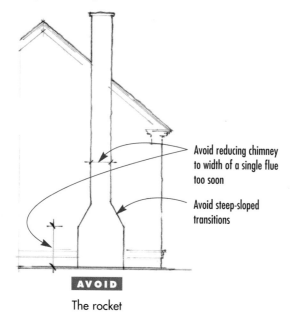

Avoid reducing chimney to width of a single flue too soon

Avoid steep-sloped transitions

AVOID

The rocket

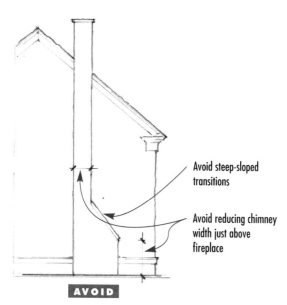

Avoid steep-sloped transitions

Avoid reducing chimney width just above fireplace

AVOID

The one-sided rocket

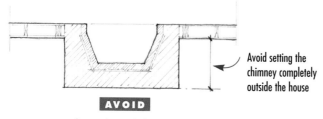

Avoid setting the chimney completely outside the house

AVOID

The outboard chimney

MASONRY CHIMNEYS

If you are going to the expense of using a masonry chimney, make sure you don't cut corners. It would be better to have no chimney at all than one that looks thin and meanly dimensioned.

Flues and Fireboxes

Traditional chimneys usually contained more than one flue. In a house of any importance, every room had a fireplace, to keep the occupants warm in the days before central heating. As the chimneys extended upward, more fireboxes would be added at each floor, with as many as four, five, or six flues emerging at the roof. The traditional chimney was by its nature a substantial construction.

Today it is unusual for more than one or two rooms in a house to have a fireplace, and these are almost always located on the first floor. Chimneys no longer need to contain fireboxes at upper levels of a house, and the chimney may contain only a single flue. Put this into practice, though, and everything will look wrong (11.5 top and center). To get the right effect we have to examine old models and use them to inform today's design.

The construction of fireboxes and chimneys is governed by a series of codes and design guidelines used to ensure safety and efficiency. But to these we must add some rules to get the design right. Follow the instructions in 11.6.

11.6 Setting out a Masonry Chimney

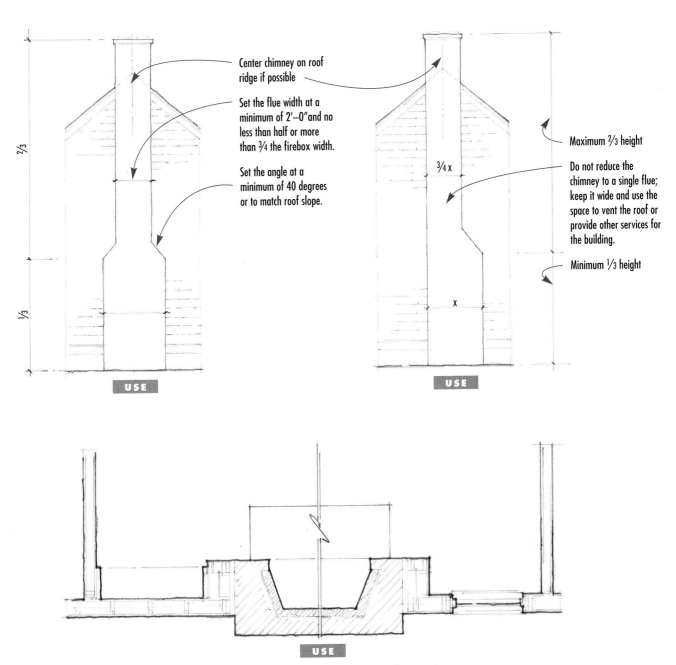

Center chimney on roof ridge if possible

Set the flue width at a minimum of 2'–0"and no less than half or more than ¾ the firebox width.

Set the angle at a minimum of 40 degrees or to match roof slope.

Maximum ⅔ height

Do not reduce the chimney to a single flue; keep it wide and use the space to vent the roof or provide other services for the building.

Minimum ⅓ height

In plan, build the fireplace into an interior chimney breast.

11.7 Chimney Caps to Avoid

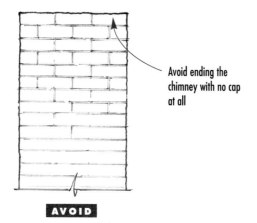

AVOID

No termination

Avoid ending the chimney with no cap at all

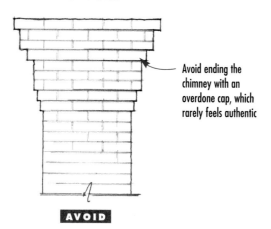

Avoid ending the chimney with an overdone cap, which rarely feels authentic

AVOID

Too much termination

11.8 Draft Inducers

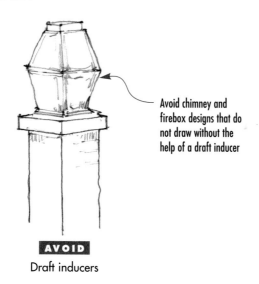

Avoid chimney and firebox designs that do not draw without the help of a draft inducer

AVOID

Draft inducers

CHIMNEY CAPS

It is worth taking time with the design of your chimney cap. Small details at this location can have a surprisingly prominent effect. Don't forget the cap or overwhelm the house with something too heavy or ornate (11.7). A simple projecting profile can have a considerable effect—the last punctuation mark before your house meets the sky.

One option is to use a stone cap, often bluestone. The stone cap should be a minimum of $2^1/_2''$ to $3''$ thick. It should project not more than $1^1/_2''$ all around (11.9).

Another option is to use one or two projecting brick courses to achieve a good termination. Don't project each course too much—$^3/_4''$ to $1''$ maximum. There are many possible variations; look to historic examples for more choices.

Draft Inducers

Be careful when designing the flue and firebox that the chimney is detailed in such a way that it will draw well. In particular, be aware of the height of the stack relative to the roof ridge, the size of the flue relative to the size of the fireplace opening, and correct make-up air. Getting it right requires careful coordination between the mason, who details the firebox and flue, and the mechanical engineer or contractor. If their work is coordinated right, a new chimney should not require a draft inducer (11.8) at the top of the stack. Draft inducers are unsightly and should only be used as a last resort.

Chimney Pots and Caps

Chimney pots can be used where additional height is required to achieve a good draft and to keep out both rainwater and birds.

Traditional chimney pots were thrown by hand. Good restoration examples, properly made, are still available and can be found by searching on the Internet. Make sure they have a lip at the top to give the right appearance. Don't choose a machine-made (extruded or cast) pot for a prominent location. Raised chimney caps (either stone or brick arch, as shown) allow for good ventilation while protecting the flue from heavy rain.

11.9 **Chimney Caps to Use**

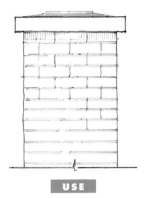

USE

Simple bluestone or concrete cap

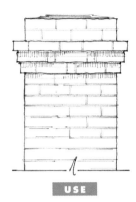

USE

Three projecting courses, stepped back above

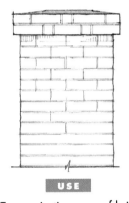

USE

Two projecting rows of brick

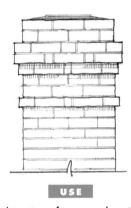

USE

Combination of steps and projections

11.10 **Decorative Chimney Caps and Chimney Pots to Use**

USE

Stone cap over brick extensions

USE

Chimney pots

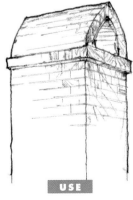

USE

Arched cap

OFFICE·SCAPE

CULTURE·SCAPE

CHURCH·SCAPE

PRIVAT·SCAPE

Chapter 12

INTERIORS

The details of traditional interiors, historically run in plaster or framed in wood, are derived from the same classical Orders as the exterior elements we have looked at in previous chapters. As with exterior details, interiors can range from a high-style, fully classical design to a modest trim selection, but even the simplest casings and baseboards must obey the Orders and relate to the size of the room and the other elements in it.

INTERIORS

THOUGH A THOROUGH EXAMINATION of the traditional interior is beyond the scope of this book, there are some clear and simple rules that everyone working with a traditional building will want to know. On the pages that follow, you will find the basics illustrated to help you get your house right on the *inside*.

Just as with the exterior, getting the interior right depends on balancing the elements and paying attention to the details, too. Even if you want the interior to have a contemporary quality, it often feels best to set modern furniture and paintings within a traditional framework. The inside and outside of your house should relate harmoniously.

Figure 12.1 shows how to lay out a simple classical interior. The crown and picture rail relate to the cornice and frieze on the outside. The door casing is the equivalent of the architrave in an Order. The chair rail, plinth (or dado), and baseboard relate to the column plinth that we first looked at in Chapter 3. Exactly the same rules that govern exterior terminating and supporting moldings apply inside.

Elegance and Purpose

The location of moldings is also based in common sense. Casings, for example, are used to cover the joint between wood door jamb and plaster wall. As the building settles over time, this is an area where cracks could open up between the two materials — at a very visible location. A casing not only serves to enrich the door and make it easier to "read" its role in the room (more important doors have grander casings than less important ones), it also has the highly practical purpose of masking a potential trouble spot.

Likewise, crown moldings not only provide an elegant termination to the room, but cover the joint between the two planes of wall and ceiling, another area susceptible to cracking. And a chair rail not only relates to the dado, but protects paint and wallpaper surfaces from chair backs—an important function in the eighteenth century, when furniture was traditionally kept pushed back against the wall when not in use.

12.1 Traditional Interior Millwork

Every element of an interior millwork package is derived from the Orders of classical architecture.

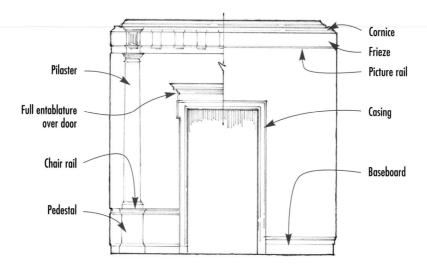

Pilaster

Full entablature over door

Chair rail

Pedestal

Cornice

Frieze

Picture rail

Casing

Baseboard

Throughout this book, we have stressed simplicity and quality rather than a lot of elaborate, poorly built detail, and this holds true for the interior of your house as well as the exterior. A door casing can be as simple as a flat board; a fire surround can be formed from a simple casing frame and a square mantel shelf supported on a bedmold. The important thing is to proportion your moldings correctly for the room and to each other.

12.2 Casings

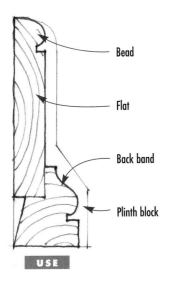

- Bead
- Flat
- Back band
- Plinth block

USE

12.3 Baseboards

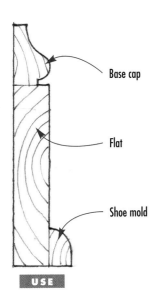

- Base cap
- Flat
- Shoe mold

USE

12.4 Molding Profiles

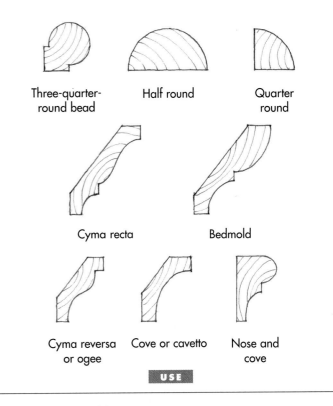

Three-quarter-round bead   Half round   Quarter round

Cyma recta   Bedmold

Cyma reversa or ogee   Cove or cavetto   Nose and cove

USE

12.5 Types of Moldings

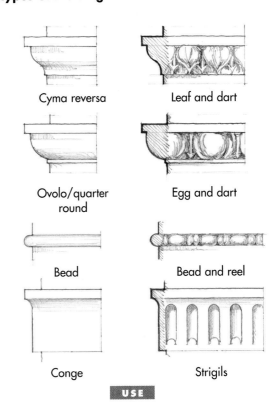

Cyma reversa   Leaf and dart

Ovolo/quarter round   Egg and dart

Bead   Bead and reel

Conge   Strigils

USE

CROWNS AND BASEBOARDS

12.6 Cornice Height and Details

Most first-floor rooms have a crown and picture rail. Full entablatures and cornices are typically reserved for high-style rooms with ceilings 11'–0" or higher. Most second-floor rooms will have only a crown; secondary rooms on the first floor often have only a crown, no picture rail. Unless there are exposed beams in the room, use a terminating molding for the crown.

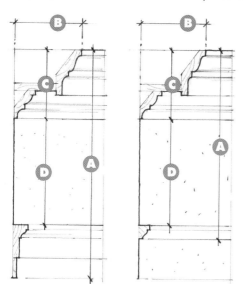
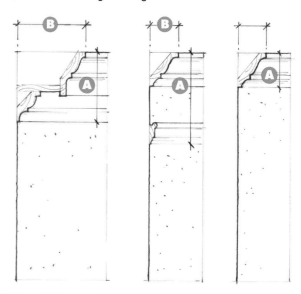

CEILING HEIGHT	FULL ENTABLATURE			CORNICE AND FRIEZE			CORNICE	CROWN AND PICTURE RAIL	CROWN
	A	B/C	D	A	B/C	D	A/B	A	A
8'	—	—	—	—	—	—	6"	8"	2½"
9'	1'-9"	7½"	9½"	1'-5¾"	7½"	9½"	7½"	9"	3"
10'	2'-0"	8	11"	1'-8"	8"	11"	8"	10"	4"
11'	2'-2"	9½"	1'-0"	1'-9¾"	8½"	1'	9"	11"	—

12.7 Crowns to Avoid

Avoid abstract combinations of moldings.

12.8 Crowns with Beams

In rooms with exposed beams, use a supporting molding, ogee, or bedmold as a crown under the beam.

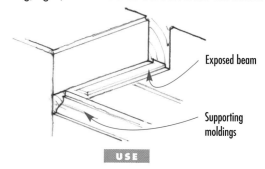

Exposed beam

Supporting moldings

12.9 Types of Base Caps

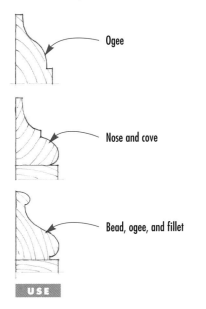

Ogee

Nose and cove

Bead, ogee, and fillet

USE

12.11 Baseboards to Avoid

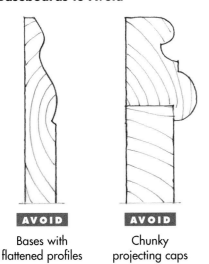

AVOID

Bases with
flattened profiles

AVOID

Chunky
projecting caps

12.12 Shoe Molds

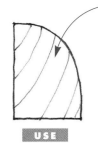

Use a shoe mold to
conceal the crack between
the floor and baseboard if
necessary; don't paint the
mold to match the
baseboard, stain it to
match the floor.

USE

12.10 Setting the Baseboard Height

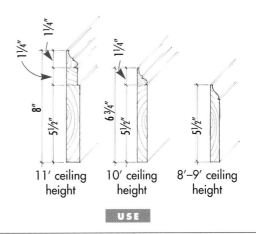

1¼"   1¼"

1¼"

8"   5½"

6¾"   5½"

5½"

11' ceiling
height

10' ceiling
height

8'–9' ceiling
height

USE

12.13 Baseboard and Plinth Block Heights

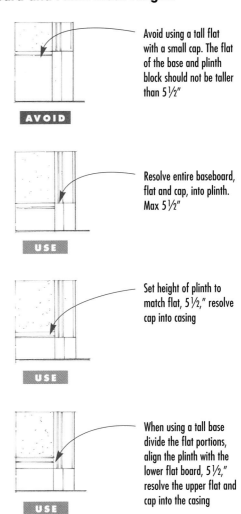

Avoid using a tall flat
with a small cap. The flat
of the base and plinth
block should not be taller
than 5½"

AVOID

Resolve entire baseboard,
flat and cap, into plinth.
Max 5½"

USE

Set height of plinth to
match flat, 5½," resolve
cap into casing

USE

When using a tall base
divide the flat portions,
align the plinth with the
lower flat board, 5½,"
resolve the upper flat and
cap into the casing

USE

CASINGS AND CHAIR RAILS

12.14 Casing Width and Details

Less is more! Don't let the profiles get away from you. Make sure that the casing has 3 distinct parts:

1. Termination: a bead, quarter round, or simple profile

2. Flat: the largest portion of the casing. In larger casings the flat may be divided into two unequal sections

3. Back band: frame for casing and door

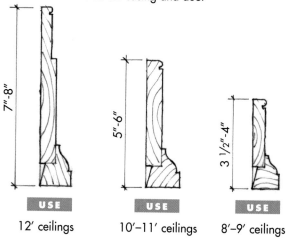

USE
12' ceilings

USE
10'–11' ceilings

USE
8'–9' ceilings

12.15 Casing Terminations to Use

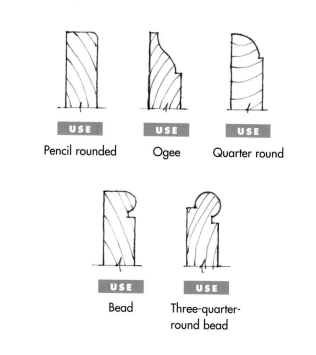

USE
Pencil rounded

USE
Ogee

USE
Quarter round

USE
Bead

USE
Three-quarter-round bead

12.16 Casings to Avoid

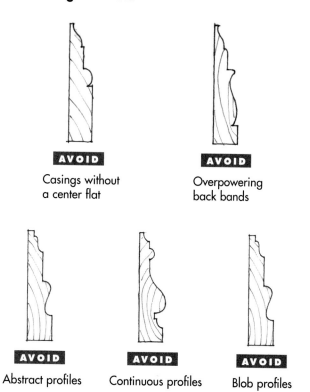

AVOID
Casings without a center flat

AVOID
Overpowering back bands

AVOID
Abstract profiles

AVOID
Continuous profiles

AVOID
Blob profiles

12.17 Back Bands to Use

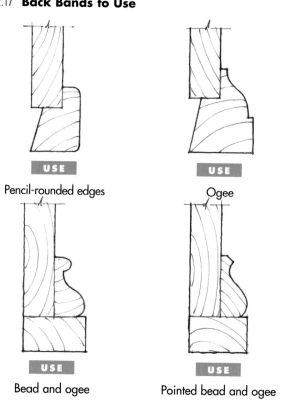

USE
Pencil-rounded edges

USE
Ogee

USE
Bead and ogee

USE
Pointed bead and ogee

12.18 **Window Sill Details**

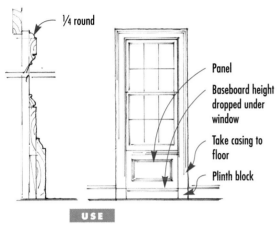

1/4 round

Panel

Baseboard height dropped under window

Take casing to floor

Plinth block

USE

Casing for formal first-floor rooms

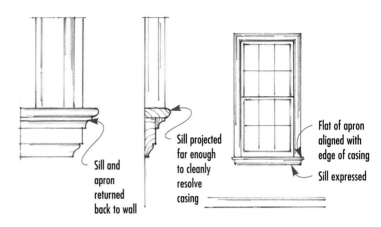

Sill and apron returned back to wall

Sill projected far enough to cleanly resolve casing

Flat of apron aligned with edge of casing

Sill expressed

12.19 **Beaded Openings**

Beaded openings provide a good alternative in applications where a casing will not fit. Avoid sheetrock openings without either a casing or bead. Use beads on openings wider than 7'-0"; casings on larger openings tend to create the optical illusion of sagging. When combining beaded and cased openings in the same room, align the top of the bead with the top of the casing.

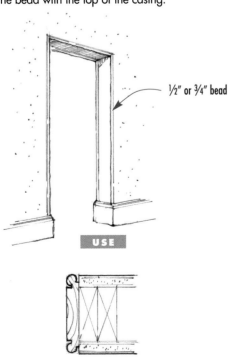

1/2" or 3/4" bead

USE

USE

12.20 **Chair Rails**

A chair rail can be as complex as a full pedestal or as simple as a board with beads.

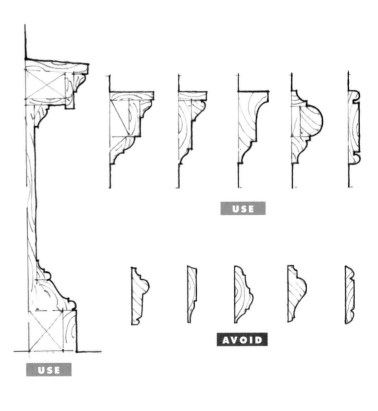

USE

AVOID

USE

FIRE SURROUNDS

12.21 Setting Out the Chimney Breast

Don't stop the chimney breast short of the ceiling or project the fireplace into the room without one. Balance the width of the chimney breast with the side bays, but avoid setting all three equal; reinforce the center by setting the center bay largest.

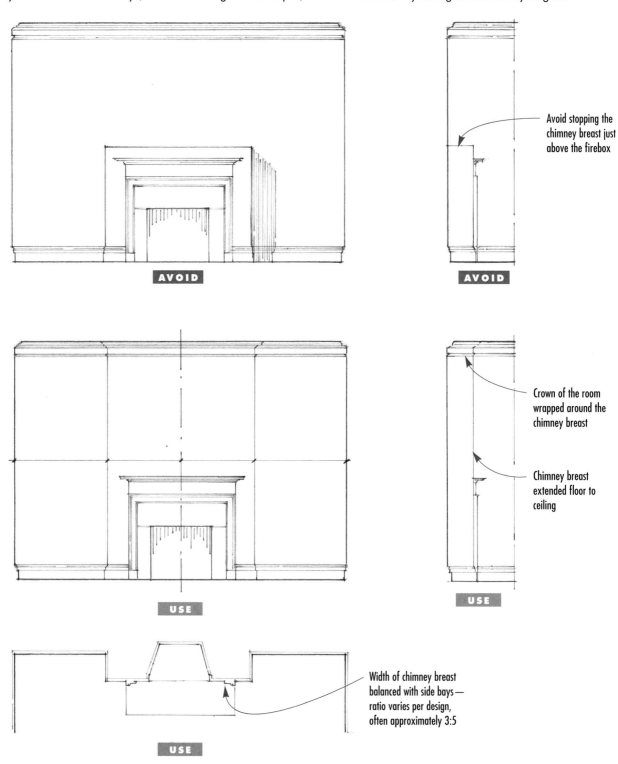

Avoid stopping the chimney breast just above the firebox

AVOID

AVOID

Crown of the room wrapped around the chimney breast

Chimney breast extended floor to ceiling

USE

USE

Width of chimney breast balanced with side bays — ratio varies per design, often approximately 3:5

USE

12.22 Fire Surround Designs to Avoid

Avoid surround designs that are abstract combinations of moldings and profiles.

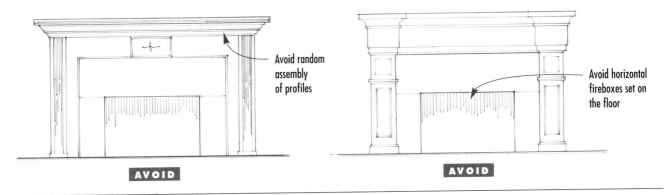

Avoid random
assembly
of profiles

Avoid horizontal
fireboxes set on
the floor

AVOID

AVOID

12.23 Fire Surround Designs to Use

Apply the basic principles of the Orders to the design of the fire surround. Use an architrave, frieze, and cornice; place supporting and terminating moldings correctly; and always use a drip under the corona.

When using a gas fireplace with horizontal proportions, raise the fireplace to the height of a masonry firebox. Infill below with slate, dark stone, or tile, darker than the slips.

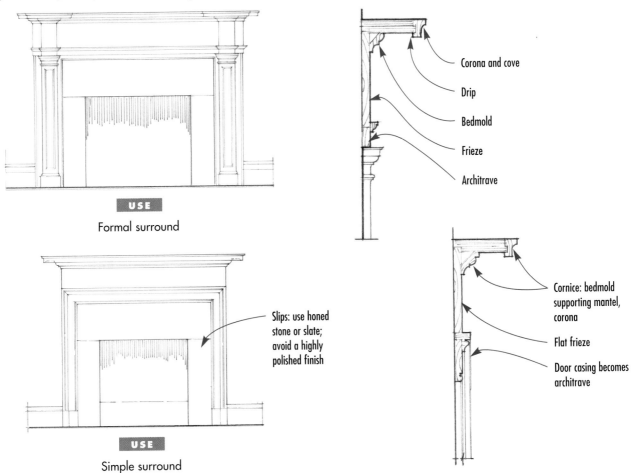

USE

Formal surround

Corona and cove

Drip

Bedmold

Frieze

Architrave

Slips: use honed
stone or slate;
avoid a highly
polished finish

USE

Simple surround

Cornice: bedmold
supporting mantel,
corona

Flat frieze

Door casing becomes
architrave

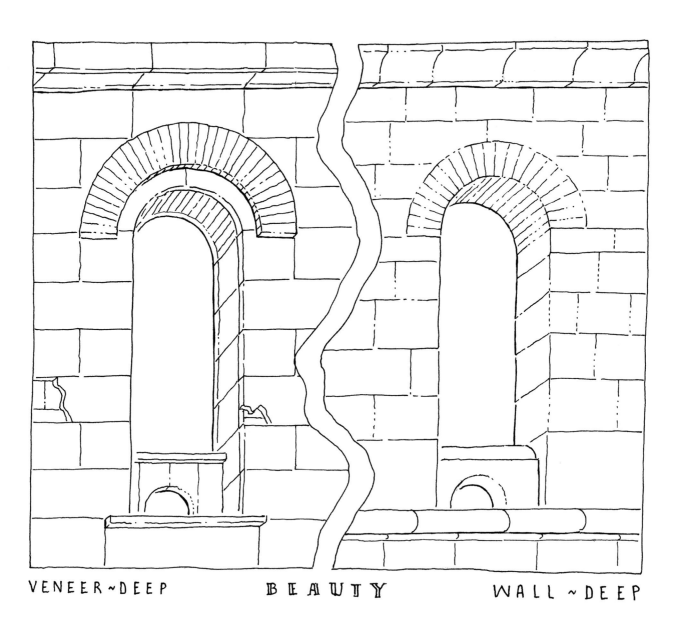

VENEER~DEEP   BEAUTY   WALL~DEEP

Chapter 13

MATERIALS AND METHODS

Good traditional architecture is not just about designing well or getting the details right. It is about sustainability and longevity. When designing a traditional building, we need to think carefully about the *way* we build and the nature of the materials we use.

MATERIALS AND METHODS

THE BUILDING PROCESS, like so many aspects of our lives, has been revolutionized in the last hundred and fifty years. Since the late nineteenth century, architectural components have been manufactured off-site and transported, often long distances, for assembly elsewhere. The process of mass-production was accelerated in the years following the Second World War, when the vast industrial capability of the war effort shifted to peacetime production.

Such methods of manufacture and supply meant that buildings could be produced faster and more easily than ever before. It is not coincidental that the Modern movement in architecture, deeply concerned as it was with the invention of new materials and methods of construction, developed entirely in parallel with this industrialization of the building process.

But by the late 1970s, an entire range of architectural design had become more concerned with the specification and assembly of pre-manufactured products than with any individual design or act of creation. We're living with the result today—a bland world of homogeneity where every office park, shopping mall, and suburban tract development looks just like the others, even hundreds of miles away.

Traditional buildings cannot ignore the world we live in. Of course, we are going to specify prefabricated items, from windows to columns to cornices and roofing materials. We are constantly trying to balance the complex equation of quality, scope, and budget, and one easy way of getting more "bang for your buck" is to select items and materials from the catalogs. Thankfully, the style known as "Contractor Colonial" has kept many building products commercially available for use in the traditional home. Indeed, one of the main purposes of this book has been to give you the criteria by which to make such choices, so that in the future you are well informed about what to use—and what to avoid.

That said, it is worth pausing to think about what really makes a good traditional building. Proportion and good detailing are important, but the materials you use can truly set your house apart, not only in terms of how good it looks, but in terms of how well it functions. We must take responsibility for the world that we are building, and this starts with the way that we build and the materials we build with. However well designed the building, if it is made of cheap modern materials it will look just like that—cheap and modern.

13.1 **Materials**

Materials define the appearance as well as the performance of a building. Even a well-designed building can look cheap and modern without the texture of carefully specified materials.

AVOID   USE

Five Rules for Specifying Materials

1. Build for the Long Term

Traditional architecture is about designing for the long term. In our Western economy, materials are cheap relative to labor. It is accepted in today's culture that it is simpler to throw something out and start again than to repair it, whether it happens to be a refrigerator, a car, or even a building. But our current cycle of constant disposal and replacement is ecologically unsustainable. Before you choose your columns or your door surround, ask yourself: "How will this look in twenty or fifty years' time?" Select materials that can be maintained so they will last.

2. "No Maintenance" Is a False Economy

Longevity is all about maintenance. "Maintenance-free" is all very well for a while. But what happens in fifteen years when the white plastic siding is beginning to crack and turn yellow, or when water, trapped behind a plastic-clad window frame, is rotting the wood inside?

Nothing can be done except to rip it all out and start over at considerable expense. For a while everything looks fine again. But the process has already started, the materials cannot be repaired or maintained, and so by definition they have a limited life. It's just a matter of time until they have to be ripped out again.

Traditional building takes the opposite approach, specifying only materials that can be easily maintained on a regular basis. New materials on the market, such as cement board siding and trim, bridge the gap between wood and vinyl. They require painting every fifteen to twenty years, but create a much longer life for the building.

3. Always Ask: "Is This a Sustainable Product?"

Look carefully at the materials you are using and the way they are made. Some—especially plastics and metals—require huge amounts of energy *and* produce harmful side effects in the manufacturing process. Others, such as wood, require very little energy to create and can even have a beneficial impact on the environment during production. The amount of energy required to produce any item is known as "embodied energy." Wherever possible, tend towards materials with a low embodied energy.

Consider also the components of your materials and how they will break down over time. The chemicals and glues in many insulation materials, or medium density fiberboard, for example, constantly breathe unhealthy gases into the rooms of your house. Conveniently, the natural materials are often the ones that look best over time *and* the easiest to maintain and repair.

4. Use Appropriate Materials: Location & Climate

Before industrialized systems of supply were developed, we had to build with whatever materials were locally available. Most structures were designed by the builders themselves, who knew from years (and often generations) of experience how to use materials and were deeply responsive to local conditions and climate.

This was all swept aside in the twentieth century. It is neither possible nor desirable to turn the clock back completely, but as we move into a post-industrial world, remember that traditional architecture is not just a question of design. It is concerned with appropriateness to place and living in harmony with our environment.

5. Always Specify the Best You Can Afford

We have returned to this point many times in this book. It is always better in traditional architecture to do something simply but do it well, rather than to be extravagant yet make mistakes. This rule applies not only to the details of your building; it should be the driving consideration behind everything you specify. When it comes to materials, learn from the examples of traditional buildings.

Always try to use the real thing rather than a cheaper substitute. Vinyl siding is cheaper than cement board, but it can't be maintained and will be more expensive in the long run. Still worse, it looks plastic, and your building will fail as a piece of convincing traditional architecture. Wire-cut bricks are inexpensive to buy, but they will never age properly. They will continue to look cheap and modern for the entire life of the building. And windows with snap-on plastic muntins will never look convincing. Sometimes you just can't cut corners with your specification.

13.2 Types of Siding to Use

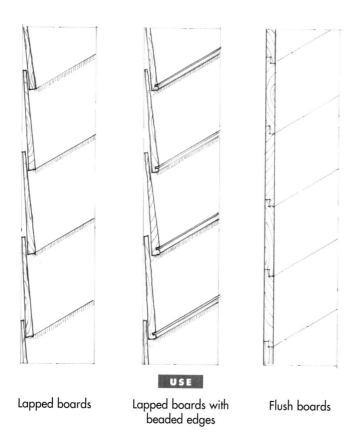

USE

| Lapped boards | Lapped boards with beaded edges | Flush boards |

13.3 Cement Board Siding

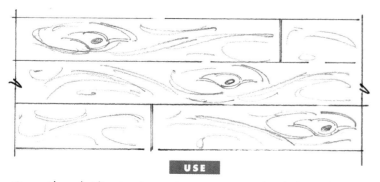

USE

Cement board siding is a low-maintenance material with the traditional look of wood. It is rot-, flame-, and termite-resistant as well as hurricane-rated.

WOOD

During the seventeenth and eighteenth centuries, American builders formed the basic language of wooden construction that has remained the touchstone for many traditional developments today. In the nineteenth century, they became ever more inventive in the use of wood, as seen in the fantastic Victorian "Painted Ladies" or Carpenter Gothic styles. Wooden construction sets few limits to the imagination of the house designer and builder.

In a heavily forested country settled rapidly by large numbers of people requiring immediate shelter, wood was the obvious choice of material, and it has remained so ever since. Today we have to deal with fast-grown wood, which is not as good a material as the slow-growth wood the settlers found in North America's virgin forests.

In many southern states, installing exposed new wood on a house is an invitation for trouble. Even with maintenance, this wood may rot away after a few years. The challenge in these markets is knowing which alternative materials to use and detailing them in a manner that looks traditional.

Siding

Wood siding, or clapboard, uses lapped boards nailed to plywood sheathing (or, even better, to battens) to protect the walls. A typical lap is between 4″ and 6″. Figure 13.2 shows three typical types of siding: lapped boards, lapped boards with beaded edges, and flush boards.

Painted wood siding works in northern climates, but is not ideal for more humid southern climates. The best alternative to wood in all climates is cement board siding, which, although thinner than wood, is similar in appearance. Cement board siding is the perfect low-maintenance material: not only is it rot-, flame-, and termite-resistant, it is also hurricane-rated. *Do not use vinyl siding* in traditional construction; it will never appear convincing.

Corner Boards

At the outside corners of a house with siding or shingles, corner boards are often used to protect the end grain of the boards and provide a termination to the wall. Avoid corner boards that are thinner than the projection of the siding, or mitered corners that open over time to expose the thin edges of the boards (13.4). When possible, use corner boards that meet with a bead or quarter-round molding (13.5). With the corner rounded, the corner boards themselves are protected and will have a longer lifespan.

Trim: Plastics and PVC

When specifying alternate materials, be careful of false economies. When possible avoid oil- and petroleum-based products. Hand-paint the trim on site; brush strokes will help these materials feel more authentic.

Shingles

Shingles are typically left to weather naturally. When exposed to air and water, white cedar shingles turn a beautiful silver gray color; red cedar shingles turn dark brown. Red cedar is typically considered more rot-resistant and is often used for roofs. Combined with fresh white painted trim, shingle has become the archetypal language of the New England coastline. When painted, evenly coursed shingles make a formal surface that can be used as an alternative to lap board siding. Painted fiber cement shingles are a good low-maintenance alternative to traditional cedar shingles.

Many early shingle houses are very simply handled, with plain, modest details and proportion. In the nineteenth and early twentieth centuries, architects developed a whole language of freestyle shingle architecture called Shingle Style, which became the predominant idiom for grand seaside "cottages" on both coasts of America. Considerable invention was used in laying out shingle patterns so that the whole wall became a decorative surface.

The exposure on a cedar shingle depends on the size of the material but is typically 7″ for most applications. Imperials (22″–24″ long) are coursed at 8–10″ exposure, but usually require (rose head) face nails at the butts, which are typically $^{3}/_{4}$″ thick.

13.4 **Corner Board Details to Avoid**

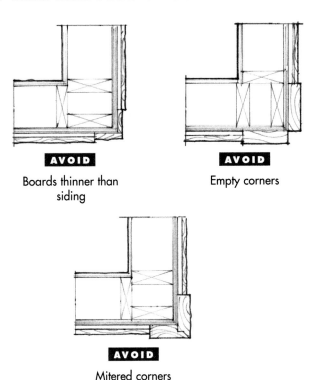

AVOID
Boards thinner than siding

AVOID
Empty corners

AVOID
Mitered corners

13.5 **Corner Board Details to Use**

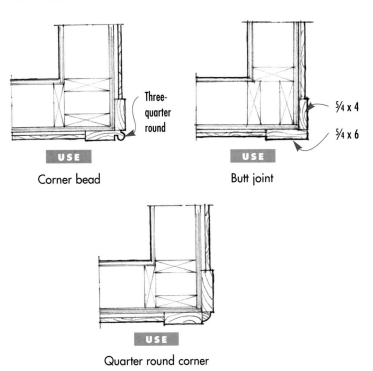

USE
Corner bead

Three-quarter round

USE
Butt joint

5/4 x 4
5/4 x 6

USE
Quarter round corner

13.6 Expansion Joint Details to Avoid

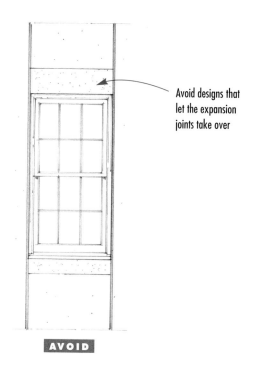

Avoid designs that let the expansion joints take over

AVOID

13.7 Expansion Joint Details to Use

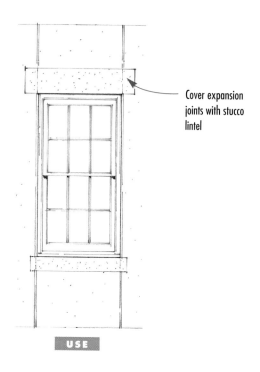

Cover expansion joints with stucco lintel

USE

STUCCO

Stucco is a common finish for Mediterranean and Spanish styles of architecture. Appropriate for use in both arid and humid climates, stucco as a finish material is often found in Florida and areas of the Southwest where masonry construction is a common building trade. It is less common in other regions of the country as a primary building finish, but found throughout the United States as a secondary material, used to finish elements such as chimneys and foundation piers.

Traditional Lime-rich Stucco

Never use a portland cement base for stucco in a traditional building. Portland cement is hard and cannot "breathe" naturally like a lime-based or plaster stucco. When water penetrates behind this hard surface, it has nowhere to go. In the winter it will freeze, expand, and crack the stucco. A lime-based stucco is much softer and some moisture can pass through it. Nothing gets trapped where it is not wanted and cracking is avoided. The plaster will last much longer and will look more beautiful with age, as lime plaster chemically reacts over time with oxygen in the air to form a durable and resilient weatherproof surface.

A pure lime-sand mix will often prove difficult to work because it can take a long time to harden. For this reason it is sometimes necessary to add a small quantity of white portland cement to speed the drying process. A suitable mix is 1:2:9 – 1 part white portland cement, 2 parts white hydrated lime, 9 parts sand. This mixture is similar to Type 'N' mortar used by bricklayers. Lime stuccos are easy to work and nearly every builder who has made the transition from Portland cement never looks back.

Stucco on Masonry

Expansion joints have become ubiquitous in modern construction. Every 10 feet or so, a thin line of flexible mastic is inserted to allow for contraction and expansion and to prevent cracking that would inevitably occur. But the effect of these lines running horizontally and vertically across your façade de-materializes the wall surface and makes the building feel fake.

Traditional lime-based construction is more flexible. The material is softer and can respond more easily to the effects of heating and cooling. Expansion joints are typically not required with lime-based plasters and mortars when used over block. Some cracking may occur without expansion joints, but adding the joints doesn't guarantee that the building won't crack. In fact, one is just as likely to find cracks in a stucco building with expansion joints.

If you use expansion joints, think carefully about how to mitigate their impact. Hide them behind a downspout or in an out-of-the-way location. Consider the relation of the expansion joint to the architecture of your façade—in particular, to openings. Avoid placing joints in line with doors or windows. The building will end up looking like an assembly of clip-on panels.

Stucco on Frame Walls

Try to avoid using stucco on frame walls. This combination of materials invites problems with leaking over time. If you do use this system, expansion joints will be necessary at all windows and doors to ensure that water can escape out of the wall. Avoid stopping the lintel at the joint (13.6). To mitigate the effect that they have on the design, overlap the lintels and sills to cover the joints (13.7). These few inches make an enormous difference.

Synthetic versus Real

Real stucco is preferable to synthetic stucco. They cost the same and there is no real difference in the required maintenance. But real stucco ages beautifully. Its uneven color and thin hairline cracks are part of the rich patina that makes traditional architecture richer through time.

Stucco Imitating Masonry

A stucco wall can be left plain, but it is common practice to score "masonry lines" to give it the appearance of a stone wall. These can be applied across the entire façade, or just to suggest door and window lintels. Properly handled, the effect can be enriching. Make sure that the details match authentic stone construction, with the joints realistically scaled for the façade and areas such as lintels handled correctly.

Finish

Generally it is best to avoid a finish that is too heavily troweled, but the wall should retain some hand-made quality—don't polish out every imperfection. It is sensible to make a number of sample panels to get exactly the right effect. The quality of sand is important. Very fine sand will yield a perfectly smooth finish, which would not be appropriate for exterior use. Instead, use a sharp or rough sand that will result in a look closer to natural sawn stone.

Color: Natural, Limewash, and Paint

Most lime renders will take on a wonderful, natural stone color if suitable dark orange or yellow sand is used. If you can't get the right sand locally, use commercially available colored stucco, but tend toward the warm stone colors. To avoid deadening the color, make sure the small amount of portland cement added to the mix is white, not gray.

Stucco walls can be whitewashed or limewashed. Colored limewash is available commercially or can be mixed and tinted on site. Several successive thin layers of limewash are brush-applied to a dampened wall surface to build up a finish that will last for decades. Limewash is an organic, natural finish and it requires little or no maintenance. As it is bleached by the sun and stained by the weather, it takes on beautiful qualities that will enhance the building over the years.

Stucco walls can also be painted using masonry paint to achieve a more uniform finish. Use historically correct colors for traditional work. Walls will require repainting every ten years or so to maintain a good, durable finish.

13.8 **Brick Bonds to Use**

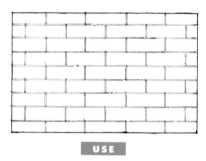

USE

Running bond

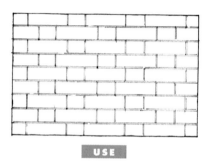

USE

Flemish bond

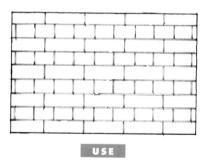

USE

English bond

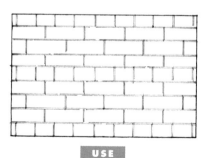

USE

English garden wall bond

BRICK

Brick is another ubiquitous American building material. Historically it was particularly popular in towns and cities, where the spread of fire was an ever-present risk. In the country, it tended to be used for grander structures—estates and plantation houses—and for kitchen outbuildings, again to avoid the risk of destruction by fire.

Bricks to Avoid

Do not use wire-cut or machine-made bricks in an exposed location on your house. For an authentic effect, it is always better to use sand-faced machine-made or a handmade brick. The brick should have a soft, slightly imperfect texture and quality.

It is not necessary—or in fact particularly desirable—to use secondhand, or "reclaimed," brick in new work. Generally, a new brick, properly laid, will look more convincing than reclaimed brick, which requires a lot of work to reinstall and tends to *look* reclaimed and therefore feels rather fake. Limit your use of reclaimed material to paths and garden walls.

Color

Brick is available in a wide variety of colors, determined both by the clay used in manufacture and by the heat of the kiln. Select according to the traditions of your region, but in general use a soft, warm color—red, brown, or yellow—to achieve the right traditional effect. Again, it is best to look at and build with a few samples before making a final choice.

In the eighteenth century it was common to use glazed or dark headers, to add interest to the wall. Victorian architects and builders made considerable use of colored bricks to form large patterns running across the wall. Some contrast detailing can be a simple way to enrich a plain brick building. Limit the use of contrast brickwork, and use historical examples to study how to get it right.

Brick Bonds

Brick walls were traditionally at least two bricks thick. To tie the entire wall together, courses of brickwork were laid using alternate headers and stretchers in different patterns or "bonds." Many of these brick patterns were developed in Europe many centuries ago according to particular local traditions (13.8).

Today, it is more common to build a brick veneer that is one brick thick over a frame construction. In terms of brick patterns, the result was that the simplest stretcher bond, where only the stretcher face of the brick is exposed, became very common. On large expanses of wall, the stretcher bond results in something bland and monotonous by comparison with the old brick bonds. A good compromise is to use cut headers, achieving the effect of the old masonry work without the expense of a full thickness of brick.

Brick Joints

The treatment of brick joints can have a dramatic effect on the appearance of a wall. Joint size and mortar selection has just as much impact on the finished quality as the choice of brick itself.

Always use a lime-based mortar with the same mix and color we described for lime-rich renders on page 236. Lime mortars are softer and more forgiving than Portland cement-based mortar, which often sets harder than the brick itself and can lead to damaging cracking as the building settles over time. Lime mortar works with the building mass rather than against it.

Joint Finish

Most traditional work looks best with a simple struck joint, without too much of the troweling and smoothing that was developed by bricklayers in the twentieth century. If possible, look at local historic examples and match these. In the eighteenth and nineteenth centuries, on formal brickwork, it was common to incise very thin lines within the joint itself—so-called "tuck" jointing—to give the impression that the brick joint was even thinner.

Painted and Whitewashed Brick

New brick buildings often feel static and inauthentic. In some cases this is the fault of the brick selection; in other cases, it comes from large expanses of running bond. Painting the brick or adding a whitewash gives a new building the texture of an older traditional building. It is not necessary to repaint the brick; over time the paint or whitewash will flake off and create a rich patina on the house.

13.9 Brick Modules

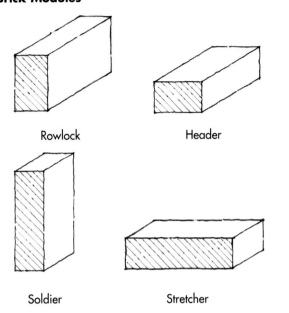

Rowlock   Header

Soldier   Stretcher

13.10 Brick Joint Sizes

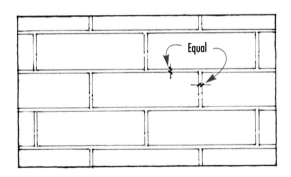

Equal

Set width of joints above and between the bricks to match

13.11 Types of Brick Joints

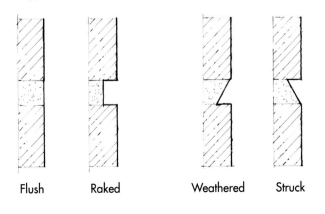

Flush   Raked   Weathered   Struck

13.12 **Types of Stone**

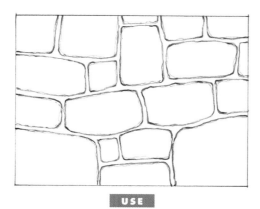

USE

Random rubble

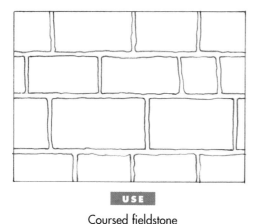

USE

Coursed fieldstone

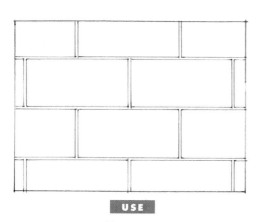

USE

Ashlar masonry

STONE

Stone is a highly durable material. Some stones, such as marble or limestone (which is relatively soft when it is first cut and hardens over time), are excellent for carved work. They would be used for ornamental work, and decorative eaves and other details. Columns, eaves, and door and window surrounds would often be made from stone. At the opposite end of the design spectrum, stone is the ultimate vernacular material, literally collected—as field-stone—from the land upon which the house is to be built.

Rough Fieldstone and Random Rubble

This is stonework at its simplest. Fieldstone—literally whatever was locally available—was lifted from fields or rivers and laid up in a wall. Fieldstone today is commercially available and comes in many different grades (13.12 top). If possible, match historical local examples and prepare samples before proceeding with work.

Coursed Fieldstone

Coursed fieldstone uses a process of selection before building work begins. The stones are laid up in courses that typically diminish slightly in size, with larger stones at the base and smaller stones at the top of a wall (13.12 center). Coursed fieldstone can be combined with dressed stone quoins or door and window jambs. If dressed stone is not available, a contrasting warm red brick is often used for opening surrounds.

Ashlar Masonry

Traditionally, more formal ashlar (dressed and cut) stonework was reserved for the most important buildings. The stone is sawn and worked before assembly and is carefully laid to horizontal courses. The joints are made as thin as possible to achieve a smooth and even finish across the wall (13.12 bottom). Today, with the invention of computer-controlled cutting machinery, sawn stone masonry (including curved work) has never been more affordable.

Grain

It is vital to cut and install stone in the right direction. Sandstone and limestone are sedimentary rocks, formed by layers of sand or calcium carbonate deposited over centuries on the seabed. Because of these layers, the stone has a distinct "grain" or "bed," like a piece of wood. The stone *must* be laid on bed— that is, with the grain of the stone running horizontally, in the direction in which it was found in the quarry. If the stone is installed on end it can spall, or chip, and may disintegrate within a few years (13.13).

Stone Veneer

Discussion of grain introduces an important point about stone veneer. *Never* apply stone to a vertical wall as you would use it in horizontal paving. The stonework is not laid on bed and will spall within a short time. Still worse, it will look just like paving stuck to your house, resulting in a totally inauthentic appearance. If it were real, such a wall could never stand up (13.14).

Tooling

An additional layer of detail can be provided with "tooling," chiseling the surface of a plain-sawn piece of stone. The tool work catches the light, casting small shadows across the entire wall and providing lively texture to the surface. Roughly worked stone done with a pick or brush hammer gives a heavy rusticated look, which can be formalized by tooling the edge with chisel work (13.15). Chiseled tooling on ashlar can be heavy (4-6 cut lines per inch) or light (10 cut lines per inch), depending on the application. Look at historical examples and insist on samples before proceeding.

Cast Stone

A popular alternative to natural stone is cast or reconstructed stone, now widely available. It allows a great deal of freedom with repetitive ornament for a sensible price. Cast stone can also be made easily to custom specifications. If this is not in the budget, be extremely careful when selecting from a catalog to ensure that the details work with the principles outlined in this book. Check and double-check that their overall scale and proportion works with the building as a whole.

13.13 **Stone Grain**

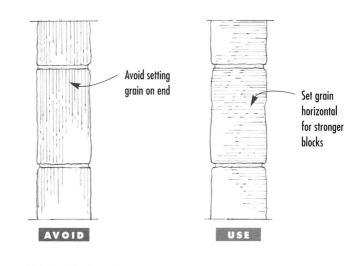

Avoid setting grain on end

Set grain horizontal for stronger blocks

AVOID   USE

13.14 **Stone Veneer—Avoid**

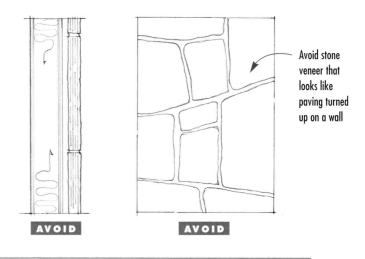

Avoid stone veneer that looks like paving turned up on a wall

AVOID   AVOID

13.15 **Tooling—Use**

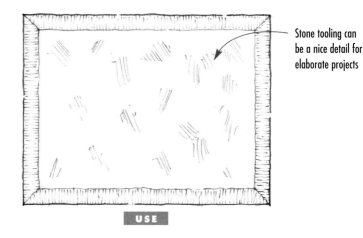

Stone tooling can be a nice detail for elaborate projects

USE

13.16 **Asphalt Shingles**

Avoid asphalt shingles in "architectural" or "historic" ranges with printed shadows and other fake detailing applied. Dark colors, such as charcoal gray, usually look the best.

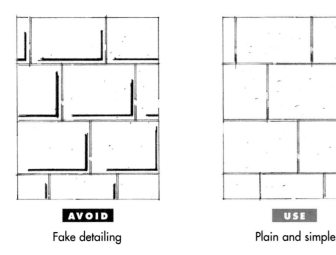

AVOID	**USE**
Fake detailing	Plain and simple

13.17 **Slate**

A well-laid slate roof can last 150 years. Use slates at least $\frac{1}{2}''$ thick to achieve an authentically traditional roof; slates any thinner may look insubstantial and fail sooner. Avoid imitation slates with obvious repeat patterns.

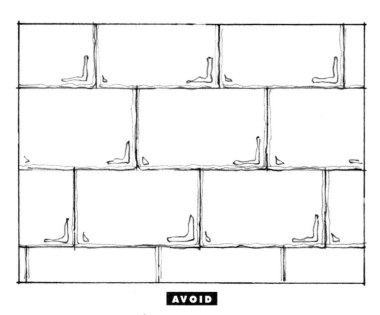

AVOID

Obvious repeat patterns

ROOFING MATERIALS

As we discussed in Chapter 9, the pitched roof is one of the key distinguishing features of a traditional building. The appearance of the roof is determined both by the design and the material selection. Traditionally, color, texture, and finish material were determined by climate and architectural style. Today, although budget guides most roofs to be asphalt shingles, there are ways to enhance appearance at an affordable price.

Shingles

Asphalt shingles, a good option for the budget-conscious project, have a long history in simple traditional work. But avoid asphalt shingles with fake detailing. An asphalt roof should be what it is—plain and relatively cheap—and not draw attention to itself (13.16).

Cedar shingles are an excellent choice for wood construction in northern climates. They are light and relatively inexpensive and they weather beautifully. Red cedar shingles are considered more rot-resistant and are commonly used in roofing. A typical exposure is 6 to 8″. Use lead or lead-coated copper at valleys, but be sure it is coated with non-patination oil or it will stain with runoff from the shingles.

Slate

A slate roof is reserved for the more expensive project; it is the best choice for a stone building as well as a building in brick veneer. A few dos and don'ts should be observed. A slightly ragged bottom edge will help to achieve a well-textured roof.

Consider laying slates in diminishing courses, particularly on a steep-pitched roof. At the eaves an exposure of 8–9″ reduces to approximately 4″ at the ridge in carefully graduated courses. A diminishing-course roof is a high-end feature, but it will transform your house into something with life and beauty (13.19).

Clay Tile

A good clay tile will last for 100 years, sometimes considerably longer. Clay tile (or "pegtile") has a very old-European quality. It can be used successfully in conjunction with painted clapboard walls and is a good palette choice to mix with brick veneer.

Pantiles were imported into North America from Holland and the Low Countries during the early days of colonial expansion. They were often used as ballast for ships crossing the Atlantic to pick up their cargoes in the New World. They can be found in traditional work in seaports throughout the Eastern Seaboard, from Salem, Massachusetts to Charleston, South Carolina.

Barrel tiles are very common in Mediterranean-style work. Use a handmade clay roman tile in soft red for traditional work and avoid anything that has too mechanical or "extruded" an appearance.

Concrete tiles provide a good budget alternative for simpler projects. They are cheap, but weather well as lichens and moss take hold over time. Concrete tiles are used convincingly on many of the buildings in Colonial Williamsburg. Lay the tiles in diminishing courses, like slate, for additional effect.

Metal

Metal roofs (13.18) are a popular material for new traditional houses, especially throughout coastal areas of the Southeast. Higher-style and more formal houses often use standing-seam roofs of copper or painted metal. On these buildings, upstanding seams are important to provide scale and shadow, especially on a larger roof mass.

Materials to Avoid

Be very careful when specifying plastic "slates." Some brands on the market are convincing alternatives to the real thing, but as with all faux materials, they are manufactured with varying degrees of effect. Avoid slates with obvious repeat patterns, especially thin profiles and shiny plastic finishes. If a good fake slate is not in the budget, use a simple asphalt shingle.

Don't use machine-made clay tiles that have too mechanical an appearance; avoid hard edges and straight lines. A beautiful roof needs some texture and imperfection.

13.18 **Metal Roofs**

Standing-seam roofs can be expensive. An affordable, but still authentic, alternative is a V-crimp roof made of galvalum, a combination of galvanized steel and aluminium that works well in coastal areas prone to salt spray and hurricane damage.

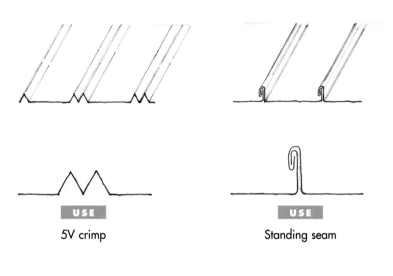

USE
5V crimp

USE
Standing seam

13.19 **Clay Tile Roofs**

Pegtiles are a good roof choice for a house of painted clapboard or brick veneer. Pantiles, larger than pegtiles with a gently curved interlocking module, require a pitch of at least 40 degrees to prevent exposure to wind-driven rain. Barrel tiles, which are installed on the roof sheathing in a cement bed, require a flatter pitch to stay in place.

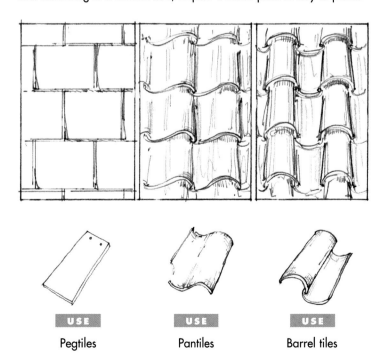

USE
Pegtiles

USE
Pantiles

USE
Barrel tiles

AFTERWORD

PUTTING IT ALL TOGETHER

IN THIS BOOK, we started by looking at the big picture of your house and its place in the world, and continued by examining each element in detail and seeing how the parts fit together.

Because this book is all about avoiding common mistakes, inevitably it involves your learning and understanding a series of rules. At times, as you have read this book, the rules doubtless seemed rather obscure, and sometimes repetitive, although we hope you will have understood that part of the beauty of great traditional architecture derives from the way in which it combines big-picture elegance and fine-grain detail, almost effortlessly, to create a perfect whole.

As you become more familiar with the rules, and with understanding the names and relationships of parts, you will also find that it's just like any language—the more you speak it, the more fluent you become.

In the chapters, we have occasionally referred you to additional sources, from nineteenth-century pattern books by architects such as Asher Benjamin to some of the great texts of architecture, such as Palladio's Four Books or Vitruvius's Ten Books— written 500 and 2000 years ago respectively, and still relevant today. A full list of books to read and learn from can be found by turning to page 253.

As you become more informed, you will also train your eye to look in a fresh way at old buildings. They will no longer appear as relics of another age, but as a rich source of material inspiration for your building today. And the more you look, the more you will understand the combination of overall design, choice of site and material, and fine detail, that makes up the careful balance of every good piece of traditional design. You will see that in so many cases, the problems you are struggling with today have been solved by your predecessors; if in doubt, look to the past to find the best way forward.

You will realize that few traditional buildings strive to be showy or extravagant, and you will understand the benefits of what we might call the "Good Ordinary"—simple, handsome buildings that combine well to make something quietly special. This is the quality that our forefathers understood when they built, and which we could usefully relearn today.

The great twentieth-century English architect Sir Edwin Lutyens, designer of hundreds of buildings from the British Embassy in Washington, D.C., to the Capitol of New Delhi in India, used to call classical architecture the "Great Game." To know how to play any game, you need to understand the rules. But to play it well, you need to learn to break the rules too. The more you look at old buildings, the more you realize how many departures they make from the rules in this book. In fact, at times, while we were writing it, we sometimes wondered if there were any hard and fast rules at all!

The reality is that this book explains the norms. It demonstrates the baseline and how, time after time, you need to work and think hard just to get to first base.

As you gain confidence and skill, feel free to break the rules. It is here that you can realize the extreme invention that the possibilities of traditional architecture offers: constantly adaptive, always fresh, and forever answering new questions with old wisdom. Good luck!

GLOSSARY

Note. Figure numbers indicate the first place in the book where an element is illustrated.

A

Abacus (3.3). The flat top of the capital of a column; usually a plain square slab, with a cove on top.

Acroterion. A decorative corner piece; a plane placed over a gable, supporting an ornament.

Alignment. An adjustment in a straight line. Theoretically, the lines that describe the position of a construction or the shape of an object (such as a curved or straight beam).

Anthemion. Sometimes called a honeysuckle; a floral or leafy decoration in the form of a radiating gathering of vegetation from the same plant.

Apron (5.3). A flat broad trim piece below a windowsill, sometimes shaped and decorated.

Arcade (4.13). A line of arches spanning piers or columns. In cloisters and courtyards, one or more sides were often "arcaded."

Arch (4.1). A construction that spans an opening; usually curved, as opposed to a lintel, which is straight. Often consists of wedge-shaped blocks called voussoirs and a keystone that converts downward thrust to outward thrust, which holds the arch in place.

Architrave (1.11). Lowest element of the Classical Entablature, literally the beam that spans between columns.

Ashlar masonry (13.12). Hewn blocks of burnt clay, shale, or stone wrought to even faces and square edges, with joints laid in mortar (as opposed to rubble or unhewn stone straight from the quarry).

Astragal (3.3). A beaded molding, usually half round, with a narrow fillet below. The classical profile consists of a small convex molding decorated with a string of beads or bead-and-reel shapes.

Asymmetrical composition (2.24). Literally, a design without symmetry, that is, without mirror imagery; a design that does not use symmetry to achieve balance.

Attenuate (7.5). To make slender, reduce in magnitude.

Attic (3.52). In classical building, the story above the main cornice. Also, more loosely, the space within the sloping roof of a house.

B

Back band (5.3). A piece of molding used around window or door casing to cover the gap between the casing and the wall.

Balance. Using the methodologies of scale, proportion, symmetry, asymmetry, light and shadow, small parts within a larger form, pattern, texture, and color to keep elements equal or in the correct proportions.

Baluster (3.52). One of the short posts or pillars used to support a handrail or coping, forming a balustrade.

Bargeboard (10.15). Board hanging from the projecting end of a roof hiding the ends of the horizontal roof timbers, or gables; elaborately ornamented in the Middle Ages.

Base (1.11). The lowest visible part of a building or column.

Baseboard (6.14). A board on the interior wall or partition at the floor, covering the gap between the floor and wall and protecting the wall from kicking, mopping, etc.

Base cap (7.11). Molding used to trim the top of a baseboard.

Bay (2.10). A regularly repeated spatial element making a vertical division in a structure defined by columns, pilasters, piers, or segments of wall between windows and/or doors.

Bay window (5.56). An angular or curved protruded window structure.

Bead (3.13). Ornamental molding resembling a string of beads; a molded strip against which a door or window closes.

Beam (3.24). In the body of a building, the main horizontal timber whose prime function is to carry transverse loads, as a joist, girder, rafter, or purlin.

Bedmold (1.11). The lowest supporting molding of the cornice of an entablature between the corona (or drip stone) and the frieze, forming the bearing plate.

Bow window. A curved bay window.

Box bay (5.59). A bay window shaped with 90-degree angles like a box. The side windows typically protrude perpendicular to the house wall, as opposed to the side windows in a regular bay, which are typically set at an angle to the house wall.

Bracket (5.33). Any small piece of stone or other material protruding from a wall to support a weight (such as a cornice).

Brick (1.7). Substance such as clay or sand molded into a form and fired in a kiln to give it mechanical strength and resistance to moisture.

Brick bonding (13.8). Laying bricks in a pattern that provides a brick wall with strength and stability.

Brickmold (5.17). Wooden molding used to cover the gap between masonry and framing for a door or window.

C

Canopy (7.3). A decorative hood suspended over a door, window, niche, or the like.

Cantilever (1.6). A structural member (a step, balcony, beam, or canopy) fixed at one end, projecting beyond its vertical support.

Capital (1.11). The head, crowning feature, or topmost structural member of a column, pilaster, or pier.

Casement window (5.3). A window that swings open along its entire length, usually on hinges fixed to the sides, swinging inward or outward.

Casing (5.3), window. Flat or molded trim around a window or doorway.

Cast stone. Concrete cast into blocks or moldings that reproduces the look and texture of natural stone.

Center point (4.9). The point that generates the arc and the angle of the individual members of an arch.

Chair rail (12.1). Strips of wood or another substance attached to walls horizontally to keep the backs of chairs from touching the wall.

Chamfer (3.31). The area resulting from cutting off the corner of a piece of stone or wood at an angle, usually 45 degrees.

Channel (3.18). An inset rectangular or concave groove such as found in rustication.

Chimney (11.1). A structure above a fireplace containing flues for drawing off products of combustion.

Chimney cap (11.7). The crowning cornice of a flue opening; a structure that protects the opening of a chimney from elements such as rain or snow.

Chine (9.14). The line where the slopes of two roof masses intersect in an obtuse angle, as in a gambrel or mansard roof.

Closed eave (7.43). A projecting eave in which the underside of the soffit is boxed in.

Column (1.11). A vertical structure, circular in cross-section, consisting of a base, shaft, and capital; can be weight-bearing as well as ornamental.

Composite (3.2). The most elaborate of the classical Orders. The capitals of composite columns are characterized by the merging of Ionic scrolls with Corinthian acanthus leaves.

Compound roof (9.11). A roof composed of more than one pitch or angle, such as the gambrel and the Witch's Hat.

Concave (3.22). Curved inward, such as the inner curve of a sphere.

Convex (3.22). Curved or rounded outward, such as the outer curve of a sphere.

Corinthian (3.2). The second most elaborate of the classical Orders. The columns are slender and the capital has acanthus stalks emerging to support volutes.

Corner board (13.4). A board used as trim on the corners of a house.

Cornice (1.11). A crowning projection where the wall and ceiling meet. In classical architecture, the projecting uppermost portion of an entablature, above the frieze.

Corona (1.11). The vertical structures that overhang a classical cornice, usually having significant projection in order to provide protection for an underlying frieze, the drip stone.

Cyma recta (3.19). Molding or structure having a profile of double curvature, both concave and convex, with the concave part uppermost.

Cyma reversa (3.21). Molding or structure having a profile of double curvature, both concave and convex, with the convex part uppermost.

D

Dado (3.3). Die or flat-faced plain block middle portion of a pedestal, between the base and the cap.

Dentil (3.34). A small tooth-like block, forming one of a long horizontal series, usually along the underside of a cornice; a characteristic ornament of classical styles.

Diameter. The measurement taken across the center of a circle or through the center of a sphere from one side to the other.

Divided light (5.2). A window sash that is separated into smaller panes.

Door (6.1). Movable, lockable barrier, usually of solid and finished construction and usually leading either from exterior to interior or between interior spaces.

Doric (3.2). The second most simple classical Order of architecture, it is characterized by a simple form and imposing scale. The Greek version has no base or pedestal, shafts with twenty shallow flutes, and an entablature with three elements.

Dormer (5.42). Projecting framed structures set upon a sloping roof, usually housing a window or ventilating louver.

Double-hung window (5.2). Windows having two vertically sliding sashes, each closing a different part of the window; the weight of each sash is counterbalanced with pulleys, lines, and weights for ease of opening and closing.

Double porch (8.9). A two-storied porch.

Drip (5.18). A projection shaped to deflect rainwater and prevent it from running back down a wall, often with an underlying channel.

Drip cap (5.18). External molding over an opening to carry rainwater away from the face of the wall.

Duality (2.8). Two equal elements without a clear hierarchical relationship.

E

Eave return (9.3). A termination of a fascia on a sloped roof.

Echinus (3.3). Convex molding underneath the abacus of a Doric capital, sometimes decorative.

Elevation. The external face of a building; a scale drawing of the facade of a building.

Elliptical arch (4.3). An arch that is half an ellipse, having an axis that lines up with the spring line.

Engaged column (3.38). A column that is partially embedded into the surface of a wall, not freestanding.

Entablature (3.3). The top horizontal structure of an Order in classical architecture, divided into cornice, frieze, and architrave.

Entasis (3.11). A subtle outward swelling of the outline of the shaft of a column, done in order to prevent the illusion of concavity in columns.

Expansion joint (13.6). A joint that allows for expansion between two adjacent surfaces of a structure due to temperature, bending from wind load, or differential settling.

F

Façade. External face of a building.

Federal architecture. Style of architecture, drawing from Palladianism and Georgian architecture, that flourished in the United States from around 1785 to 1820.

Fieldstone (13.12). Loose stone or rubble found on the ground.

Fillet (3.18). Small, narrow band of molding, square in section, used to separate or terminate a series of moldings; or the flat surfaces between flutes on column shafts.

Flat arch (4.3). Arch lacking curvature.

Flute (3.18). Closely spaced vertical grooves or channels used to ornament columns and pilasters.

Frame wall. Any skeletal structure made up of metal or wood studs that serves to enclose a room, house, or other space.

French doors (6.4). A pair of floor-length casements hinged on one side to open in the middle so they may function as doors.

Frieze (1.11). Middle section of an entablature, above the architrave and below the cornice.

Fulcrum (2.23). A fixed point or pivot on which a lever moves.

G

Gable (9.3). The triangular area of a wall immediately under a double-sloping roof.

Gambrel (Dutch and English) (9.2). A symmetrical double-sloping roof in which the upper slope is at a shallow angle and the lower slope is steep.

Gauged brick (5.24). A series of bricks spanning an opening, each cut at a slightly different angle, all set to a single center point.

Georgian (2.26). The style in architecture, interior design, and decorative arts in Britain and its colonies between 1714 and 1830. Classical forms and motifs dominate, but the style also encompasses Renaissance and Rococo forms as well as a range of Neoclassical styles.

Giant Orders (3.49). Architectural Orders where columns, pilasters, or piers extend over two or more stories.

Glazed door (6.4). A door with glass windows or coverings.

Glazing. Glasswork for a door or window.

Glazing bar (5.3), *see also* **Muntin.** A strip, usually of wood or metal, that holds or separates panes of glass within a window.

Golden section (2.15). Canon of proportion based on the ratio between two unequal parts where the ratio of the smaller to the larger is the same as the ratio of the larger to the whole.

Gothic arch (4.3). An arch having two centers and equal radii so that the apex of the arch is a point.

Gothic sash window (5.4). A window with a sharp pointed arch.

Grain. Texture due to the arrangement of particles or fibers; alignment of wood fibers in woodworking.

Guttae (3.32). Pendant ornaments resembling truncated cones found on the underside of mutules and regulae in Doric entablatures.

Gutter (1.11). Shallow channel beneath the eaves of a building for collecting and diverting water from a roof.

H

Half round gutter (10.5). A gutter having a semicircular profile.

Head height (2.16). The dimensions from the floor to the top of a window or door opening.

Hierarchy. A system of organization by which every element is subordinate or dominant to another.

Hip (9.2). In roofs, the meeting or joining of four pitched slopes, without gables.

I

Impost (4.6). The block set into a wall or above a pier at which is the spring point for an arch.

Inflection (2.20). Adjusting the spacing of bays to create a visual rhythm.

Intercolumniation (3.45). The spacing between columns, which affects both proportion and the perception of scale.

Ionic (3.2). The classical architectural style characterized by columns that are fluted with large volutes on the capitals.

J

Joint (4.6). The gap between masonry units. Also, an apparatus used to join, or the manner of joining, two or more parts so they interlock.

Joist. One of a series of parallel beams spanning the space between walls to support floor and ceiling loads.

K

Keystone (4.6). The top wedge-shaped voussoir in an arch or vault.

L

Lancet window (5.4). Slender window with a high pointed arch at the top, common in early Gothic architecture.

Light (5.3), *see also* **Pane.** Most commonly, the glass between mullions in a window; an opening through which daylight may cross.

Lime mortar. A mixture to bond stones, made with burnt limestone, sand, and water.

Limewash. One of the original types of paint employed for both exterior and interior surfaces; made primarily of water and lime paste, often colored with natural oxides. Also called whitewash.

Lintel (5.20). Horizontal piece of wood or stone that spans an opening in a wall, such as a door or window, and that supports the weight of the wall over the opening.

Lock rail (5.3). A horizontal piece of a window between the upper and lower sashes into which the lock is fastened.

M

Mansard roof (9.2). A hip roof in which all four sides have two slopes, the lower slope nearly vertical, in order to allow for habitable space in an attic; named after seventeenth-century French architect François Mansart.

Masonry. Construction composed of cut, carved, shaped, or molded units composed of stone, ceramic brick or tile, concrete, glass, adobe, or other similar material.

Massing (2.2). The relationships between different volumes of a building or structure.

McMansion (2.3). A pejorative term for a type of home that is both large and mass-produced; often refers to a home that is perceived to be too large for the lot on which it is built.

Metopes (3.32). The space between triglyphs in the Doric frieze, either plain or adorned.

Modillion (3.33). An ornamental bracket, often in the form of a scroll with acanthus, used in a series to support a cornice.

Molding, supporting (3.19). A type of trim that carries an implied weight, emphasis up.

Molding, terminating (3.19). A type of trim that is the last before an edge, emphasis out.

Molding, separating (3.22). A type of trim that aids in moving from one condition to the next, emphasis side to side.

Molding, transitioning (3.22). A type of trim that connects between two vertical planes, emphasis up and down.

Mortar. A gluey building material, composed of sand and lime, or cement mixed with water, which hardens as it dries; used to bed or separate stones and bricks.

Mullion (5.13). A vertical bar between windows or doors that gangs them together.

Muntin (5.3), *see also* **Glazing bar.** Wood strips that hold a pane of glass in a glazed door or a window.

Mutule (3.32). A wide, flat bracket under the soffit of the Doric cornice, usually decorated underneath with rows of six drops or guttae; appears over each triglyph and each metope of a frieze.

N

Neck (1.11). The uppermost part of a column shaft, below the capital.

Newel (8.14). The central upright posts supporting the handrail at the top and bottom of a stairway or at the turn on a landing; the main posts about which circular staircases wind.

O

Ogee (12.9). *See* **Cyma Recta.**

Ogee arch. A pointed arch composed of two reversed curves.

Ogee gutter (10.5). A gutter with a profile composed with a cyma reversa, also known as a K-gutter.

Open eaves (7.44). Eaves with visible supporting members that are not boxed or enclosed; often found in the Arts & Crafts style.

Openings. Breaks or discontinuity in the surface of a wall or other architectural element; for example, windows and doors.

Orders. In classical architecture, unique styles of column and entablature, each having standardized details and proportions. The five Orders are Tuscan, Doric, Ionic, Corinthian, and Composite.

Ornament. Decorative form that is part of a building or object but not essential to its structure.

P

Palladio, Andrea (1508–1580). Influential architect of the Italian Renaissance; developed the classical style of architecture known as Palladian.

Pane (5.3), *see also* **Light.** Individual plate of glass set in a frame within a window or other opening.

Panel (3.54). Flat plane, section, or division of a surface, generally sunk below or raised above the level or enclosed by a frame or border. Common on walls, ceilings, doors, and furniture pieces.

Panel mold (6.1). Molding that frames a panel.

Parapet (3.52). Low wall projecting from the edge of a platform, terrace, roof, or exterior wall of a building.

Pedestal (3.3). Solid, fixed support found under such architectural elements as columns or balustrades, often built to hold sculpture.

Pediment (3.3). Triangular, low-pitched gable wall across a portico or facade in classical architecture.

Perspective. Means of producing an object graphically in three dimensions, as it appears to the eye.

Pier (3.36). A solid vertical element of a wall between two openings; a heavy mass used for support, such as at either side of a gate or supporting either side of the arch of a bridge.

Pilaster (3.36). Flat, shallow pier or rectangular column fixed against a wall and, in classical architecture, conforming to one of the Orders

Plan. The formal concept of the layout of spaces and elements in the built environment, such as of a building or city; a drawing showing the horizontal area of a building and illustrating the layout of rooms.

Plate, see also Bedmold (1.11). Supporting molding located beneath the corona and above the frieze in classical architecture; a horizontal structural element used to distribute point loads of a joist or rafter along the wall.

Plinth (3.3). Rectangular or square support for columns, pilasters, or door framing.

Plinth block (7.11). A rectangular plane element at the base of the trim of a door. A transitioning element that allows vertical (casing) and horizontal (baseboard) trim to resolve into one another.

Pointed arch (4.3), *see* **Gothic arch.**

Porch (8.1). A roofed space, open along one or more sides and connected to a building, often used to shelter an entrance or employed as a living space.

Portico (7.3). A roofed porch-like space, open along at least one side and connected to an entrance, supported by columns; can protrude from the main building mass or be recessed within it.

Post (3.42). A vertical timber that supports a lintel or provides a solid point of lateral attachment. Also, a stiff, vertical,

relatively isolated member of considerable length that is support for a superstructure.

Profile. Side view of a figure, especially when a clear outline is emphasized; outline of a building illustrating heights and projections.

Proportion. Relationship between respective parts and between a part and the whole in a building or structure.

Pulvinated frieze. Frieze with a convex face, similar to a pillow or compressed cushion.

Punctuation (2.18). Modulation of an element at its extreme providing visual termination.

PVC. Polyvinyl chloride, a widely employed thermoplastic polymer used in construction for trim.

Q

Quarter round (3.21). Molding that presents a profile that is a quarter of a circle.

Quarter-round window. Window openings that form a quarter circle, often found in Federal and Colonial Revival houses.

R

Radius. A line segment joining the center of a circle or sphere to the edge of the circle or sphere.

Radiused eave (10.2). An eave that has a curve at the edge.

Rafter (9.3). One of a series of parallel long, rectangular, sloping members that support the roof covering.

Rafter tail (7.44). The exposed end of a structural member of a sloped roof.

Rail (door) (6.1). The horizontal member that runs between the posts of the frame of a door or between panels.

Railing (5.58). Parapet or balustrade of a lightweight, partly open, usually metal or wood construction.

Raking cyma (4.5). Projecting molding with a double curvature that forms an inclined plane.

Reflected ceiling plan (3.32). A drawing of a ceiling, displayed as if it were a plan.

Regula. In a Doric entablature, a series of short bands under the triglyph and beneath the taenia, from which the guttae hang.

Regulating lines (2.14). Diagonal lines describing the geometrical relationships and proportions of a plan or elevation.

Ridge (9.3). Apex of a pitched roof where two sloping sides intersect; the top of a pitched roof.

Roof. The overhead enclosures of buildings or other structures that protect the interior from the weather.

Roof pitch (9.7). The amount of slope in a roof.

Rough stone (13.12). Stone that is not hewn, sawn, or worked.

S

Sash (5.3). The frame that holds window lights.

Scale. Graphic representation or model of an object that is larger or smaller than the actual size of the object being represented and accurately represents relative size.

Schematic design (2.1). Drawings or diagrams done early in the architectural design process, showing the initial design intent.

SDL, Simulated Divided Light (5.16). The effect of making a single piece of glass look as if it is divided into smaller panes. Bars of plastic, wood, or another substance are attached to the interior and exterior of a window with an element placed in between to create the appearance of glass that is separated into small panes.

Segmental arch (4.3). An arch in which the inner circle is less than a semicircle.

Segmental arch window (5.4). An arched window in which the inner circle of the arch is less than a semicircle.

Semicircular arch (4.3). An arch with an inner circle that is a full semicircle.

Semicircular transom window (5.10). An arched window above a door in which the inner circle is a semicircle.

Shaft (3.3). Main vertical part of a column between the base and the capital.

Shed roof (9.2). A roof with only one sloping plane.

Shingles (5.54). Material such as wood, slate, tile, or concrete, cut or molded to flat dimensions; used for roofing and in some cases on walls.

Shoemold (12.12). Small trim used where a wall meets the floor.

Shutter (5.35). Movable panels, covers, or doors that cover an opening, especially a window.

Shutter dog (5.36). Ornamental catch used to hold an opened shutter back against the wall.

Sidelights (6.3). Fixed areas of glass framing a door or window opening, often narrow in dimension.

Siding (13.2). The nonstructural exterior wall covering of buildings.

Sill (2.17). Horizontal beam or timber at the bottom of the inner structure of a wall to which posts and studs can be attached.

Sill (5.3), window. Lower horizontal member of a window frame; prevents water from falling on the wall below.

Sill height (2.17). The height of the windowsill above the floor.

Simulated Divided Light. *See* **SDL.**

Slate (9.4). A very fine-grained stone easily split into thin slabs used for roofing, flooring, and other construction needs.

Soffit (3.24). The exposed underside of a part of a building, such as an overhang, ceiling, staircase, cornice, or entablature.

Spall. The hard face crust of a brick that begins to flake off and deteriorate due to weathering; also, to splinter or chip.

Specification. Detailed and specific statement of particulars, especially prescribing materials, dimensions, and workmanship for something to be built, installed, or manufactured.

Split fillet (4.5). The fillet that extends both horizontally and at an angle along the cornice of a pediment.

Spring point (4.7). The point at which an arch or slope begins, located above the impost.

Stile (6.1). The main vertical element of a frame of a door, a sash, or a chest of drawers.

Stilt (4.7). Post or pier that raises a structure above ground or water level; of an arch, an elevation of the spring point.

String course (2.19). Horizontal band extending across the face of a wall.

Stucco (13.7). A type of light, malleable plaster used on the surface of walls, moldings, and ornamentations.

Stud wall. A skeletal vertical-plane structure made up of wood or metal vertical members.

Stylobate (3.5). The top step of a three-step foundation on which columns are placed in classical Greek architecture; also, any floor or base upon which a row of columns stand.

Superimposition (3.47). The stacking of the Orders in between multiple stories of a building.

Sustainable (1.10). Term describing design that is environmentally conscious, taking into account construction methods and materials that are locally available and renewable as well as the building's efficient use of resources, including systems of heating, cooling, power, water, and waste.

Symmetry. Exact matching of parts on either side of an axis; unity, proportion, and affinity in the design of the parts of a building and the whole.

T

Taenia (3.3). Narrow raised band, particularly the topmost member of the Doric architrave.

TDL, True Divided Light (5.16). Modern term describing the condition of a window sash divided into small panes by muntins (as opposed to SDL, Simulated Divided Light).

Tectonics. The consideration of loads and stresses in architectural designs.

Tile. Flat, solid, and relatively thin durable material generally used for roofing, flooring, or wall and ceiling covering.

Tooling (13.15). Intentionally leaving the marks of a tool on a surface, especially on leather or stone.

Torus (3.3). Bold, projecting, semicircular, convex molding, often constituting the lowest member of a base of a column over the plinth.

Tower of the Winds (3.17). A simplified variant of the Corinthian Order derived from the portico of the Tower of the Winds in Athens.

Trabeated (7.1). Having upright posts or columns that support horizontal beams or lintels.

Transom (5.10). Opening above a window or door.

Transom bar (6.3). Horizontal member across a window or door separating the main opening from a smaller opening above.

Triglyph (3.31). The characteristic ornament of the Doric frieze, consisting of a slightly raised block of three vertical bands separated by V-shaped grooves.

True Divided Light. *See* **TDL.**

Truss. Arrangement of elements such as beams, bars, or rods, organized in a triangle or combinations of triangles to form a rigid framework (as for supporting a load over a wide area).

Tudor arch (4.3). A four-centered arch with arcs in each corner joining nearly straight lines to the center.

Tuscan (3.2). The simplest of the five classical Orders of architecture, Tuscan, developed in Rome, is a simplified variant of the Doric order.

U

Unity (2.8). The quality of a design in which nothing can be added or removed without adversely affecting the composition.

V

Veneer (13.14). A thin layer of material, often wood or plastic, used to cover an inferior material.

Vignola, Giacomo (1507–1573). One of the foremost late Renaissance architects; succeeded Michelangelo as chief architect for St. Peter's in Rome and is widely known for his treatise on the five Orders of architecture.

Vinyl. Short for polyvinyl chloride (PVC), a tough plastic ubiquitously used in modern construction.

Voussoir (4.7). One of the wedge-shaped stone pieces that form the curved part of an arch.

W

Wall. One of the sides of a room or building, presenting a continuous surface, except where pierced by doors, windows, or other features.

Window. An opening in the wall of a building, serving to admit light, air, or both; typically fitted with a frame in which are set movable sashes containing panes of glass.

Window head (5.13). The uppermost horizontal member of a window frame; also called a header.

Window sill (5.3). The horizontal member at the bottom of a window frame.

RESOURCES

RECOMMENDED READING: ARCHITECTURE

Benjamin, Asher. *The American Builder's Companion*. Dover Publications, 1969.

Benjamin, Asher. *The Architect, or Practical House Carpenter*. Dover Publications, 1989.

Chambers, William. *A Treatise on the Decorative Part of Civil Architecture*. Dover Publications, 2003.

Institute of Classical Architecture & Classical America. *Classical Architecture: A Handbook of the Tradition Today*. W.W. Norton & Co., 2008.

Mouzon, Steve. *Traditional Construction Patterns*. McGraw-Hill, 2004.

Palladio, Andrea. *The Four Books of Architecture*. Dover Publications, 1965.

Ramsey, Charles George, and Harold Reeve Sleeper. *Traditional Details: For Building Restoration, Renovation, and Rehabilitation: From the 1932-1951 Editions of Architectural Graphic Standards*. Wiley, 1998.

Susanka, Sarah. *The Not So Big House: A Blueprint for the Way We Really Live*. Taunton, 1998.

Ware, William. *The American Vignola*. Dover Publications, 1994.

Vitruvius. *The Ten Books on Architecture*. Dover Publications, 1960.

RECOMMENDED READING: URBANISM

Duany, Andres, Elizabeth Plater-Zyberk, and Jeff Speck. *Suburban Nation*. North Point Press, 2000.

Jacobs, Jane. *The Death and Life of Great American Cities*. Random House, 2002.

Hegemann, W., and E. Peets. *The American Vitruvius*. Princeton Architectural Press, 1996.

Krier, Leon. *Architecture: Choice or Fate*. Andreas Papadakis Publishers, 1998.

ORGANIZATIONS & WEBSITES

The Institute of Classical Architecture & Classical America: classicist.org

Congress of the New Urbanism: cnu.org

The Prince's Foundation for the Built Environment: Princes-Foundation.org

The Library of Congress: Historic American Building Survey (HABS): memory.loc.gov/ammem/collections/habs_haer

INSTITUTE OF CLASSICAL ARCHITECTURE & CLASSICAL AMERICA

Get Your House Right: Architectural Elements to Use and Avoid is part of the Classical America Series in Art and Architecture, published by the Institute of Classical Architecture & Classical America.

Since its inception with the republication of *The American Vignola* by William R. Ware in 1977, the Classical America Series in Art and Architecture has been a leader in the publication of important books related to classical design, architecture, painting, and sculpture. The mission of the Series is to promote understanding and appreciation of classical art and architecture and encourage the application of the historical principles and techniques of the tradition in new works for our own time. The intended audience of the Series includes design practitioners and students as well as the interested layman or potential patron.

For a list of other titles in the Classical America Series in Art and Architecture, please visit: classicist.org/publication.html

INDEX

ABOUT THE AUTHORS

MARIANNE CUSATO is an expert in the field of architectural design. Her work focuses on the elements of good design in homes and communities and how design impacts the quality of our lives and the sustainability of the earth's resources.

Ranked the No. 4 most influential person in the home building industry in *Builder Magazine's* annual "Power on 50" list, Cusato and her design principles are changing the landscape of the housing industry. In 2006, the Smithsonian Institution's Cooper-Hewitt National Design Museum honored Cusato with the first annual "People's Design Award." Cusato leads a team of designers that has partnered with Lowe's in a licensing agreement to sell the plans and material packages for the Lowe's Katrina Cottage Series. In June 2006, Congress appropriated $400 million for an alternative emergency housing program, based on the idea of the Katrina Cottage.

Born and raised in Anchorage, Alaska, Cusato is a graduate of the University of Notre Dame School of Architecture and is currently based in New York's Greenwich Village.

BEN PENTREATH is one of the leading young classical designers working in Britain and runs his own architectural practice based in Bloomsbury, London. Much of the firm's work is concerned with improving the quality of new housing in the United Kingdom. Ben has designed many buildings at Poundbury, H.R.H. The Prince of Wales's urban extension to Dorchester, where in 2006 his Crescent was commended in the Georgian Group's Best New Classical Buildings award. In 2004, he won the design competition for Phase B of Upton, Northampton, and he is currently working on a number of substantial projects throughout the U.K. with the Duchy of Cornwall and others.

Ben read History of Art at the University of Edinburgh and studied at the Prince's Institute. He has worked as Urban and Architectural Designer at the Prince's Foundation, and he worked for five years with Fairfax & Sammons Architects in New York.

RICHARD FRANKLIN SAMMONS is President of Fairfax & Sammons Architects, P.C., New York and Palm Beach, founded in 1992. He received a B.A. from Denison University and a Master of Architecture degree from the University of Virginia. He is an internationally recognized expert in the field of architectural proportion and he lectures widely on the subject. His monograph "American Houses: The Architecture of Fairfax & Sammons" was released in 2006.

LEON KRIER was born in 1946 in Luxembourg. His architectural projects have been built in the United States, Italy, France, Portugal, Belgium, Germany, and the United Kingdom. His theories on architecture and urbanism form part of the urban development recommendations of the OECD and the European Union and have been widely applied in the United States, via the New Urbanism. Leon Krier is a personal adviser to H.R.H. the Prince of Wales, for whom he is master planning the new cities of Poundbury in Dorset and Chapel Town in Cornwall, both in the United Kingdom. Krier is the author of numerous books and papers, including *Architecture: Choice or Fate* in 1997.